1787

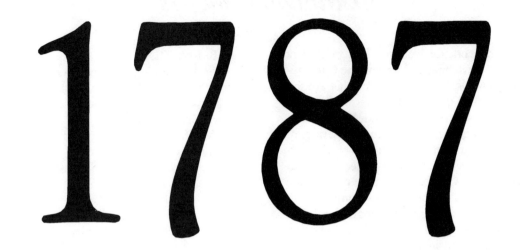

1787

the day-to-day story of the
CONSTITUTIONAL CONVENTION

compiled by historians of the
Independence National Historical Park
National Park Service

Exeter Books

NEW YORK

Acknowledgments

The historians at Independence National Historical Park have been engaged in researching and writing the Constitutional *Bicentennial Daybook* for three years. This edition includes less than one-third of the material in the *Bicentennial Daybook*. The entire project, which includes every day in 1787, required extensive research and the gathering of materials from local and national repositories, private collections and papers, and various publishing projects on delegates to the Constitutional Convention. In the process, the staff has gathered thousands of documents—from the well-known letters of George Washington to biographical data on the elusive William Houstoun (a delegate from Georgia).

We are grateful for the many individuals who contributed essays to the complete *Bicentennial Daybook* project. Although many of their essay contributions could not be used in this abridged edition, their work is deeply appreciated and acknowledged:

Penelope Hartshorne Batcheler, INHP Staff
Frank W. Bobb, Grand Lodge of Pennsylvania
Lee Boyle, Hopewell Furnace NHS
William Brookover, INHP Staff
Jane Bush, Western Reserve, Historical Society
Toni E. Collins, Elfreth's Alley Association
Rev. George L. Curry, St. George's United Methodist Church
Karie Diethorn, Friends of INHP
Dr. John Duckett, University of Pennsylvania
W. Joan Marshall Dutcher, Valley Forge NHP
Emma Edmunds, free lance writer, Philadelphia
Doris Devine Fanelli, INHP Staff
Joseph Foster, Temple University
Curt Gaul, INHP Staff
Eleanor Gesensway, INHP Staff
Rev. Gerald Gillette, Presbyterian Historical Society
Robert L. Giannini, III, INHP Staff
Jennifer Lord Gallogly, Carpenters Company
James Green, Library Company of Philadelphia
Thomas A. Horrocks, The College of Physicians of Philadelphia
William C. Kashatus, III, INHP Staff

Jane B. Kolter, INHP Staff
Gordon Lloyd, University of California, Redlands
Margie Lloyd, University of California, Riverside
Mark Frazier Lloyd, University of Pennsylvania Archives
Sandra Mackenzie Lloyd
John M. Dickey, F. A. I. A., Staff
Catherine Lojewski, INHP Staff
Rev. John G. McKevitt, St. Joseph's Roman Catholic Church
John Calvin Milley, INHP Staff
D. Roger Mower, The John Bartram Association
Charles E. Peterson, Carpenters' Company of Philadelphia
Susan Alexander Popkin, Philadelphia Maritime Museum
Denise Rabzak, INHP Staff
David Seipt, INHP Staff
Anne Verplanck, INHP Staff
William Ward, Philadelphia Maritime Museum
Rev. David J. Wartluft, Lutheran Theological Seminary at Philadelphia
Carol Wojtowicz, Mutual Assurance Company and The Philadelphia Contributionship
Martin I. Yoelson, Chief Historian (retired) INHP

Special thanks for research assistance go to Dorothy Bauer, Temple University; Hope Fleischman and Roger Friedlander, Vermont Academy; and Stephen Wright, INHP Staff. We especially appreciate Theresa Hyett, who transcribed, organized, typed and edited the several drafts of this daybook. Her assistant Wendy Pope kept pace with this voluminous product. Shirley Mays is commended for her cooperation in assembling illustrations from the Park photo collection. Any errors of fact or omission in this text are our responsibility.

Bicentennial of the Constitution Research Team:
David C. Gillette Dutcher
David A. Kimball
Robert K. Sutton
Anna Coxe Toogood
March 1987

342.73
S 497
79417

Produced by
Combined Books,
26 Summit Grove Avenue,
Suite #207,
Bryn Mawr, PA 19010

and

Wieser & Wieser, Inc.,
118 East 25th Street,
New York, NY 10010.

Printed in the United States of America

Project Director: Robert L. Pigeon
Project Coordinator: Antoinette Bauer
Photographs: Robert Fanelli
Layout: Lizbeth Hoefer-Nauta
Consultant: Anna Coxe Toogood,
David C. Gillette Dutcher

Introduction

In 1787, the United States of America already had a working document which provided *some* governmental structure. Six years earlier, Congress had ratified the Articles of Confederation which formally recognized the authority which Congress had been exercizing for over five years. But the authority that Congress enjoyed was limited to the necessities of the war against Britain. Congress only had the power to raise and maintain an army, and negotiate loans and treaties.

In essence, the federal government was the Congress, which was also the legislative and executive, and established the judiciary whenever a judiciary was needed. The Congress prior to 1787 had a Secretary, Charles Thompson, and several clerks to help organize its work and record its decisions, and it had a President, elected annually from among its members, and housed and supported by Congress, as the nation's titular head of state. It also had a rudimentary executive branch—a Secretary of Foreign Affairs, a Secretary of War, a Postmaster General, a Treasury Board, and a few ministers abroad. Still, every single significant action had to be initialed and approved by the Congress.

This government did not work very well. It had no power to tax; it had to ask the states for money, and it got very little of what it asked for. It had to make all decisions affecting the nation, including such decisions as to whether or not the claim of a private for pay due him for fighting in the Revolution was valid, but had trouble keeping enough of its members present to make any decision. It could never agree upon and carry out a consistent policy on any subject. And it was unable to pay its debts.

Still, it was served by capable people. No nation could have better representation abroad than John Adams, Minister to Great Britain and the Netherlands, and Thomas Jefferson, Minister to France. Few Secretaries of State have had a clearer perception of our relations abroad than Secretary of Foreign Affairs, John Jay.

But the United States in Congress Assembled provided by the Articles of Confederation had no authority over people. It had authority only over the thirteen states. It could not levy taxes: it could only ask the states to give it money. It could not enforce treaty provisions unless it wished to go to war with the state or states responsible for violating the treaties. Increasingly, Congress, which had to initiate every government action, couldn't even get enough members together to act legally.

These weaknesses disturbed many Americans—and states. Early in 1786, Virginia invited all the states to send delegates to Annapolis, Maryland, to discuss trade and its problems. While only five states sent delegates in time, the Annapolis meeting decided to call for a convention "to meet at Philadelphia on the second Monday of May next, to take into consideration the situation of the United States, to devise such further provisions as shall appear to them necessary to render the constitution of the Federal Government adequate to the urgencies of the Union, and to report . . . to the United States in Congress Assembled."

There was no provision in law for this convention, and Congress had not yet agreed that it was necessary. However, New Jersey, Virginia and Pennsylvania had already appointed delegates.

The Annapolis Convention probably didn't think at all before it chose Philadelphia as the site of the Federal Convention. With 40,000 inhabitants (about the size of Burlington, Vermont, or Hutchinson, Kansas, or Corvallis, Oregon), it was the nation's largest city by 15,000. It was also the most accessible and boasted the best convention facilities—large public meeting rooms, taverns, boarding houses, amusements and a notoriously hospitable upper class to entertain delegates at dinner and tea. It had hosted the First Continental Congress and the Second Continental Congress, and intended to reclaim the Federal government later in 1787.

Like all other cities of its time, Philadelphia was a hopeless mix of land uses, with stables, breweries, blacksmith shops, soap boilers and tanyards intermixed with taverns, offices, shops and opulent residences. Unlike other cities, it had been planned, and its streets followed a regular grid pattern which struck some visitors as monotonous. A center of foreign trade, it was a great place to shop for china, silks, stays and wine, for wimble bits and pickled mangoes, for weathervanes, stoves and venetian blinds. It was also a center of medicine, the arts of science and literature— among its temporary residents in 1787 were inventor

John Fitch and lexicographer Noah Webster. It also boasted a summer climate which daunted even coastal South Carolinans, although 1787 would have some unusually cool weather.

* * *

All 13 States appointed delegates except Rhode Island, an insufficient number of whose leaders sympathized with the nationalistic goals of the Convention. A total of more than 70 individuals were originally nominated, but a substantial number of them did not accept the assignment or did not attend. Their reasons included opposition to constitutional revision, poor health, family illness, and the press of personal or professional business.

Some of the men in this category were prominent, including Richard Henry Lee, Thomas Nelson, Jr., and Patrick Henry of Virginia; Abraham Clark of New Jersey; George Walton of Georgia; Henry Laurens of South Carolina; and Maryland's Thomas

Stone and Charles Carroll of Carrollton. All these individuals except Henry and Laurens had signed the Declaration of Independence. Part of the group who rejected nomination or did not take part in the Convention later favored the new frame of Government and supported ratification of the Constitution; others opposed it.

Various national leaders and eminently qualified people were not even elected. Among these were such men as Thomas Jefferson and John Adams, who were on diplomatic duty in Europe; Samuel Adams, whose political fortunes were temporarily on the decline; and John Hancock, who was busy as Governor of Massachusetts.

New York named the smallest delegation, three; Pennsylvania the largest, eight. Attendance ranged from New York, which for much of the time had only one unofficial representative (Hamilton) on hand, and New Hampshire, with two late arrivals, to Pennsylvania, whose eight delegates all participated throughout most of the Convention. The States usually paid all or part of their representatives' expenses, and apparently in some instances compensated them.

Each State specified what portion of its delegation needed to be present to act for it and cast its vote. The credentials of all the delegates except those from thinly populated Delaware authorized them to approve such changes in the Articles of Confederation as they deemed desirable. Delaware directed its emissaries not to agree to any changes in the basis of congressional representation from the one State-one vote system in the Continental Congress, though during the Convention the Delawareans disregarded these instructions when the large and small States reached a compromise on this matter.

Attending all or practically every session were 29 men: Bassett, Bedford, Blair, Brearly, Broom, Butler, Clymer, Fitzsimons, Franklin, Gerry, Gorham, Ingersoll, Jenifer, Johnson, King, Madison, Mason, Mifflin, Robert Morris, Charles Pinckney, Charles Cotesworth Pinckney, Randolph, Read, Rutledge, Sherman, Spaight, Washington, Williamson, and Wilson. Ten individuals missed only a few weeks: Baldwin, Davie, Dayton, Dickinson, Ellsworth, Livingston, Alexander Martin, Luther Martin, Gouverneur Morris, and Strong. Twelve persons were away for long periods: Blount, Carroll, Few, Gilman, Hamilton, Houstoun, Langdon, Lansing, McClurg, McHenry, Paterson, and Yates. Four men attended for extremely short stretches: Houston, Mercer, Pierce, and Wythe. Reasons for absences included personal and family illness, service in Congress, other professional or personal business; late appointment, early departure, boredom or a feeling of uselessness, faith in the views and actions of fellow State delegates, and opposition to the prevalent nationalism.

Although the group hardly matched Jefferson's characterization as an "Assembly of demigods," it was a distinguished one. Statesmen, legislators, patriots, and leaders in commerce and agriculture for the most part, the men were as a whole highly talented and well educated. They also enjoyed extensive political and worldly experience.

Between May 25 and September 17, except for Saturday May 26 and during the two adjournments (July 3–4 and July 26–August 6), sessions were held 6 days a week. The hours usually ranged between 10 or 11 a.m. and 3 or 4 p.m., though sometimes they were shorter or longer. But the expenditure of time in sitting on committees, drafting papers and speeches, and otherwise preparing for the sessions made for long days for most of the group.

The following is the day-to-day story of the men who met in Philadelphia and drafted a lasting framework for a government of the United States of America.

The number of delegates who served at Philadelphia totaled 55, though they were not all on hand for the entire Convention. Some arrived late, left early, or were temporarily absent for various lengths of time. The 55 men, 39 of whom signed the Constitution, were as follows (non-signers indicated by asterisks):

Baldwin, Abraham (GA)
Bassett (Basset), Richard (DE)
Bedford, Gunning, Jr. (DE)
Blair, John (VA)
Blount, William (NC)
Brearly (Brearley), David (NJ)
Broom, Jacob (DE)
Butler, Pierce (SC)
Carroll, Daniel (MD)
Clymer, George (PA)
Davie, William R. (NC)*
Dayton, Jonathan (NJ)
Dickinson, John (DE)
Ellsworth, Oliver (CT)
Few, William (GA)
Fitzsimons, Thomas (PA)
Franklin, Benjamin (PA)
Gerry, Elbridge (MA)*
Gilman, Nicholas (NH)
Gorham, Nathaniel (MA)
Hamilton, Alexander (NY)
Houston, William C. (NJ)
Houstoun, William (GA)*
Ingersoll, Jared (PA)
Jenifer, Daniel of St. Thomas (MD)

Johnson, William S. (CT)
King, Rufus (MA)
Langdon, John (NH)
Lansing, John, Jr. (NY)*
Livingston, William (NJ)
McClurg, James (VA)*
McHenry, James (MD)
Madison, James (VA)
Martin, Alexander (NC)*
Martin, Luther (MD)*
Mason, George (VA)*
Mercer, John F. (MD)*
Mifflin, Thomas (PA)
Morris, Gouverneur (PA)
Morris, Robert (PA)

Paterson, William (NJ)
Pierce, William L. (GA)*
Pinckney, Charles (SC)
Pinckney, Charles Cotesworth (SC)
Randolph, Edmund J. (VA)*
Read, George (DE)
Rutledge, John (SC)
Sherman, Roger (CT)
Spaight, Richard D., Sr. (NC)
Strong, Caleb (MA)*
Washington, George (VA)
Williamson, Hugh (NC)
Wilson, James (PA)
Wythe, George (VA)*
Yates, Robert (NY)*

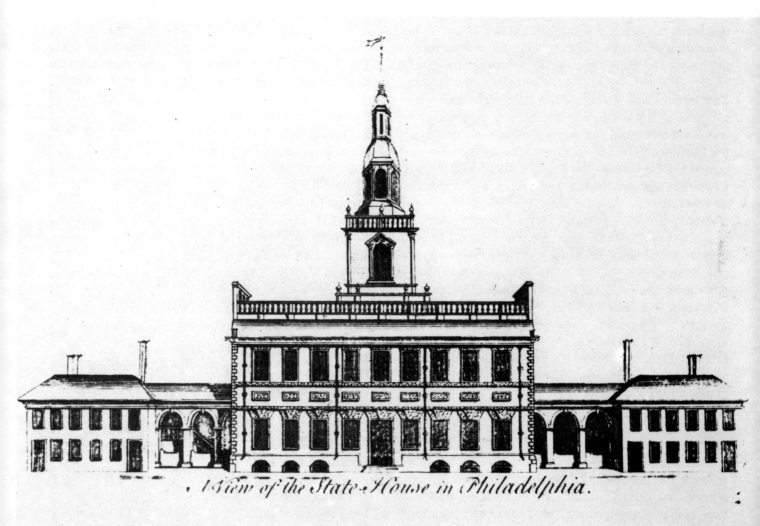

A View of the State House in Philadelphia.

Friday, May 25, 1787

The day was cool and overcast with occasional light rain and variable winds.

Convention

When the delegates gathered at the State House, as they had since May 14, it was evident that seven states had a quorum of their delegates present. And so finally, eleven days after the date set, the Convention began.

Someone, probably Governor Randolph as the ranking state officer present, assumed the chair. Credentials were presented by Rufus King (MA), Robert Yates and Alexander Hamilton (NY), David Brearley, William Churchill Houston and William Paterson (NJ), Robert Morris, Thomas Fitzsimons, James Wilson, and Gouverneur Morris (PA), George Read, Richard Bassett and Jacob Broom (DE), George Washington, Edmund Randolph, John Blair, James Madison, George Mason, George Wythe and James McClurg (VA), Alexander Martin, William Richardson Davie, Richard Dobbs Spaight and Hugh Williamson (NC), John Rutledge, Charles Cotesworth Pinckney, Charles Pinckney and Pierce Butler (SC) and William Few (GA).

Robert Morris, acting for Benjamin Franklin who was too ill to attend, nominated George Washington as chairman. Rutledge seconded. Because this nomination came from the only possible alternative (Dr. Franklin), the General was unanimously elected, and escorted to the chair by Morris and Rutledge.

Thus officially opened, the Convention chose William Jackson as its Secretary, appointed Thomas Claxton and Nicholas Weaver as its doorkeeper and messenger, named Wythe, Hamilton and Charles Pinckney a committee to prepare rules, and adjourned until Monday.

Delegates

General Washington invited himself to breakfast with the Meredith family, returned many visits in the afternoon, dined at Mr. Thomas Willings', and spent the evening "at my quarters" in the Robert Morris residence.

George Read wrote to John Dickinson in Wilmington. Governor Randolph had rented a couple of rooms elsewhere so his room—"on the first floor, up one pair of stairs, on Fifth Street . . ."—was available for Dickinson. Elbridge Gerry also had applied for it. Read closed with the admonition, "You shoud be here at the first opening of the Budget."

James Madison, who continuously spoke for the national interest in the Convention, was primarily responsible for the Virginia Plan which promoted a strong national government. He was the only delegate who consistently kept notes on each day's proceedings.

James Madison, Junior

JAMES MADISON was one of the leading advocates for assembling this Convention to revise the Articles of Confederation. He significantly contributed to the Virginia Plan, the first and foremost proposal for drafting a new, central government. At the Convention his voluminous notes and strong arguments for an improved political system helped establish Madison's place in American history. But it was his essays in favor of ratification in *The Federalist* that firmly etched Madison's name in the political annals of the nation. From 1787 Madison's career followed a direct path to the White House.

James Madison grew up in Virginia, the eldest of ten children. His education came mostly from home tutors until he entered the College of New Jersey at Princeton in 1769. Madison was only twenty-five when he helped draft Virginia's first state constitution in 1787.

After the Convention in Philadelphia, Madison vigorously prodded a reluctant Virginia through the ratification process. He, John Jay and Alexander Hamilton authored *The Federalist,* the authoritative essays which swayed the course of ratification and are still considered landmark contributions to political science.

In the first Congress under the Constitution he helped to create the executive departments and authored the amendments that we revere as the Bill of Rights. Madison served in the House of Representatives from 1789 to 1797.

In 1794 Madison was introduced by Senator Aaron Burr of New York to a young Philadelphia Quaker widow, Dolley Payne Todd. Their extraordinarily happy marriage created a legend. After his appointment as Secretary of State by President Jefferson in 1801, Mrs. Madison became the leading lady of the capital, as both the President and Vice President were widowers. On March 4, 1809, James Madison was elected our fourth President and Dolley Madison became First Lady of the land. She set the high standard which guided subsequent First Ladies. The President died in 1836, survived by Dolley and a step-son, John Payne Todd, a long-time sorrow to his parents.

Saturday, May 26, 1787

Today was cool and fair with a westerly breeze.

Convention

Having met and organized yesterday, the Convention was in recess until Monday. For the delegates, it was the last Saturday off until July 28.

Delegates

General Washington finished returning visits in the morning, dined with a club at City Tavern (a club was a group of men who dined together and split the check equally), and spent the evening in his room writing letters. Although he dated the letter "May 27," George Mason wrote his son George Junior today. He asked whether it had rained in Virginia, and how the wheat and tobacco crops looked. About Philadelphia society, he said, "I begin to grow heartily tired of the etiquette and nonsense so fashionable in this city. It would take me some months to make myself master of them, and that it should require months to learn what is not worth remembering . . . is . . . discouraging. . . ."

Dr. William Shippen in a letter to his son reported that Gouverneur Morris at about 4 P.M. "came into Mr. Willing's with the news that Gen. Washington was elected President to the Convention and Major W. Jackson Secretary; with which he [Jackson] is extremely delighted and thinks his fortune and fame are both established. Old Dr. F. [Franklin] much mortified he had not interest [influence] enough to procure the place for his Grandson."

Maryland's legislature this day appointed James McHenry, Daniel of St. Thomas Jenifer, Daniel Carroll, John Francis Mercer and Luther Martin the state's delegates to the Convention.

Daniel of St. Thomas Jenifer

JENIFER grew up in the lush farm country of Charles County Maryland. In his youth he was employed by the last proprietors of Maryland, the Calverts. From 1773 to 1776 he sat on the Governor's council.

Known as a conservative, Jenifer, nonetheless, was prominent in revolutionary activities. He sat on Maryland's Council of Safety and was president of the state's first Senate from 1777 to 1780. He also represented Maryland in the Second Continental Congress for four years after 1778.

Jenifer continued to support the idea of a strong national government during the 1780s. In 1785 he represented Maryland at the Mount Vernon Conference—first stop on the road to the Philadelphia Convention.

In the Convention he attended nearly every session but seldom spoke. After the Convention he never again held public office. Daniel of St. Thomas Jenifer died three years later—a confirmed bachelor. He was a good friend of George Washington and his nieces and nephews were frequent visitors at Mount Vernon.

The City Tavern (detail from a 1799 print) was the place where many delegates dined together as a club. It was the location of a farewell dinner attended by the delegates on September 11.

Sunday, May 27, 1787

The wind swung around to the WNW, and brought cold and clouds.

Convention

The Convention was in Sunday recess and its members were initiating what became a Sunday habit—catching up on their letter writing.

Delegates

General Washington and several of his colleagues attended Mass at St. Mary's, then dined, drank tea and spent the evening at his lodgings. He used the evening to write a long letter of instructions to his nephew and farm manager, George Augustine Washington.

James Madison wrote his father on business (the iron his father wanted was not available from the Andover Furnace; the Virginia legislation requiring cargo bound for Fredericksburg to enter first at downriver ports was hurting trade), and to summarize the first day of the Convention. He also wrote Edmund Pendleton, a long-time friend who had been a Revolutionary leader in Virginia, to report on attendance and the election of officers. Madison's old friend Governor Randolph wrote Acting Governor Beverly Randolph also to report on the Convention.

Nor were Virginians the only letter writers; Rufus King of Massachusetts wrote Secretary of War Henry Knox and Massachusetts Congressman Nathan Dane to report on the Convention and ask for information about events in Massachusetts. King's colleague, Nathaniel Gorham, turned 49.

Nathaniel Gorham

NATHANIEL GORHAM was born on this day in 1738 in Charlestown, Massachusetts, of ancestors who had arrived on the *Mayflower*. He was locally educated and then apprenticed to a merchant when he was fifteen. In 1759 he began his own mercantile business. Four years later he married Rebecca Call and they had nine children. Four years service in the colonial legislature was succeeded by two years in the State House of Representatives. After helping draft Massachusetts' constitution in 1780 Gorham again served in the legislature, and was three times its Speaker.

In 1782 he went into Congress where he served five years. From June 1786 until January 1787 he was President of Congress—making him the sixth head of state of the United States under the Articles of Confederation.

His political service ended with the Convention. In the year following the Convention Gorham became a partner with Oliver Phelps in the largest land speculation in the history of Massachusetts to that date. In 1786, as part of a boundary settlement worked out between New York and Massachusetts, New York ceded title to all land in the state west of Ithaca, in return for which Massachusetts gave up its claim to jurisdiction over the land. In 1788, Massachusetts sold this land—over 6,000,000 acres—to Gorham and his partner, Oliver Phelps, for about $1,000,000 payable in state consolidated notes in three annual installments.

Incredible though it may seem, Phelps and Gorham were unable to make the required payments. Gorham

Nathaniel Gorham served on the Committee of Detail which composed the final version of the Constitution. During the discussion of the Virginia Plan, he was chairman of the Committee of the Whole. He suggested that the President appoint judges with the Senate's consent and proposed staggered terms for Senators.

died in 1796, insolvent but still highly esteemed in his native town.

Monday, May 28, 1787

The weather stayed cool, but there was no wind, and skies were fair.

Convention

Nathaniel Gorham and Caleb Strong both from Massachusetts, Oliver Ellsworth from Connecticut, Gunning Bedford, Esq. from Delaware, James McHenry from Maryland, and Benjamin Franklin, George Clymer, Thomas Mifflin and Jared Ingersoll from Pennsylvania appeared and took their seats.

Mr. Wythe (VA) reported from the Rules Committee appointed the previous Friday. Most of the report was approved and became the Convention's rules of procedure. Rufus King (MA), Pierce Butler (SC) and Richard Dobbs Spaight (NC) all made motions aimed at keeping debates secret until the Convention finished its work. These motions were referred to the Rules Committee and the Convention adjourned for the day.

Delegates

General Washington dined "at home" (use of this phrase says a lot about Robert and Mary Morris as hosts) and drank tea with many others at Tench Francis'.

Dr. Franklin received a visit from lexicographer Noah Webster "and ladies."

South Carolina's Charles C. Pinckney tried out a pair of sorrel horses owned by Jacob Hiltzheimer. Pinckney, like the Morrises, Jenifer, Washington and others, loved a good horse race and was probably a good judge of horses.

Connecticut's Roger Sherman, still in New Haven, bought blankets, linen, calico and thread worth 17 pounds twelve shilling two pence from Pearsall and Glover.

Caleb Strong

CALEB STRONG, the tall, blue-eyed delegate from Massachusetts, presented a different picture from the stereotype of the boisterous New England politician. Strong possessed a gentle and scholarly air that enabled him to be an effective public official. Born in Northampton, Strong's parents sent him to Samuel Moody, a teacher in York, for his primary education. Strong then attended Harvard and graduated with the highest honors in 1764. A devout Congregationalist, he began preaching a few years later in Conwey.

He went to Cambridge, and upon his return contracted smallpox which weakened his eyes greatly. With family help in reading he then studied law under Joseph Hawley.

During the year 1772 Strong took a very active part in public life. He was town treasurer, selectman for the county government, and member of the Committee of Correspondence. During the Revolution, Strong unfortunately signed the lawyers' address welcoming General Gage into the city. Later that year in August when three thousand people stormed a Springfield courthouse, Strong signed a petition agreeing not to hold office or execute commissions under an act of Parliament.

In 1770, Caleb Strong had married Sarah Hooker, daughter of a prominent Northampton family. The couple had nine children, two of whom graduated from Harvard. Strong continued to build his career in law, and took a stand for negro rights. He represented Quok Walker and other former slaves whose owners tried to disclaim responsibility for their support. Strong also advocated female education and joined several others in the construction of a coeducational school in Northampton.

When in the wake of slackening economic condition in January 1787, Captain Daniel Shays led a rebellion against a Springfield armory, Governor Bowdoin appointed Caleb Strong and several others to a committee to decide the punishment of the insurgent. In April one of the men arrested in the uprising was brought before Strong, in his position as Justice of the Peace.

That same month Governor Bowdoin appointed him a delegate to the Federal Convention. He ac-

Caleb Strong joined with Gerry on several issues to split the vote of the Massachusetts delegation. The effect on the vote for the Connecticut Compromise was to discourage the larger states' determination to seek more power.

cepted the nomination, albeit reluctantly. During the Convention Strong maintained a low profile. In the spirit of conciliation, he voted for equality of representation in the Legislature. He supported adoption of a similar method of election for both houses, and voted in favor of the Connecticut Compromise. Along with his colleague Elbridge Gerry, he refused to lodge the powers of revising the law with the federal judges. Concerning appropriations, Strong proposed that money bills originate only in the lower house. In terms of renumeration for federal congressmen, he advocated a four-dollar-a-day salary. Though dedicated to the work of the Convention, Strong left the Convention suddenly when his wife became ill.

Tuesday, May 29, 1787

After morning fog, the day turned very fair, and warmer, with a mean temperature of 59°.

Convention

John Dickinson (DE) and Elbridge Gerry (MA) took their seats.

Mr. Wythe reported more rules for the Convention session:

> *That no member be absent from the House so as to interrupt the representation of the State without leave.*
> *That Committees do not sit whilst the House shall be, or ought to be, sitting.*
> *That no copy be taken of any entry on the journal during the sitting of the House without the leave of the House.*
> *That members only be permitted to inspect the journal.*
> *That nothing spoken in the House be printed, or otherwise published, or communicated without leave.*

Mr. Randolph and Mr. Pinckney each proposed a plan of government and the Convention decided to refer both to itself meeting as a Committee of the Whole.

Delegates

General Washington "dined at home," after which he accompanied Mrs. Morris to the benefit concert of a Mr. Juhan. An apologetic Charles Wilson Peale wrote asking him to pose for another portrait (Peale completed seven life portraits of him). The General agreed,

Charles Wilson Peale painted George Washington during the summer of 1787 (He did six additional Washington protraits.). He also maintained a natural history museum where he had such curiosities as dinosaur bones and mounted golden pheasants.

whereupon Peale suggested, "by bringing my Pallette and Pencils to Mr. Morris' that you might sett at your leisure and that if any interruptions by Visitors or business took place I would wait convenient to you."

John Dickinson wrote "My dear Polly" (his wife of nearly seventeen years, Mary Norris) to report a pleasant journey and send his "tenderest love to our precious children."

James McHenry also wrote to his wife of three years, Margaret Allison Caldwell, "We are beginning to enter seriously upon the business of the Convention, so that I shall have but little time to give my Peggy."

The Course Charted

AT first glance, the Convention didn't do much today—adopted a few additional rules, received a couple of schemes for strengthening the Confederation, referred the plans to a Committee of the Whole, and adjourned. But these few actions in large part determined the course the Convention would follow and its destination.

Secrecy contributed significantly to the work of the Convention. There were no daily leaks about what the Convention was doing and what the individual delegates thought about each issue. When the Constitution was finished, the various alternatives to each provision had not been publicized or attacked by the press. Nor were individual delegates locked into a position that, on further reflection, they wished to change but couldn't because their earlier position had been widely publicized. Although the general outlines of the Convention plan became known early on (a government divided into executive, judicial and legislative branches), the details of its various provisions were kept remarkably confidential. The fifty-five delegates could—and did—keep their mouths shut.

But the most significant action was the referral to a Committee of the Whole of the Virginia and Pinckney plans. By considering these plans the Convention committed itself to a new government, not a patched-up version of the Articles of Confederation.

Wednesday, May 30, 1787

The day was cool with an ENE wind and a hard steady rain.

Convention

Roger Sherman of Connecticut appeared and took his seat. The Convention "went into a Committee of the Whole on the State of the Union." Nathaniel Gorham of Massachusetts was elected to the chair. After debate the committee agreed "that a national government ought to be established consisting of a supreme Legislative, Executive and Judiciary," although New York was divided and Connecticut voted no. Discussion then turned to how many votes each state should have in Congress. After a number of unsuccessful motions, Madison moved "that the equality of suffrage [that is, one vote for each state] established by the Articles of Confederation ought not to prevail. . . ." George Read (DE) moved to postpone because the Delaware deputies had been instructed not to approve such a change

and, if it was approved, they might have to leave the Convention. Several members said that the Delaware delegates could stay even if the motion were approved, but eventually Read's motion to postpone was agreed upon and the Committee recessed.

Delegates

General Washington dined with Mr. Samuel Vaughan, a former London merchant, Jamaica landowner, and friend of America. He drank tea and spent the evening at the home of John and Elizabeth Laurence. He also found time to write a long letter to Thomas Jefferson promoting Alexandria as a principal depot for the fur trade, pointing out some errors in a French article on the Society of Cincinnati ("nothing can be more ridiculous than the supposition . . . that the Society was instituted partly because the Country could not then pay the Army"), and announcing, somewhat apologetically, his presence at the Federal Convention.

Dr. Franklin wrote his sister, Jane Mecom, to describe his new houses.

William R. Davie of North Carolina wrote from Philadelphia to James Iredell, future Supreme Court Justice, asking for Iredell's opinion on whether executive and judicial powers should be added at the federal level.

Richard D. Spaight wrote from Philadelphia to John Gray Blount of North Carolina asking him to remit additional cash if the Governor approved, since the Convention would last much longer than Spaight had thought originally.

Charles Pinckney wrote from Philadelphia to Secretary of Congress Thomson telling him that the boundary dispute between Georgia and South Carolina was settled and the judges that Congress had appointed to settle the dispute weren't needed.

William Samuel Johnson

WILLIAM SAMUEL JOHNSON was one of the best educated and scholarly of all the delegates, with a BA degree from Yale, an MA from Harvard, and an honorary doctorate from Oxford. He also was the only loyalist from the revolutionary era—actually he was neutral, but was considered a loyalist since he did not support the American cause. Another distinction was that he lived to the ripe old age of 92, which was older by several years than any of his fellow 55 delegates.

Although Johnson did not participate in the Revolution, he spent much of his life in politics. He was a member of the Connecticut General Assembly and Governor's Council in the 1760s; he opposed the crown's taxation policies as a representative of the Stamp Act Congress in 1765: and he served as his colony's agent to London for two years. During 1787 he was one of his state's representatives in Congress, and following ratification he was selected as one of Connecticut's first United States senators. During the Constitutional Convention, Johnson was not a frequent speaker. Yet most of his points carried a great deal of weight. For example, one of his proposals that was adopted stated that the Senate should be elected by the state legislators and the House by the people.

Johnson obviously was respected by the Convention—for he was selected chairman of the Committee of Style, which drafted the final version of the Constitution. In November 1787 he accepted the presidency of Columbia College and served there until his retirement in 1800.

William Samuel Johnson was the chairman of the committee which presented the Constitution in its final form. He also made proposals concerning conviction for treason.

Thursday, May 31, 1787

The temperature rose markedly from the morning's 69° and there was an afternoon thundershower.

This view of Market Street is what George Washington saw from his second story quarters in the home of Robert Morris. Conestoga wagons are parked beneath Lombardy poplars introduced by William Hamilton, colonial horitculturist.

Convention

William Pierce of Georgia appeared and took his seat. The Convention resolved itself into a Committee of the Whole and:

1. Decided on a bicameral (two-house) legislature.
2. Agreed on an election of the first house by the people.
3. Agreed not to have the second house elected by the first house.
4. Agreed that either house could initiate legislation.

Delegates

General Washington dined at Mr. Tench Francis' and drank tea with Mrs. Meredith, whose husband Samuel was a member of Congress and an old friend of the General. Washington also wrote a note to Henry Knox expressing pleasure that "Miss Lucey's eye" was better and that he expected to see the General and Mrs. Knox in Philadelphia soon.

Several delegates attended a party given by Nancy Shippen, whose father had been Director General of Hospitals for the Continental Army and whose uncles had signed the Declaration of Independence.

Governor Bowdoin wrote from Boston to Elbridge Gerry, enclosing a new commission as a Convention delegate.

William Pierce, a Happy Man

WILLIAM PIERCE is something of a mystery. Students of the Constitution know he prepared written sketches of his fellow delegates. Students of the Revolutionary War know he served as General Nathaniel Greene's aide, and that Congress voted to give him a sword for his heroism at the Battle of Eutaw Springs. Students of Alexander Hamilton know that Pierce challenged an English debt collector, John Auldjo, to a duel while the Convention was meeting—Hamilton was Auldjo's second and worked out a settlement.

Pierce was born in 1740, probably in Virginia. Nothing is known about his early years. However, at 26 he was a captain in the First Continental Artillery, and served with distinction throughout the Revolution. Either before the war began, or in 1782 and 1783, he may have studied at the College of William and Mary. By 1783 he was in Georgia as a planter and merchant, and in 1785 he married Charlotte Fenwick, by whom he probably had two children. He was an active member of the Georgia Society of the Cincinnati and wrote frequently to several of the men with whom he had served in the army. His career as a merchant was disasterous.

Pierce made no significant contribution either in Congress or to Convention, although his character sketches of fellow Convention delegates have endeared him to historians of the Convention. By 1787, he was bankrupt. Yet, his letters reveal a warm, friendly, well-educated and perceptive man, a man perhaps more interested in the well-being of his friends and his country than himself. He died in 1789, saying, "Farewell, farewell, now dies a happy man."

Friday, June 1, 1787

Today was fair and warm with a stiff wind from the WNW.

Convention

Mr. William Houstoun of Georgia took his seat.

The Convention, meeting in the Committee of the Whole, debated on the question of a national executive and agreed to give that branch the power to effect national laws and to appoint officers who were not provided for elsewhere. Further the Committee agreed on a seven-year term for the office.

The body also accepted chairman Nathaniel Gorham's decision that, during the Convention, a divided vote of 5 state delegations "for," 4 "against," 1 "divided" was a "yes" vote. This decision set a precedent for the remainder of the Convention, and was especially important on July 16, when the same breakdown decided the critical issue of representation in Congress.

Delegates

Dr. Johnson arrived in Philadelphia at seven o'clock and lodged at Dickinson's (unidentified, but not fellow delegate John) house.

General Washington dined with John Penn, the last proprietary governor of Pennsylvania and "spent the evening at a superb entertainment at Bush-hill given by Mr. (William) Hamilton—at which there were more than a hundred guests." He also wrote to François Claude Amour, Marquis de Boille, to congratulate

him on being elected to the Society of Cincinnati.

George Mason of Virginia wrote at length to his son concerning plastering, a legal case, the progress of the Convention, and the delegates. He added a postscript which should endear him to the disorganized among us. He asked his son to send a couple of documents. He thought one was "among the loose Papers in the right hand division of the second Drawer in my desk . . ." and that the other was "among the loose Papers in one of the dining Room windows; . . ."

New York delegate Robert Yates wrote his uncle, states' rights extremist and member of Congress Abraham Yates, that Convention debates were secret but he was keeping notes of the debate.

David Brearley, William Churchill Houston, and William Paterson of New Jersey petitioned the state legislature to authorize payment for their share of Convention expenses, including messenger, doorkeeper and stationery costs. They estimated New Jersey's share would be five shillings per day for two or three months.

George Mason

GEORGE MASON, a sixty-two-year-old from Virginia, was one of the leading statesmen and constitutionalists at the Philadelphia Convention. Ten when his father died, Mason was raised by his mother, with his uncle John Mercer, as guardian. Mason's first cousin, John Francis Mercer, served as member of Maryland's delegation to the Convention.

George Mason personally owned several hundred slaves, but in the Convention spoke ardently against slavery and voted against all proposals that would benefit the slave trade.

When George Mason came of age he inherited 5,000 acres of land from his father's estate. Shortly thereafter he married Anne Eilbeck who bore him nine children. Anne died in 1773 leaving George Mason with several children. In 1780 he married Sarah Brent.

In 1775 Mason wrote the Declaration of Rights, a major part of Virginia's first constitution and a key source for Jefferson when drafting the Declaration of Independence. During the rest of the decade Mason worked with Jefferson and Wythe to build the new government of Virginia. His disgust with public affairs caused him to retire in 1780. He emerged from retirement to attend the Mount Vernon Conference in 1785. At the Philadelphia Convention Mason was among the five most frequent speakers. Of consuming interest to him was the guarantee of individual rights for the people. Despite arguments that those rights were implied, Mason refused to sign the Constitution and campaigned actively against its ratification in Virginia. The Bill of Rights—the first ten amendments to the Constitution—are a tribute to Mason's position, and, indeed, a vindication. Mason died in 1792, survived by his second wife, Sarah.

Saturday, June 2, 1787

The day dawned cloudy with rain and cold toward evening.

Convention

William Samuel Johnson of Connecticut, Daniel of St. Thomas Jenifer of Maryland and John Lansing, Jr., of New York took their seats.

Resolved into a Committee of the Whole, the delegates debated on the executive. Wilson (PA) moved to divide the states into districts and have the people (that is, adult white males) in each district elect electors who in turn would elect the president. Gerry (MA), like Wilson, opposed election by the national legislature but thought Wilson's plan was too innovative. Williamson (NC) couldn't understand why selecting electors to choose the executive was an advantage over having the state legislatures choose. Wilson's motion lost, 8 states to 2 (PA and MD). The Committee then agreed to have the executive chosen by the national legislature for a term of seven years, and went on to discuss executive pay, removal from office, eligibility for a second term, and whether the executive should be one man or a committee.

Arch Street and Second was the location of Dennison's (sign of St. George) where Dr. Johnson dined.

The Second Presbyterian Church was located at Arch and Third Streets.

Delegates

Dr. Johnson made some visits in the morning, then took his seat in the Convention. He dined at Dennison's (the sign of St. George at Second and Arch Streets) and in the evening took lodgings at City Tavern. Dennison's bill and his other daily expenses came to 15 shillings Pennsylvania lawful money.

General Washington "dined at the City Tavern with the Club and spent the evening at [his] own quarters."

A Key Decision: A Salaried President

WE can see in today's Convention activities, as we can on many other days, how quickly—often without much debate—the Convention made decisions which would later have profound consequences. For example, on this day the Convention discarded, without a discussion or vote, Franklin's motion that the executive (President of the United States) serve without pay.

This was not a hare-brained scheme proposed by a senile revolutionary. Every delegate present, even James Wilson, would agree that the political elite—those qualified by education, experience, and success—should fill the key offices of government. This political elite should be able to afford such service, they would say; in fact, every delegate present was serving without salary. Earlier, Washington had served as commander in chief for over eight years without a salary, Sherman had served in Congress for six years without salary (and was nearly broke as a consequence), and so on.

But let us suppose that Franklin's motion had been adopted. Would Washington have been willing to serve a second term? Could Jefferson or Madison, or Polk, or Lincoln, or Truman have afforded to be President? If not, would their political party, or their friends, or others provide enough money to make up for the lack of a salary?

Sunday, June 3, 1787

Cool wind from the NE with clouds and rain in the morning; in the evening, clear and cold.

Convention

The Convention was adjourned until Monday. Its delegates could look back over a week in which they had adopted rules, been presented with two differing plans for a new government, tacitly decided to restructure rather than amend the government, and reached some decisions concerning the legislature. However, the most astute among them must have been worried about Delaware's obvious determination not to give up that state's equal vote.

Delegates

General Washington dined with his fellow delegate and long-time friend George Clymer and stayed on for tea. The setting may have brought up memories: Clymer was renting the house of Dr. William Shippen the younger. Back in 1774 and 1775, Washington and his Virginia colleagues in Congress frequently visited Dr. Shippen and his wife, Alice, who was the sister of the Virginia Lees. At any event, the General stayed longer than intended and didn't finish his weekly letter of instructions to General Augustine until 11 P.M.

Connecticut nationalist Jeremiah Wadsworth wrote from Hartford to Rufus King with second thoughts about the Connecticut delegation.

I am satisfied with the appointment—except Sherman, who, I am told, is disposed to patch up the old scheme of Government. This was not my opinion of him, when we chose him: he is as cunning as the Devil, and if you attack him, you ought to know him well: he is not easily managed, but if he suspects you are trying to take him in, you may as well catch an Eel by the tail.

Rufus King

RUFUS KING, Massachusetts delegate, was born in Scarboro, MA (now part of Maine), in 1755. He graduated from Harvard in 1777 and soon thereafter entered the law firm of Theophilus Parsons in Newburyport to read law. He had a brief and uneventful military career during the Revolutionary War. Shortly after the war, he began a political career that would last for most of the remainder of his life. He was elected to the Massachusetts General Court and House of Representatives in the 1780s. He was appointed as one of Massachusetts' delegates to Congress from 1784–86. During his term in Congress, he served on a committee dealing with American territories and in this capacity he recommended that slavery should be outlawed in the Northwest Territories. His suggestion was adopted as part of the Northwest Ordinance in 1787.

Rufus King served on six of the twelve Convention committees. He had a special talent for clarifying issues and spoke frequently on the Convention floor.

While in Congress, King met and married Mary Alsop, the only daughter of a wealthy New York merchant. With this union, King's interests shifted, and not long after the Constitutional Convention he moved to New York. But, he served his state's interests well in the Convention and was one of the Federalist leaders in the ratification battle in Massachusetts. He was an eloquent orator, and made several effective speeches in the Convention. He served on the Committee of Style and was a signer.

King's political career blossomed after the Convention and his move to New York. He was one of the first United States senators elected from that state. In this office he consistently defended the Washington Administration's programs, such as Hamilton's economic plan. Partly because of his loyalty, Washington appointed him as minister to England in 1796, an office which he held until 1803 when he resigned to run as vice presidential candidate with Charles Cotesworth Pinckney. His ticket lost in 1804 and again in 1808, and after a short retirement, King returned to the Senate in 1813. He served another term in that body, returned to the New York Assembly in 1820, then in 1825 returned to England as United States ambassador. King left this post after one year due to poor health, and died in 1827 in New York.

Monday, June 4, 1787

Today was clear and cool with a strong west wind.

Convention

Resolved into a Committee of the Whole, the Convention resumed the debate on Pinckney's motion for a single executive. Wilson supported the motion. Sherman agreed, if the executive would have council of advice. Williamson asked Wilson if he meant to have a council; Wilson said no. Gerry couldn't see the advantage of a three-member executive. The Convention agreed on a single executive; 7 aye and 3 no (NY, DE, MD). The committee then considered an executive veto and agreed to give the executive a veto which could be over-ridden by two-thirds of the legislature. At the end of the day, the committee also agreed that there should be a national judiciary with a supreme tribunal and one or more inferior courts.

Delegates

Doctor Johnson spent the afternoon at Noah Webster's and had expenses of seven shillings and sixpence.

General Washington reviewed the Light Infantry, Cavalry and part of the Artillery of the City. He later dined with Gen. Mifflin and drank tea with Miss Cadwallader.

The New Jersey General Assembly considered a petition from its delegates for permission to draw on the State Treasurer to help pay the Convention staff and stationery bill. It authorized them to draw on the Treasurer for a sum not to exceed 30 pounds for this purpose.

Paying the Bills

TODAY, if Congress wants something done, it first passes legislation authorizing the action and, then (usually), appropriates money to pay for it. It does both in advance of the action. This was not the procedure in 1787.

Congress called the Convention on February 21, but it had not yet appropriated money to pay Convention expenses. Nevertheless, fifty-five delegates traveled to the Convention, hired a secretary, doorkeeper and messenger, and purchased record books, paper and so forth. Who paid for this? For delegates' salary and expenses, the answer was simple. Nobody paid their salary—they didn't get one. The Pennsylvanians, all from Philadelphia, didn't get an expense allowance either. The other eleven delegations did receive expense money—from $4 per day (New Jersey) to 40 shillings per day (Delaware)—paid by the state. Some of the states advanced expense money, others paid as soon as the delegates got home, and New Hampshire paid its delegates within a year.

Despite New Jersey's effort to help, nobody paid staff salaries and bills for office supplies and printing

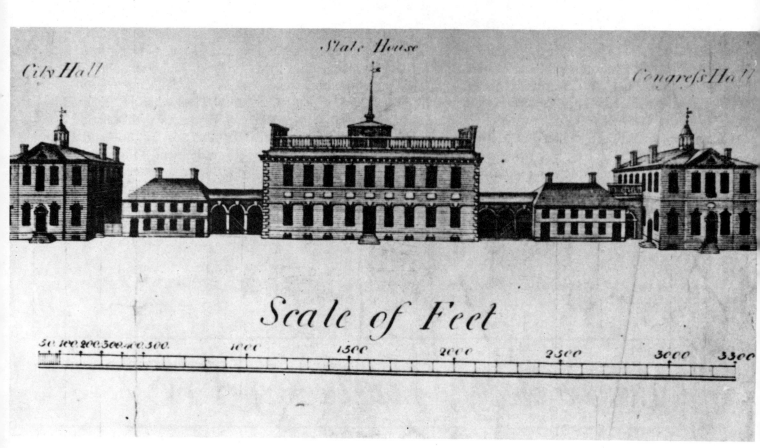

City Hall   State House   Congress Hall

Scale of Feet

50 100 200 300 400 500   1000   1500   2000   2500   3000   3300

until after the fact. The secretary, doorkeeper, messenger, and stationer waited until September 20, 1787, for their money; the printer was finally paid in March 1793. The total cost to the Federal taxpayer for getting the Constitution written was $1,586.00.

The Pennsylvania State House (as it appeared in 1794) was the destination of the fifty-five delegates who traveled to the Convention, hired a secretary, doorkeeper and messenger, as well as purchased record books and paper, before Congress had appropriated money to pay expenses.

Tuesday, June 5, 1787

After a clear and pleasant morning there was an evening shower.

Convention

Governor William Livingston of New Jersey took his seat with his state's delegation.

The Convention, meeting as a Committee of the Whole, considered the proposal that the judiciary be appointed by the national legislature. Wilson (PA) favored their appointment by the executive; he argued that intrigue, partiality and concealment would be a consequence of selection by the legislature. Rutledge (VA) was against any national court system except a single supreme court; otherwise, he felt the state courts could be used. Dr. Franklin, perhaps sensing tension, suggested the model used in Scotland—let the lawyers choose. They would choose the best of the bar to be judges in order that the largest law practices would be left to share among them. Madison and Wilson moved to leave the method of appointment open until later; the motion passed.

The delegates then agreed that the judiciary should have a long tenure and a fixed salary. They also resolved to make a provision for admitting new states to the union.

Several other proposals were taken up before the committee recessed for the day.

Delegates

Dr. Johnson (CT) was not feeling well while he attended at the State House. His expenses, including "Bark" (quinine), were six shillings and ten pence.

General Washington dined with a large company at the Robert Morrises, and spent the evening there.

Jared Ingersoll, A Prominent Attorney

INCONSPICUOUS during the Convention and the ratifying process, Jared Ingersoll is a difficult person to place within the Constitution-making process. He delivered only one speech during the Convention—on the last day—and he did not write any letters, or articles, or make any speeches during ratification.

Ingersoll was the son of one of the most famous (or infamous) loyalists during the Revolution. Jared Ingersoll, Sr., served the colonies in various posts under the crown, including judge of the Philadelphia vice-admiralty court. He remained loyal to the king and was forced out of Philadelphia during the war. His son, Jared, Jr., broke with his father and supported the revolutionary cause. He became a prominent attorney in Philadelphia, served as a member of the Continental Congress in 1780, and was active in the movement to revise the Articles of Confederation.

Ingersoll represented Pennsylvania with impressive credentials. He graduated from Yale in 1776 and studied law at the Middle Temple in the 1770s. Under the new Constitution, Ingersoll became one of the more prominent attorneys in the country. He was the attorney for Stephen Girard, a wealthy Philadelphia merchant and banker; he defended Senator (and former delegate) William Blount against impeachment charges in 1797; Ingersoll was counsel for Georgia in the case of *Chisolm vs. Georgia* which led to the 11th Amendment; and he was the first attorney to test the constitutionality of *Hylton vs. United States*.

Ingersoll later served in several Pennsylvania offices. He was considered as a candidate for vice president in 1812 and ran for a Senate seat from Pennsylvania in 1814. But he was not elected for either.

John Ingersoll appeared on the Convention record only two times. He signed the Constitution "As a recommendation, of what, all things considered, was the most eligible."

25

Wednesday, June 6, 1787

After a cloudy morning rain began about 11 A.M. and continued all day.

Convention

On the motion of Pinckney and Rutledge of South Carolina the Convention in Committee of the Whole considered having the state legislatures instead of the people elect the lower house. Gerry (MA), Wilson (PA), Mason (VA), Madison (VA), Dickinson (DE), Read (DE) and Pierce (SC) opposed; Sherman (SC) and General Pinckney (SC) supported it. Gerry didn't like popular election because in Massachusetts "the worst men get into the legislature," but, he admitted, one house had to be so elected. He hoped the other house would be filled with men of merit. Sherman wanted the states to retain most of their authority and, thus, saw this motion as helpful. Dickinson felt one house had to be elected by the people but the other should be elected by the state legislature. Read went further. "Too much attachment is betrayed to the state governments . . . A national government must soon of necessity swallow all of them up . . . The Confederation was founded on temporary principles. It cannot last; it cannot be amended; if we do not establish a good Government on new principles, we must either go to ruin, or have the work to do over again . . ." The motion lost; Connecticut, New Jersey and South Carolina, aye; the other eight, no.

Delegates

Dr. Johnson (CT) spent the day in Convention and dining at Dr. Franklin's.

General Washington also dined at Dr. Franklin's, drank tea there, then went home and wrote letters to France. One of them was a rueful letter to Lafayette.

You will I dare say, be surprised, My dear Marquis, to receive a letter from me at this place [Philadelphia], you will probably be more so, when you hear I am again brought, contrary to my public declaration, and intention, on a public theatre. Such is the vicissitude of human affairs, and such the frailty of human nature that no man I conceive can well answer for resolutions he enters into.

Madison wrote to Thomas Jefferson and William Short reporting in general terms on the Convention and who was attending. Governor Randolph (VA) wrote Acting Governor Beverly Randolph, asking him to deliver thirty pounds to Mrs. Randolph, who was about to leave for Philadelphia.

Nathan Dane wrote from New York to Nathaniel Gorham (MA), observing that although he was glad to hear of the determination to divide the powers of Government into distinct and independent hands, ". . . what hands to lodge the Legislative and executive powers so as to collect in the federal Government the greatest strength and stability, and general confidence, is a work, I think, the Convention will find of vast consideration." Dane was correct in this.

William Livingston

WILLIAM LIVINGSTON was the seventh child born to Philip and Catherine Livingston of Albany, NY. Upon graduation from Yale in 1741, he began the study of law with the liberal James Alexander. In 1745, before the completion of his legal studies, he married Susanna French by whom he had thirteen children. He began to champion popular causes and to oppose the established order. In 1751 he fought the founding of King's College because it would increase the influence and power of the Anglican Church in New York. His appeal served to strengthen the liberal party, and by 1760, Livingston was playing a major role in colonial politics. By the end of that decade, however, his attempts to reconcile the street mobs to the leadership of the wealthy moderates cost him his political power in New York.

In 1772 Livingston retired to his country estate, Liberty Hall, in Elizabethtown, NJ, but ended his retirement almost immediately, quickly plunging into the political life of that colony. Livingston served as delegate from New Jersey to the First Continental Congress where he joined his son-in-law John Jay in drafting an address to the American people.

He continued his work during the Second Continental Congress, and in 1776 the New Jersey legislature elected him first governor of the state, a position he continued in until his death in 1790. In 1787,

Livingston traveled to Philadelphia to take his seat as a member of the New Jersey delegation to the Federal Convention where he worked for compromise and signed the Constitution. He thereafter exerted his influence and helped to produce the speed and unanimity with which the New Jersey ratifying convention adopted the Constitution.

Livingston read and spoke Dutch fluently, as his mother was Dutch. He liked to pun, and several of his letters give delightful examples of this trait. He saw himself as a plain and unassuming individual as a

William Livingston is said to have selected the members of the New Jersey delegation. He was chairman of the Committees on Navigation Acts and the Slave Trade and on State Debts and Militia.

description of him by a French diplomat indicates: "You may have an idea of this respectable man, who is at once a writer, a governor, and a ploughman, on learning that he takes pride in calling himself a New Jersey farmer."

Thursday, June 7, 1787

The day was cool and rainy.

Convention

"The Clause providing for the appointment of the 2d branch of the national Legislature, having lain blank since the last vote on the mode of electing it, to wit, by the 1st branch," Mr. Dickinson now moved, "that the members of the 2d. branch ought to be chosen by the individual [state] legislatures." Sherman seconded this motion.

James Wilson countered by proposing that the people elect the Senate and a lively debate ensued. Certainly Madison, and probably most other delegates, realized that election of Senators by the states ensured a larger role for the states in the new government than the nationalists wanted them to have, and it tended to work against proportional representation in the Senate. After a lengthy debate, a motion to consider Wilson's motion lost: ten states against, Pennsylvania for. Dickinson's motion was then approved unanimously.

Delegates

Dr. Johnson (CT) dined at Mr. Clymers' (PA) and visited the Binghams. His daily expenses were seven shillings six pence.

General Washington dined with a club of Convention members at the Indian Queen and spent the evening in his lodgings at the home of Robert and Mary Morris.

John Rutledge (SC) wrote to Jefferson in Paris to introduce his oldest son, who would present the letter in person.

The New Jersey legislature resolved to appoint Jonathon Dayton "a commissioner on the Part of this State" to attend the federal Convention. Dayton wrote David Brearley to announce his appointment.

Jonathan Dayton

JONATHAN DAYTON, the youngest of the delegates, was born on October 16, 1760, in Elizabethtown, NJ. His father was a militia veteran and storekeeper named Elias Dayton. Jonathan Dayton graduated from Princeton in 1776 (fellow delegate William Richardson Davis was a classmate), and promptly joined the 3d New Jersey Regiment, commanded by his father, as an ensign and paymaster. Thereafter, he was promoted to lieutenant, then captain, serving at Brandywine, Germantown, Valley Forge, and Yorktown.

Upon his discharge, Dayton was admitted to the bar and became active as a lawyer and business man. He was elected to the New Jersey Assembly in 1786 and was serving in that body when he was elected a delegate to the Convention.

During the Convention he spoke frequently for one so young and relatively inexperienced. He supported the small states' position on representation, opposing proportional representation in the House until after the Connecticut Compromise, and thereafter watched to safeguard the prerogative of the Senate. Otherwise, he was a moderate nationalist who opposed state payment of Senators, supported a motion to have only free inhabitants represented in the House, and favored reasonable Federal control over state militia.

Jonathan Dayton opposed slavery and fought for the small states' demand for equal representation.

Friday, June 8, 1787

Convention

The Convention meeting as a Committee of the Whole reconsidered the provision giving the national legislature a veto over state laws which were "contrary to the articles of Union, or Treaties with foreign nations." Charles Pinckney (SC), seconded by James Madison (VA), moved to strike the qualifying clause and thus give the legislature power to veto *any* state law.

Madison (VA), Wilson (PA) and Dickinson (DE) spoke in support of the motion. Gerry (MA) and Sherman (CT) thought it went too far, although Gerry thought Congress should have an exclusive right to issue paper money. Williamson (NC), Bedford (DE) and Butler (SC) vehemently opposed the motion; Bedford because he viewed it as a further attack on the small states, Butler because he viewed it as against the interests of the more distant states. The motion was defeated: 3 aye (MA, PA, VA), 7 no, 1 (DE) divided.

Delegates

Dr. Johnson (CT) dined at home (City Tavern), and had expenses of 8 shillings. He also paid Mr. Sherman 18 pounds 12 shillings 7½ pence.

After attending the party at the Morris' yesterday, General Washington dined, drank tea and spent the evening at his lodgings.

General Charles C. Pinckney (SC) bought two six-year-old bay geldings from Jacob Hiltzheimer. He paid 55 pounds a piece for them.

William Few observed his thirty-ninth birthday.

William Few

WILLIAM FEW who observed his thirty-ninth birthday two hundred years ago was one of the least active members of the Convention. He presented his credentials on May 25, was elected to the Committee of Eleven on preventing discrimination between ports in trade regulations on August 25, signed the document on September 17, and in between is absent from extant records.

He is, however, one of the more interesting delegates and a typical American success story very much like Jackson and Lincoln.

Few was born on a tobacco farm in Hartford County, Maryland, in 1748. His father, having lost two or three consecutive crops to frost, moved to Orange County, North Carolina, in 1758 and Few was put to work on the frontier farm. In 1760 a schoolmaster appeared. Earlier, before the family left Maryland, Few had been sent to a schoolmaster, and in his words, "I detested the man, the school, and the books, and spent six or eight months at that school in terror and anxiety, with very little benefit." He had better luck with the new master from whom he recovered the one year of schooling he ever had.

In 1764, the family moved to a farm near Hillsboro, which was a county seat complete with a church, court house, jail, and a couple of lawyers. Few learned a lot from listening to trials and reading the few books his family could buy or borrow—the Bible, Tillotson's *Sermons,* Barclay's *Apology,* Dyche's *Dictionary,* and *The Spectator.*

Within five or six years of the move to Hillsboro, Few's father had legal problems and moved to Georgia, leaving William to settle affairs in North Carolina. He moved to Georgia himself in 1776 and was promptly elected to the state constitutional convention. Thereafter, he served in various military and political capacities in Georgia and was twice a member of the Congress before being elected a delegate to the Convention. In 1786, while in New York to attend Congress, he met, courted and married Catherine Nicholson, who seems to have stayed in New York during Few's service in the Convention.

William Few made no concrete contribution to the Convention and was irregular in his attendance.

Saturday, June 9, 1787

The morning dawned clear and fine, but the day became cloudy toward noon and remained cloudy all afternoon.

Convention

The Pennsylvania *Evening Herald* printed a story about the Convention which was almost entirely false:

> *We are informed that the Federal Convention, among other things has resolved that Rhode Island should be considered as having virtually withdrawn herself from the union, and that the right of emitting paper money by the states jointly or severally, ought to be abrogated. It is proposed in the first case, that for the proportion of the federal debt now due from Rhode Island, she shall be held, and, if gentler means will not avail, she shall be compelled to be responsible; but upon no account shall she be restored to her station in the Union. And in the other case, it is proposed to establish a mint for the receipt of Bullion, from which the states are to draw coin, in proportion to their respective contributions. The Convention has sent to New York for the last return of the accounts between the individual states and the confederated body.*

Mr. Luther Martin (MD) appeared and took his seat.

Mr. Gerry (MA) moved to reconsider the method of electing the Executive, and to have the Executive elected by the governors of the states with their votes weighed in proportion to the vote of their state in the Senate. Randolph argued strongly against this motion and it lost: ten states no, Delaware divided. Mr. Paterson (NJ) then moved to resume consideration of the clause concerning suffrage in the National Legislature. Brearley (NJ) seconded in a speech which bristled with arguments about the injustice of proportional representation. Paterson followed Brearley with still more argument. Wilson (PA) and Williamson (NC) then spoke in favor of proportional representation. At that point, at Paterson's request, the vote was postponed until Monday.

Delegates

Dr. Johnson (CT) paid Edward Moyston, the proprietor of City Tavern, 3 pounds, 7 shillings and 6 pence for his room for the week and dined with William White who had recently returned from England where he was consecrated a Bishop in the Protestant Episcopal Church.

General Washington dined with a club of his fellow delegates at City Tavern and drank tea and visited at Mr. Powels until 10 P.M. He also wrote Governor George Clinton of New York he would arrange to pay Clinton the 365 pounds, 6 shillings balance he owed him for land he purchased in 1782.

Dr. Franklin wrote to Granvill Sharp, a British anti-slavery leader and enclosed the constitution of the Pennsylvania Society for Promoting the Abolition of Slavery and the Relief of Free Negroes.

Luther Martin

IT was only fitting that the Maryland delegate, Luther Martin, should take his seat on the day when the small states launched their attack on proportional representation. Luther Martin is today only known for his extreme states' rights stand and the two-day speech on the subject which exhausted his fellow delegates and their patience. He was actually more constructive during the Convention.

Born in the Raritan Valley of northern New Jersey in 1744 (or 1748), Martin graduated from Princeton in 1766 in the same class as Oliver Ellsworth and received his MA in 1769. After teaching for several years on the Eastern Shore of Maryland and Virginia, he was admitted to the Virginia bar in 1771. Within two years he moved to Somerset County, Maryland. He was active on the committees of the early Revolution and, in 1778, was named Maryland's Attorney General. In 1783 he married the daughter of the noted frontiersman Thomas Cresap, and by 1787 they had three daughters. By that time, he had also acquired a reputation for excessive drinking.

In the Convention, Martin stood with the most ardent supporters of states' rights. He opposed a bicameral national legislature, proportional representation and wanted the states to decide how to choose members of the Federal lower house. He was against letting Congress veto state laws and allowing the Federal government to suppress rebellions within a state. He wanted the executive chosen by electors appointed by the state legislators, opposed a Federal court system except for a Supreme Court, wanted Senate votes cast by state, supported requiring a two-thirds vote in Congress for duties or acts regulating commerce, wanted a constitutional limit on the size of the Federal army in peacetime, and wanted ratification to be by unanimous vote of the state legislatures.

As a member of the Committee on Representation, Martin supported the Connecticut Compromise. He didn't like it but was willing to try it rather than do nothing. He was the delegate who moved to include the provision known today as the Supremacy Clause. Finally, even though he owned six slaves, Martin proposed a tax on slave imports, noting with regard to the provision on the slave trade that "it was inconsistent with the principles of the revolution and dishonorable to the American character to have such a feature in the Constitution." He opposed ratification of the Constitution.

Luther Martin fought for states' rights, but also supported the Supremacy Clause and wanted to exclude judges from the President's veto.

Sunday, June 10, 1787

The day was clear and pleasant, and warmer than recent days.

Convention

The Convention was in recess and its members were, perhaps, looking back at its second week of work. Progress had been made. On Monday, it had agreed to a single executive who would have a veto subject to override by a two-thirds majority, and to a national supreme court, although it was vacillating on whether lesser Federal courts were necessary. Later, it had agreed to judicial tenure during good behavior and to admit new states. It had agreed to have the state legislatures elect the Senate and had rejected the pro-

posal to extend the Federal veto to all state laws except those contrary to the Constitution. Probably only a few delegates had noticed in Saturday's debate about the upper house of the national legislature the small states' insistence on an equal vote in the legislature—an issue which threatened the very existence of the Convention.

Delegates

General Washington breakfasted with former Mayor Samuel Powel and then rode with him to Bartram's garden. From there, they rode to a farm to see the effect of using lime in agriculture. They then visited Powel's farm, after which the General went to the Hills and dined with Mr. and Mrs. Morris. Returning to the city after dark, he wrote his weekly letter of instructions to George Augustine at Mt. Vernon. Seeing no end to his stay in Philadelphia, he asked for the "Blew Coat with the Cremson collar and one of those made of the Cloth sent me by the Spanish Minister, to wit that without lapels and lined with white silk, . . ."

James Madison wrote James Monroe apologizing for not writing earlier and citing the Convention's secrecy rule.

William Churchill Houston

WILLIAM CHURCHILL HOUSTON, one of the sixteen delegates who did not sign the new Constitution, is unknown today, even to Princeton alumni. Yet he had had a relatively distinguished career.

Born in the Sumter district of South Carolina [some sources say Cabarrus County, North Carolina] sometime in 1746, Houston entered the College of New Jersey, Princeton today. He was immediately appointed a teacher in the college grammar school; after he graduated in 1768, he served as master of the grammar school (1768–69), tutor (1769–71), professor of mathematics and natural philosophy (1771–83), librarian (1770–86) and treasurer (1779–83). In 1775 he was appointed deputy secretary of the Continental Congress, serving until September 1777. In 1777–1779 he served in the New Jersey legislature, and from 1779–85 as a delegate to Congress. In 1781 he was admitted to the bar, moved to Trenton, and was appointed clerk of the New Jersey Supreme Court, an office he held until his death. He also served as a commissioner in the Connecticut/Pennsylvania boundary dispute, as a delegate to Congress again (1784–85), as Receiver of Continental taxes for New Jersey (1782–85) and as a delegate to the Annapolis Convention of 1786, forerunner of the Philadelphia Convention. In between, he found time to marry Jane Smith, by whom he had five children.

Houston appears once in the records of the Constitutional Convention on May 25, when he presented his credentials. Thereafter, while he signed a letter asking the state assembly to authorize a share of Convention expense, and signed the letter transmitting the Constitution to the state, the record does not indicate his presence. Either he was absent or seconded no motions and made no speeches or remarks.

While Houston was probably already suffering from the tuberculosis from which he died in August of 1788, he seems to have been present and fulfilling an important role at least through June, and perhaps thereafter. In the act authorizing attendance at the Convention, New Jersey set a quorum of its five-member delegation at three. Jonathan Dayton did not appear in the Convention until July 21. Prior to that time, the absence of any two of the four other delegates would have deprived New Jersey of its vote. Since Brearley, Livingston and Paterson were almost certainly absent on at least a few occasions, Houston must have been present to preserve the New Jersey quorum.

The Hills was a mansion in the country owned by Robert Morris. General Washington rode out into the country on Sunday, June 10, and had dinner with the Morrises.

The day was very pleasant, clear and warm.

Convention

Abraham Baldwin of Georgia appeared and took his seat. The Committee of the Whole reconsidered the rule of suffrage in the legislature. Sherman (CT) moved that the legislature be proportional in the first house, and by state (each state one vote) in the Senate. Rutledge and Butler wanted representation based on how much money each state contributed. After extensive and heated debate, the committee decided that representation should be based on the free population plus three-fifths of "all others," and, finally, that it should be the same in both houses. Sherman's motion that each state have an equal vote in the Senate was defeated.

The bedroom of General Washington was a quiet retreat where he wrote numerous letters and sent instructions for the operation of his plantation, Mount Vernon.

Delegates

General Washington dined, drank tea and spent the evening in his own room, and must have found it a welcome break!

Elbridge Gerry (MA) wrote to James Monroe to report that the "Convention was at work, that secrecy was enjoined on the delegates and that . . . unless a system of government is adopted by Compact, Force I expect will plant the Standard, . . ."

The Reverend James Madison wrote from Virginia to thank his cousin James for a copy of John Adams' *Defence of the Constitutions.* The Reverend then attacked Adams' political theories, many of which cousin James was working to get included in the proposed new government.

David Brearley of New Jersey observed his forty-second birthday.

David Brearley

DAVID BREARLEY was born on Spring Grove Farm in Mercer County, New Jersey. He attended but did not graduate from the College of New Jersey. He was licensed as an attorney on April 15, 1767, and began practice in Allentown, New Jersey. At about this time he married Elizabeth Mullens, with whom he had at least one son and three daughters. In 1771, he was already active in politics.

At the outbreak of the Revolution he was reportedly commissioned as a captain in the New Jersey Line (October 28, 1775) and in 1776 was chosen to be a member of the state Constitutional Convention.

Promoted to lt. colonel in November 1776, he served until August, 1779, when he resigned to accept appointment as chief justice of New Jersey. After his first wife died in 1783, he married thirty-two-year-old Elizabeth Higbee, with whom he had three sons by 1787. An active Episcopalian, he was a deputy to that church's general convention of 1785, and represented St. Michael's Church, Trenton, in the diocesan convention of 1785. In 1787 he was vice president of the New Jersey Society of Cincinnati and grand master of the state's Masonic Order. He was a judge in the boundary dispute between Pennsylvania and New Jersey—William Samuel Johnson and James Wilson argued the case before him.

William Pierce's impression of Brearley may have been that of most delegates: ". . . a man of good rather than of brilliant parts . . . and . . . very much in the esteem of the people. As an orator he has little to boast of, but as a man he has every virtue to recommend him."

Tuesday, June 12, 1787

Convention

The Convention meeting in a Committee of the Whole had a busy day. The day before it had solved the problem of presentation in Congress—both houses were to be elected on the basis of their population. Today it approved the ratification process—the conventions were to be elected by the people. Also today agreement was reached on a three-year term for members of the house; a fixed salary for legislators (until Franklin objected, the salary had been described as "fixed and liberal,") drawn from the Federal Treasury; and an age restriction of thirty years for Senators.

Delegates

Dr. Johnson dined at home, bought four shillings and six pence worth of snuff, and had other expenses of seven shillings and six pence.

General Washington dined with the Morrises and attended a benefit concert for Alexander Reinagle at City Tavern.

Richard Dobbs Spaight wrote to John Gray Blount to inform him that the North Carolina delegates had asked Governor Caswell for another advance of two months salary and to ask Blount to "receive, exchange and remit the money to me."

The Conventional Dinner

MOST delegates ate their dinner—the main meal—around two or three o'clock. Some ate at local inns. The Indian Queen, a block away from the State House, was a favorite spot. Others particularly favored the City Tavern. During the Convention the City Tavern was as much a center for "club" dining as it had been in 1776 when independence was the issue.

"Clubs" offered a fixed price and the meals were eaten family style. Serving dishes and platters were passed around the table. Most of the delegates received invitations to attend dinner with friends.

These dinners were a slightly restrained version of the finest home cooking, offering fish, soup, two or three meats, vegetables, and a variety of desserts. Rock fish (sea bass), veal, and beef were likely to appear in

The Indian Queen, a block away from the State House, was frequented by Convention delegates. Stables were located behind the inn where it adjoined the property of Benjamin Franklin.

INDIAN QUEEN HOTEL

one guise or another. Ann Warder described a "usual" dinner she enjoyed: "chickens, ducks, mock turtle, ham [and] plenty of vegetables." After this simple meal, a dessert course of pastries, floating island and fruit was often set out. The simplest family dinners were "a rump of beef, apple pie and vegetables."

When the Convention closed on September 17, someone recorded that, "the members adjourned to the City Tavern, dined together and took a cordial leave of each other." While this was surely a memorable meal, it could never equal the entertainment given General Washington and many delegates two days earlier by the First Troop Philadelphia Cavalry. In that meal, the Tavern served "55 Gentlemans Dinners & Fruit" with the necessary "Rellishes, Olives etc." With dinner, the celebrants drank fifty-four bottles of madeira and sixty of claret; along with fifty bottles of assorted "Old Stock," porter, beer, cider, and seven large bowls of potent punch. The party must have gotten a little out-of-hand, for the innkeeper added a breakage fee of nearly two percent to this ninety pounds extravaganza.

Wednesday, June 13, 1787

The day was fair and warm; brewer Thomas Morris noted that it was 80° at noon.

Convention

Today, the Convention meeting as a Committee of the Whole gave the federal judiciary jurisdiction in cases concerning the national revenue, impeachment of federal officers, and questions involving the national peace and harmony. The Committee decided that the Senate would appoint federal judges, defeated a proposal to prohibit the Senate from originating money bills, and rose to report to the Convention.

Delegates

Dr. Johnson (CT) dined with fellow delegate Jared Ingersoll (PA), bought gloves for seven shilling and six pence, and had daily expenses of six shillings and three pence.

General Washington dined at George Clymer's (PA), drank tea there, then spent the evening across the street at the Bingham's.

Dr. Franklin left the Convention in time to meet with the Supreme Executive Council, the judges of the Supreme Court and the attorney general about some resolutions of a recent meeting in Easton, Pennsylvania.

James Madison wrote his brother Ambrose. He wrote that he was disappointed to receive only eight hogsheads of tobacco instead of the ten he'd asked for, and, whereas, the best tobacco had sold as high as forty-five shillings, his was being sold for forty-two shillings and six pence. He thought the session of the Convention would be of considerable length.

The Report of the Committee of the Whole

HAD today's Committee of the Whole report been accepted without change, our Constitution would provide:

1. A national legislature of two houses. The members of the first House would be elected by the people for a term of three years, paid a fixed salary from the National treasury, and ineligible for any other state or Federal office during their term. Members of the second House would be required to be at least 30 years old, elected for seven year terms by the states legislature, receive fixed salaries and be ineligible for other offices.

2. That the national legislature could "legislate in all cases to which the separate states are incompetent, or in which harmony of the U. S. may be interrupted by the exercise of individual legislation."

3. That Congress could veto state laws which in its opinion violated the Constitution or any treaties

made by the Federal government.

4. Representation in both houses based on population.

5. A national Executive of one person, chosen by Congress for a seven year term, ineligible for re-election and removeable on impeachment, and required to execute national laws.

6. An executive veto, subject to a two-thirds override.

James Madison, although a conscientious contributor to the Convention, was also concerned with the price he was receiving for his tobacco.

7. A national judiciary of one supreme tribunal and other tribunals as Congress may provide. Judges elected by the Senate to serve during good behavior at a fixed salary not to be increased or diminished during their term.

8. Provision should be made for admission of new states "with the consent of a number of voices in Congress less than the whole," for a transition from the Articles to the new government, for a guarantee of a republican form of government in each state, for submission of the new Constitution for ratification to conventions and for amending the new government when necessary.

Several changes would be made in the months ahead. How many of them can you identify?

Thursday, June 14, 1787

Convention

According to Madison:

> *Mr. Patterson, observed to the convention that it was the wish of several deputations, particularly that of New Jersey, that further time might be allowed them to contemplate the plan reported from the Committee of the Whole, and to digest one purely federal, and contradistinguished from the reported plan. He said they hoped to have such a one ready by tomorrow to be laid before the Convention: and the Convention adjourned that leisure might be given for the purpose.*

The small states were about to rebel.

Delegates

General Washington dined at Major Moore's (probably Major Thomas Moore) and spent the evening at his lodgings.

Dr. Johnson (CT) dined at home, then walked around the city looking for lodgings somewhat less expensive than City Tavern.

Dr. Franklin attended a meeting of the Supreme Executive Council in the Council's Chamber in the State House. Later, Noah Webster and Mr. Greenleaf called on him.

North Carolina's William R. Davie wrote to Mrs. Mary Edwards in New York to discuss a legal case in which he was her attorney. He reported that the Jones family, into which he had married, were well when he left North Carolina.

The Virginia Plan

UNTIL NOW the Convention had been considering the plan for a government introduced on May 29 by Governor Randolph of Virginia—the so-called "Virginia" or "Randolph" plan. In a series of fifteen resolutions, this plan proposed a government consisting of a legislative, executive and judiciary. The legislature would have two houses. In both houses the vote of each state would be proportioned to its population or contribution to the federal treasury; for example, Virginia would have ten votes to Delaware's one. The lower house would be elected by the people and would in turn elect the second upper house. The legislature would have the same powers of the existing Continental Congress plus that of legislating "in all cases to which the separate states are incompetent," and the power to veto state laws.

The executive would be chosen by the Congress for a fixed term and inelligible for a second term. With "a convenient number" of the judiciary, the executive would have a veto, subject to an override by more than half of each house of the legislature. The judiciary would consist of one Supreme Court and inferior courts. Judges would be chosen by Congress and serve during good behavior.

The Virginia Plan also laid the groundwork for state governments. Each state would be guaranteed a republican form of government and territorial integrity, but state officers would be bound by oath to support the Constitution. Ratification of the Constitution would be by special conventions in each state.

Since the Virginia Plan so closely parallels the the-

The Pennsylvania State House (1778 view) was the meeting place of the Constitutional Convention. The state officers after 1787 were bound by oath to support the Constitution, which guaranteed each state a republican form of government and territorial integrity.

ory of government that James Madison held, he almost certainly prepared it. The plan was then discussed with the Virginia delegation, and probably with a sympathetic South Carolinian, Charles Pinckney, and possibly Pennsylvanians, Thomas Fitzsimons and Robert Morris. On May 28, the head of the Virginia delegation, Governor Edmund Randolph, presented it. Its acceptance as the vehicle for organizing the Convention's work was of incalculable significance in shaping the content of the Constitution.

Friday, June 15, 1787

Convention

Robert Yates' (NY) notes on the Convention for today are more complete than Madison's. The following is his description of today's activities:

Met pursuant to adjournment. Present 11 states. Mr. Patterson, pursuant to his intentions as mentioned yesterday, read a set of resolves as the basis of amendment to the confederation.

He observed that no government could be energetic on paper only, which was no more than straw—that the remark applied to the one as well as to the other system, and is therefore of opinion that there must be a small standing force to give every government weight.

Mr. Madison moved for the report of the committee, and the question may then come on whether the convention will postpone it in order to take into consideration the system now offered.

Mr. Lansing is of the opinion that the two systems are fairly contrasted. The one now offered is on the basis of amending the federal government, and the other to be reported as a national government, on propositions which exclude the propriety of amendment. Considering therefore its importance and that justice may be done to its weighty consideration, he is for postponing it a day.

Col. Hamilton cannot say he is in sentiment with either plan—supposes both might again be considered as federal plans, and by this means they will be fairly in committee, and be contrasted so as to make a comparative estimate of the two.

Thereupon it was agreed, that the report be postponed, and that the house will resolve itself into a committee of the whole, to take into consideration both propositions tomorrow.

Then the convention adjourned to tomorrow morning.

William Paterson introduced the plan that would have given equal representation to each state in a unicameral Congress, and fought against proportional representation in Congress.

Delegates

General Washington dined and drank tea at Mayor Powel's. He wrote a note to George Augustine to acknowledge receipt of his letters of June 10 and 11, and asked him "to let your Aunt [Martha Washington] know that the buckles and knives mentioned as having been sent, were not forwarded." He added that letters mailed from Alexandria on Tuesday mornings did not get to Philadelphia until Thursday evening (about the same as 1987). He also added a request to have an umbrella sent when the two coats he had asked for earlier are sent.

Dr. Franklin met with the Supreme Executive Council.

William Blount (NC) still in New York wrote his brother John Gray telling him that Major Pierce (SC) returned to New York last night from the Convention and thought it would last until mid-October. "I have not learned from him what in particular is done but he says in general terms very little is done and nothing definitive, indeed I suppose he would not like to descend to particulars even to me who am a member . . ." He added that he would leave with Hawkins and Pierce for Philadelphia on the 18th.

William Paterson

WILLIAM PATERSON celebrated his forty-second birthday on Christmas Eve 1787 at his plantation in Raritan, NJ. Paterson, who had been born in County Antrim, Ireland, emigrated with his parents in 1747 at the age of two. (Some sources contend that he was born during the voyage over to America.) He entered the College of New Jersey when he was fourteen or fifteen, and received his AB degree in 1763, and his MA in 1766. He then studied law under Richard Stockton.

Paterson thought often of his humble background, his father being a tin peddler and a shopkeeper. His family prospered, but he did not like the fact that his father's general store was across the road from the college's Nassau Hall where he and his classmates graduated. Paterson cultivated a pleasing disposition marked by a good sense of humor, kindness, and affection that appealed to many.

In 1779, he married Cornelia Bell, a member of a prestigious family in Perth Amboy. His marriage suffered from the political turmoil of the day because is father-in-law John Bell harbored strong British sentiments, while Paterson participated actively for the colonial cause and served on the New Jersey Provincial Congress. After the wedding Mr. Bell broke off communications with his daughter.

The couple had two children, however four days after the birth of her son in 1783, Cornelia died. Paterson remained at the Raritan plantation following her death, and resumed his law practice. In 1785 he married Euphemia White, the daughter of Judge White in whose house he had been originally married.

Paterson continued to pursue an active role in politics and was selected to attend the Federal Convention. With David Brearly and William Churchill Houston of New Jersey, he gathered with various state delegates, many of whom were Paterson's fellow college alumni. They listened to Edmund Randolph's Virginia Plan which outlined a national government divided into three distinct branches, and called for proportional representation of the bicameral legislature. Paterson feared the "disparity of votes" that proportional representation would incur, and the ambition of the large states to take advantage of such a system at the expense of the small states.

On June 15th, Paterson presented his New Jersey Plan and stated clearly his intention to revise the Articles of Confederation as Congress proposed originally. His plan provided for a single house legislature to be elected by the state legislatures. The laws were in the hands of the state except those concerning the regulation of commerce, levying duties and providing the means of war. It gave a plural executive the power to compel the states by force and allowed the majority of the states to remove the executive.

The New Jersey Plan did not fair well. James Wilson delivered incisive remarks against it and James Madison dealt it a final blow on June 19th. Parts of the plan, though were lodged in the minds of the delegates. The provision for equal representation in the Senate resurfaced during the Great Compromise. Paterson fought vehemently in support of the clause and insisted that small states would not assent to the compromise unless they adopted it. After considerable debate and haranging, the delegates accepted the provision.

Saturday, June 16, 1787

Today was cooler with an east wind and noon temperature of 76°.

Convention

The Convention resolved itself into a Committee of the Whole to consider the Virginia and New Jersey plans. Lansing (NY) called for reading the first resolution of each plan. New Jersey's plan sustains state sovereignty, Virginia's destroys it. He gave several reasons for preferring the New Jersey plan; so did Paterson (NJ). Both stressed that the New Jersey plan was compatible with the delegates' instructions and with the wishes of the people.

James Wilson (PA) responded with a point-by-point comparison of the two plans and arguments in favor of the Virginia plan. Charles Pinckney (SC) cynically but presciently observed that "the whole comes to this, . . . give New Jersey an equal vote, and she will dismiss her scruples, and concur in the national system." The debate which would take up the rest of June had begun.

Delegates

General Washington dined with "the club" at the City Tavern and drank tea at Doctor William Shippen's with Mrs. Livingston's party. Mrs. Livingston was Dr. Shippen's daughter Ann Home, the estranged wife of Robert R. Livingston's son Henry Beckman Livingston.

Dr. Johnson again dined at City Tavern and went out walking to find cheaper lodgings. His expenses were nine shillings.

Rufus King wrote to Nathan Dane in New York indicating that he was prohibited from writing about the Convention, even to obtain Dane's views on points of consequence.

George Wythe wrote Governor Randolph from Williamsburg. His wife was very ill, and he felt compelled to resign from the delegation to be with her.

Gouverneur Morris wrote from "Morrisania," his New York City estate, where he had been for three weeks, to thank Jeremiah Wadsworth for his assistance.

The New Jersey Plan

WE will probably never know for sure to what extent the New Jersey Plan was put forward as an alternative to the Virginia Plan and to what extent it was a tactic to preserve an equal vote for the small states. While far less thorough-going than the Virginia proposals, it would have markedly strengthened the Articles of Confederation. A comparison of the two plans found among the papers of James Wilson is almost certainly the notes from which he spoke two hundred years ago this day. They read as follows:

Propositions

from Virginia	from New Jersey
1. A Legislature consisting of two or three branches.	1. A single Legislature.
2. On the original Authority of the People.	2. On the derivative Authority of the Legislatures of the States.
3. Representation of Citizens according to Numbers and Importance.	3. Representation of States without Regard to Numbers and Importance.
4. A single Executive Magistrate.	4. More than one Executive Magistrate.
5. A Majority empowered to act.	5. A small Minority able to control.
6. The national Legislature to legislate in all Cases to which the State Legislatures are incompetent, or in which the incompetent, or in which the Harmony of the Union may be interrupted.	6. The United States in Congress vested with additional Powers only in a few inadequate Instances.
7. To negative Laws contrary to the Union or Treaties	7. To call forth the Powers of the confederated States in order to compel Obedience.
8. Executive removeable on Impeachment and Conviction.	8. [Executive Removeable] by Congress on Application by a Majority of the Executives of the States.
9. The Executive to have a qualified Negative.	9. [The Executive] to have none.
10. Provision made for inferior national Tribunals.	10. None.
11. The Jurisdiction of the national Tribunal to extend to Cases of national Revenue.	11. [Jurisdiction] Only by Appeal in the dernier Resort.
12. [Extend] to Questions that may involve the national Peace.	12. [Jurisdiction] Only limited and appellate Jurisdiction.
13. The national Government to be ratified under the authority of the People by Delegates expressly appointed for that Purpose.	13. The Alterations in the Confederation must be confirmed by the "Legislatures of every State."

The City Tavern was the location of the "club" with which General Washington dined. Today an awning shields the sidewalk outside in the summertime.

Sunday, June 17, 1787

Today was cloudy with an occasional sprinkle.

Convention

The Convention was in recess after its third full week of meetings. By the end of three weeks its members had completed committee review of a plan of government and, one might assume, could look back with satisfaction at the work they accomplished and look forward to a speedy conclusion.

But that was not the case. Delegates were already grumbling about the lack of progress and bracing themselves for a long summer in Philadelphia. Why?

Perhaps the members sensed that the issue of an equal vote for each state in the legislature would not be easily resolved, and that days of debate and committee meetings would pass before a compromise would be reached. Perhaps they sensed that many other issues would require long hours of debate and countless votes before they could be resolved.

Christ Church, the earliest Episcopal church, is still standing today. General Washington worshiped there, as did Robert Morris, Pierce Butler, James Wilson, as well as other delegates.

Delegates

Dr. Johnson (CT) worshiped at St. Paul's Episcopal, on Third Street below Walnut Street, dined at home, and went for a walk. He used some of his time to write his son Charles. Charles was to tell Mrs. Clark that he thought he had settled accounts with her father, but, if not, would settle them with her when he got home. Juba had very little appearance of having smallpox but the doctor insisted that he had it. Apparently Juba had been inoculated to give him a mild case of smallpox. Medicine in 1787 was a risky business.

General Washington attended at Christ Church where he heard Bishop White preach and saw him ordain two deacons. He then rode eight miles into the country to dine with John Ross.

William Richardson Davis (NC) reported to Governor Caswell. This report could well serve as a model for government memo writers. It read, in its entirety:

Philadelphia June 17, 1787

Sir
We move slowly in our business, it is indeed a work of great delicacy and difficulty, impeded at every step by jealousies and jarring interests.

I have the Honor to by
Your Excellency's Most
Humble Servant William
R. Davie

Eighteenth Century Medicine

MEDICINE in the eighteenth century was a risky business—for the patient. The leading physicians of Philadelphia, many of whom trained in England or Scotland, prescribed remedies for dropsy, coughs, or fevers that included bleeding, cupping or the use of leeches to extract the "sick" blood from the patients. Ingredients for medicines taken internally included herbs, spirits, narcotics, lead, mercury, iron fillings, and spermacetti oil. At best, such treatments and medicines relieved rather than cured symptoms; at worst, they actually caused the patient to get sicker.

In the home, women often served as nurses to the ill and surviving recipe books are filled with concoctions to treat all kinds of complaints. Philadelphia resident Hannah Haines recommended "A Cure for Cholick," perhaps inspired by the birth of her first child, Reuben, in 1786. She wrote,

> *Take the rinds of four fresh China Oranges, four Pints of good Spirits of Brandy, twelve or fifteen Cloves, two Nutmegs, grated fine, a quarter of a Pound of Raisins, one teaspoonful of aniseed, mix and steep the above two days, shaking it the first when made and after settling, it is fit for use. Take a tablespoonful with a little water. If that does not ease repeat it again.*

It is hard to know whether the anise, which does relieve nausea and related stomach distress, or the well-fermented brandy and fruit best relieved her cholicky child. But if he survived that treatment he may have lived to get his grandmother's cure for worms which was a mixture of "Corosive sublimate of Mercury" and brandy.

Less drastic and probably more soothing were cures for coughs and colds which required liberal doses of syrups made with horehound and honey. Fox glove, the source of digitalis, was properly prescribed for scarlet fever, but headaches were treated with bleeding, cupping, or purging. Hannah Haines also noted that "In periodical head-aches arsenic has been found very efficacious." Teas made out of sage, balm, rosemary, rose, oatmeal, bran, linseed, flaxseed, malt, or camomile were recommended for invalids as were paps, broths and soups. If Reuben Haines survived colic, colds, scarlet fever, headaches, and their "cures," he might have been treated, as an elderly invalid, with a delicacy recommended especially for the aged. According to *The Nurse's Guide*, published in Philadelphia, it required

> *six small eels washed clean & the skin stript off . . . cut them, put them into a pint of water with a little salt . . . add two blades of mace, six whole peppercorns, and a little parsley, then let them stew about half an hour, and the broth will be fit for use.*

Monday, June 18, 1787

Today was warm, with an afternoon shower.

Convention

When the Convention returned to business, they again formed a Committee of the Whole with Mr. Gorham (MA) in the chair.

On a motion from John Dickinson (DE) the Committee agreed that the Articles of Confederation should be so amended "as to render the Government of the United States adequate to the exigencies, the preservation and the prosperity of the union." Mr. Hamilton (NY) then rose, and began a speech which lasted the rest of the day. He didn't like either plan, ". . . being fully convinced that no amendment to the confederation leaving the states in possession of their sovereignty could possibly answer the purpose." He proceeded, at length, to compare the Virginia and New Jersey plans against what he viewed as the essentials of a sound government. He then proposed a plan of his own: a bicameral legislature with power to pass all laws; a House elected by the people for three years; a senate elected by electors from electoral districts to serve for life; a federal Governor to be chosen by the people voting in electoral districts; and state governors to be appointed by the federal government.

Delegates

Only twice during the year did Dr. Johnson (CT) indicate in his diary what had occurred in the Convention. Today he followed the routine notation "In Convention" with one word, "Hamilton."

General Washington dined at the quarterly meeting of the Friend's sons of St. Patrick at City Tavern and drank tea at Dr. Shippen's with the doctor's daughter, Ann (Nancy) Shippen Livingston.

Gorham wrote to Theophilus Parsons of Newburyport to express pleasure at Parsons' election to the Massachusetts House, and to suggest that that body not comply with Congress' requisition except for that part of it requesting cash, since six or seven states had refused to comply with earlier requisitions, and he presumed none would comply with the 1786 requisition. Gorham noted that, "In short, the present Federal Government seems near its exit, and whether we shall in the Convention be able to agree upon mending it, or forming and recommending a new one is not certain."

John Blair

JOHN BLAIR was born in Williamsburg, VA, educated at William and Mary College and afterwards became a student of law at Middle Temple in London. He served in Virginia's House of Burgesses, helped draw up the new state constitution in 1776, and in 1778 became a judge of the general court. In 1780 he became the first appeals court judge in Virginia.

Judge Blair was a firm supporter of the new constitution in the turbulent ratification conventions in Virginia. President Washington appointed him an associate justice of the U.S. Supreme Court in 1789 where he served until 1796. Retiring to Williamsburg as a widower, he lived out his four remaining years in solitude.

John Blair added his vote to that of Washington and Madison to give Virginia's sanction to the Constitution.

Tuesday, June 19, 1787

Convention

The Convention again resolved itself into a Committee of the Whole, with Mr. Gorham (MA), in the chair. The New Jersey plan came again to the floor.

Madison (VA) then spoke at length pointing out that the New Jersey Plan wouldn't prevent treaty violations by the states, encroachments on Federal authority, or conflicts between states. Moreover, it wouldn't secure the internal tranquility of the states, good internal legislation for any particular state, nor the projection of the Union against the influence of foreign powers over its members. It would, however, saddle the small states with the expense of their congressional delegation. Madison further warned that if no plan was approved and the union dissolved, the small states would be at the mercy of their larger neighbors.

A motion to postpone the first proposition of the New Jersey Plan carried. A motion to use and re-report the Virginia Plan carried, and the Committee rose. The small states had lost again.

Delegates

General Washington dined with the Morris family and spent the evening there. The Morris family consisted of Robert, 53, and his wife Mary White Morris, 38, and five children, Henry, almost 3, Maria, 8, Charles, 10, Hetty, 13, and William, 15. Thomas, 16, and Robert, 18, were at the University of Leipzig. The family may also have included other house guests.

Kitty Livingston, Governor William's daughter, had lived with the family for several years earlier in the 1780s.

Robert Morris (PA) wrote Horatio Gates. He wasn't angry when he wrote last time, just busy. He couldn't undertake to collect the interest on Gates' certificates; he was trying to cut back his own business. ". . . Your Friend [Richard] Peters is as much a recluse as you are and is not much oftener in Philad. altho it is now alive with respectable characters from the several states. . . . Thank Fortune [they] cannot make it worse than it is, do what may."

Mixing Medicine and Politics

THREE DELEGATES to the Convention were medical doctors. All three had seen active service in the War for Independence. Dr. James McClurg was a Virginia delegate, Dr. James McHenry represented Maryland, and Dr. Hugh Wiliamson was a North Carolina delegate. Williamson had practiced medicine in Philadelphia in the 1760s after he received his medical degree from the University of Utrecht. He was by no means Philadelphia's only doctor to turn to politics. Fellow physicians William Shippen and Benjamin Rush became heavily involved in the Revolution—Shippen as chief physician of the Continental Army hospitals west of the Hudson and Rush as a member of the Second Continental Congress.

Both Rush and Williamson resided for a time in London where they met Benjamin Franklin. All three were fellow members of the American Philosophical Society. During the Revolution, Doctor Rush accused Doctor Shippen of maladministration. General Washington ruled in favor of Shippen whereupon Rush resigned and in July 1776 became a member of the Continental Congress. He signed the Declaration of Independence with fellow Pennsylvanian Benjamin Franklin. In January 1776 Rush married Julia Stockton, daughter of New Jersey signer Richard Stockton.

Pennsylvania Hospital (larger here in 1799 than it was in 1787) made Philadelphia a medical center in the late eighteenth century. Three delegates to the Convention were doctors.

Julia recounted to an uncle:

> *. . . mama received a letter from Dr. R. begging to know whether there was any obstacle in the way from a previous engagement . . . and whether he might have permission to try to make himself agreeable. He answered that . . . I was at my own disposal entirely, that they would never say a word to influence me in behalf of any man whatever. However, he soon found his way to make himself agreeable, and every day that I am more acquainted with him I have found him the more so. We were married the 11 day of January.*

Sixteen-year-old Julia and Doctor Rush had thirteen children. Nine of them survived at their father's death in 1813. Julia survived the doctor for another thirty-five years after thirty-seven years of marriage.

Doctor Rush was long associated with America's first hospital, Pennsylvania Hospital. He was one of the few Philadelphia physicians who remained in the city during the terrible yellow fever epidemic of 1793 in which thousands perished. Always working for the relief of the miserable, Rush pioneered the humane treatment of the insane. At the same time, he pursued his keen interest in politics. To a friend in London, Rush wrote in 1786:

> *Most of the distresses of our country, and of the mistakes which Europeans have formed of us, have arisen from a belief that the American Revolution is over. This is so far from being the case that we have only finished the first act of the great drama.*

Wednesday, June 20, 1787

Today was very pleasant with a high in the low 80s.

Convention

William Blount (NC) appeared and took his seat.

The Convention took up the resolution ". . . that a National Government ought to be established, consisting of a supreme Legislative, executive and Judiciary."

Ellsworth (CT) and Gorham (MA) moved to change "National Government" to "Government of the United States." Ellsworth didn't want to abrogate the Confederation, and he wanted the new plan to be ratified under it. This passed without controversy.

A second resolution, that the legislature of the United States have two branches, was taken up. Lansing (NH) moved instead that "the powers of Legislation be vested in the United States in Congress."

He contended that neither the powers given the Convention nor public opinion supported abandoning the Confederation. George Mason ridiculed Lansing's motion; Luther Martin and Roger Sherman supported it. It lost; six states opposed, four small states for, and Maryland divided. The Articles of Confederation would not be retained.

Delegates

General Washington dined next door at Mr. Samuel Meredith's and drank tea there.

Robert Morris wrote from Philadelphia to New York merchant and financier Nicholas Low at the request of James Bruce Nickolls, to vouch for Nickolls' credit. Within a week, Morris's own credit would be shaken when fifty thousand pounds worth of his Bitts of Exchange would be returned unpaid.

William Richardson Davie

WILLIAM RICHARDSON DAVIE observed his thirty-first birthday.

Born in England, William Richardson Davie had been brought to the Waxhaw area of the Carolinas by his father at the age of seven. He was then adopted by his uncle, William Richardson, a Presbyterian clergyman. In 1776, Davie graduated from Princeton (where fellow delegate Jonathon Dayton was a classmate and fellow delegate W. C. Houston had taught mathematics and natural philosophy).

On returning to North Carolina, Davie studied law until April, 1779. On April 5 he was commissioned a lieutenant in a troop of cavalry. Soon promoted to captain, then major, Davie served with distinction in the bitter partisan warfare of 1779–80, and was wounded in action at the Battle of Stono. On the arrival of General Greene, who knew both the importance and the difficulty of supplying an army from personal experience, Davie was appointed commissary general, a post he held throughout the remainder of the Revolution.

Davie was admitted to the bar while recovering from his wounds. After the war, he settled in Halifax, married Sarah Jones, whose uncle Willie was one of the state's political leaders, and managed his plantation while practicing law. In 1786 he was chosen to the state legislature and, in 1787, to attend the Federal Convention.

Leaving his wife and the one or two of their six children who would have been born by then, Davie left in time to arrive in Philadelphia on May 22 and be present for the opening session.

Thereafter, he seconded the motion to subject the executive to impeachment, served on the committee which proposed the Connecticut Compromise, and argued strongly for representation of at least three-fifths of the South's slaves. Satisfied with the new government as it took shape and with the views of his

William Richardson Davie had no great role in the Convention although he attended from the end of May to August.

fellow North Carolina delegates Davie left Philadelphia on August 13 to be home for the opening of the fall term of courts.

Thursday, June 21, 1787

The day was cloudy and unpleasantly humid with heavy gusts from the south.

Convention

Jonathon Dayton (NJ) appeared and took his seat. Having yesterday voted not to abandon the Virginia Plan for a much less centralized government, the Convention resumed work on it. Dr. Johnson (CT) said that the New Jersey Plan protected the states better, but was willing to be convinced otherwise. Wilson (PA) tried, as did Madison (VA). The Convention then resolved that the Legislature would have two branches (seven aye, three no, and Maryland divided) and went on to discuss the first branch of the legislature.

General Pinckney (SC) moved for election in such manner as the state legislature directs "instead of by the people." Luther Martin (MD) seconded. Hamilton (NY) and Mason (VA) opposed the motion. Sherman (CT) preferred election by the legislatures but was content with the plan as it stood. Rutledge (SC) favored the motion—he saw no difference between election by the people and by representatives elected by the people except that the latter chose better men. Wilson and King (MA) explained the difference. General Pinckney proposed making the state governments part of the general system. The motion lost; Connecticut, New Jersey, Delaware and South Carolina aye, six no, Maryland divided. The provision for popular election of the first branch then passed (nine aye, New Jersey no, Maryland divided).

Term of service was discussed next. The committee report said three years. Randolph (VA) moved for two. Dickinson (DE) preferred three, Ellsworth (CT) preferred one year, and was seconded by Strong (MA). Wilson agreed.

Madison felt that annual elections in so large a country would be extremely inconvenient. Sherman preferred annual elections but would be content with biennial. Mason preferred biennial. Hamilton argued for three years. The motion for striking "three years" passed; seven aye, New York, Delaware and Maryland no, New Jersey divided.

A two year term was then agreed to, none contrary.

Delegates

For the second of only two times in 1787, Dr. Johnson indicated in his diary what was happening in the Convention. He followed the stock phrase "In convention" with "argt." for "argument." He dined at Dr. William Shippen's and paid his City Tavern bill for six pounds, fifteen shillings.

General Washington dined at Mr. Prager's, a Philadelphia merchant and leader in the Jewish community,

The eighteenth-century office of a merchant was a busy place with many men occupied keeping records of the shipments with quills. Fitzsimons and both of the Morrises were merchants. In 1787 Congress was important in determining trade and financial regulations.

and spent the evening in his room.

William Blount wrote his brother John.

I am not at Liberty to say what is doing in Convention and if I was the Business is so much in Embryo that I could say nothing that would be in the least satisfactory. All the Members agree that the Convention will sit at least six weeks and it is generally supposed eight or ten from this Time, hence the Necessity for more Money to be remitted to me. Since my arrival I am favoured with your's by Mr. Mackie.

Inventing Federalism

WEBSTER'S dictionary defines "federal" as "pertaining to a state consolidated from several states which retain limited powers; as, a federal government." In 1787 none of the delegates would have given the quoted definition. They were still in the process of inventing the concept of divided sovereignty on which the quoted definition rests.

Earlier the thirteen states had formed a league or confederation which had limited powers to maintain an army, conduct relations with foreign countries, and govern and dispose of the public domain. They operated under the assumption that in any given geographical area only one sovereign could rule. While the Confederation ruled in this way, its government had no power to force the individual states to conform; consequently, by 1787, Congress was important only in matters of great import to the nation—international

relations, finance, and trade regulations. The states, on the other hand, were vying for power and conceding very little to the federal government.

The Virginia Plan which the Convention was debating implied that the new national government would rest directly on the people of the nation, and not on the states. It explicitly recognized, however, that the states would continue to exist and would draw their authority from the people, too. There would be one national government and a number of state governments, each sovereign within its defined area of authority.

This concept was new to the world, but the Convention accepted it with very little debate. Defining the area of sovereignty of the national government and those of the states, and spelling out how the sovereigns would relate to each other and the precise role the states would play in determining national policy and vice versa would occasion a lot of debate. It still does, despite the amazing success of the Convention's invention of the federal system.

Friday, June 22, 1787

After last night's heavy thunder shower, the day was clear and cool.

Convention

The Convention resumed discussion on the first branch of the national legislature. The clause providing "fixed stipends to be paid out of the National Treasury" was taken up. Ellsworth (CT) wanted members of Congress to be paid by the states. Williamson (NC) agreed; he reasoned that the new western states (Kentucky, Tennessee, Ohio, etc.) would pay little in taxes and their representatives would oppose the original thirteen states' interests, and why should the original states pay for the new states opposing them? Gorham (MA), Randolph (VA) and King (MA) opposed state payment because it meant state control. Sherman (MA) wanted the states to determine the salary and pay it. Wilson (PA) and Hamilton (NY) opposed fixing the salary in the Constitution; Madison favored it. Wilson moved that salaries be determined by the national legislature and paid from the national treasury; his motion was defeated: New Jersey and Pennsylvania aye, seven no, New York and Georgia divided. Ellsworth's motion also lost. It was then agreed to change "fixed stipends" to "adequate compensation."

Next the Convention agreed that members of the lower house should be at least twenty-five years old. Gorham then moved to strike out a provision making members of the first branch ineligible for office during their term and one year after it. Butler (SC) thought the provision necessary to prevent intrigue and collu-

sion with the Executive. The motion failed: four aye (Massachusetts, New Jersey, North Carolina, Georgia), four no (Connecticut, Maryland, Virginia, South Carolina), three divided (New York, Pennsylvania, Delaware).

Alexander Hamilton was in favor of a very centralized government, a proposal unpopular with most delegates. He rarely attended the Convention after mid-July. It is recorded on June 22 that he voted against fixing the salary of the Congressmen in the Constitution.

Delegates

Dr. Johnson (CT) dined with Mr. John Anstey, commissioner from England for ascertaining the claims of the refugees. Anstey had visited Mt. Vernon in December 1786.

General Washington dined at Mr. Morris' (PA) and drank tea with Francis Hopkinson, lawyer, musician, designer of flags and a signer of the Declaration of Independence.

How Much Will We Pay Us?

WOULD you like to set your own pay, and have the power to levy taxes so you could be sure that the money to pay you was always available? Representatives and senators do this, but they often wish they didn't.

The members of the Constitutional Convention didn't really want congressmen to set their own pay, but they couldn't find a better method. Franklin wanted members to serve without pay, but that wasn't practical. Madison wanted to spell out congressional salaries in the Constitution, but others foresaw inflation and decided that it wouldn't work. Madison then suggested that a congressional pay be set into the Constitution but linked to some commodity price, such as the price of wheat which would change with the rate of inflation. Most delegates didn't think that was practical either. Having salary determined by popular vote was so impractical it wasn't even brought up. Thus, Article I, Section 6: "The Senators and Representatives shall receive a compensation for their services, to be ascertained by law, and paid out by the Treasury of the United States."

Historically, a congressman's vote for a large salary increase has been a good way to get defeated in the next election. Congressional salaries have risen from $5 per day of actual work in 1789 to $75,100.00 plus office expenses and a travel allowance.

Saturday, June 23, 1787

Today was clear and warm.

Convention

The Convention resumed consideration of pay and qualification of the first branch or House of the legislature.

Madison (VA) moved and was seconded by Alexander Martin (NC) to make members ineligible for other federal office during their term and for one year after. The debate on this took most of the day. Butler (SC) said the motion didn't go far enough. Mason (VA) agreed and appealed to Madison as a witness to the shameful partiality of the legislature of Virginia for its own members. Rutledge (SC) supported the motion as did Wilson (PA). King thought the motion was too refined. Sherman (MA) and Gerry (MA) agreed that members should be barred from all federal offices. Madison defended his motion as a middle ground between encouraging corruption and excluding the most qualified appointees. Jenifer (MD) remarked that the Maryland senators were excluded from holding other offices during their five-year terms and that this had gained them the confidence of the people. Madison's motion lost; Connecticut and New Jersey aye, Massachusetts divided, eight no. Spaight (NC) moved to divide the issue into two parts: ineligibility during the term for which they were elected (passed—eight aye, Pennsylvania and Georgia no, Massachusetts divided) and extending eligibility for a year after the term (lost,—New York, Delaware, Maryland, South Carolina aye, Pennsylvania divided, six no).

Delegates

General Washington dined at Doctor Thomas Ruston's and drank tea at Mr. Morris' (PA).

New Hampshire was still trying to find delegates who would serve. The state Senate considered a House resolution for a joint session to "chuse four persons either two of whom to represent this state in the Grand Convention now sitting a (sic) Philadelphia." All agreed, but then reconsidered their agreement.

Alexander Martin—More Expectation than Performance

ALEXANDER MARTIN, when chosen to represent North Carolina in the Federal Convention, was among the state's leaders.

Born in Hunterdon County, New Jersey, sometime in 1740, Martin attended Princeton (BA 1756, MA 1759) before moving to Virginia and then to North Carolina and a career as a merchant, lawyer, and politician. By 1766 he was deputy king's attorney and in 1773 was elected to the North Carolina legislature. While he never married, by 1773 he had fathered a son.

Commissioned a lieutenant colonel early in 1775, Martin fought in the Moore's Creek campaign. Sent north to join Washington's army, he fought at Brandywine before being court-martialed for cowardice at Germantown. Acquitted by the court, Martin resigned his commission and returned to North Carolina. There he was promptly elected a state senator, then speaker of the senate, and in 1782, 1783, 1784, governor.

In 1787 he was an experienced political leader from whom much could be expected. However, his only recorded contribution to the Federal Convention was to second motions to prohibit Congressmen from serving in any Federal office created during their term, to allow North Carolina six representatives in the first Federal Congress instead of five, and to prohibit Congress from choosing a state capital as the national capital. When North Carolina delegate Hugh Williamson mentioned the imminent departure from the Con-

Alexander Martin left the Convention in early August. His political experience prior to the Convention was an asset, but his only recorded contributions were seconds made to motions.

vention of William R. Davie and Governor Martin, he added a somewhat bemused assessment: "Perhaps you may wonder at my saying that I would rather lose the assistance of the last than the first of these Gentlemen, but things of this Sort will often happen."

Sunday, June 24, 1787

The day was cloudy with showers beginning at 3 P.M. and continuing into the evening.

Convention

The Convention was in recess following its fourth full week of work. The week just past began with a masterful speech by Hamilton (NY) on the need for an effective central government which seems to have impressed all of the delegates but convinced few, if any, of them. Then, after a thorough analysis by Madison of the weaknesses of the Paterson Plan, it rejected the plan that was intended only to patch up the Articles of Confederation, revived the Virginia

Plan as amended, and began the second round of discussions on the Virginia Plan. One day after changing "national government" to "Government of the United States," it again discussed whether to patch up the Articles or provide a new government, reaffirmed its decision to do the latter, and resumed on the Virginia Plan.

Delegates

Dr. Johnson (CT) worshiped at St. Paul's, dined at City Tavern, and spent five shillings in miscellaneous expense.

General Washington dined at Mr. Morris' (PA) and spent the evening at Mr. Meredith's drinking tea. Samuel Meredith was a Pennsylvania delegate in Congress, and George Clymer's (PA) brother-in-law.

General Charles C. Pinckney and his second wife, Mary Stead Pinckney, of South Carolina observed their first wedding anniversary.

Massachusetts delegate Rufus King wrote the state treasurer asking for pay owed him.

Charles Cotesworth Pinckney

Charles Coatsworth Pinckney was against any provision that was against slavery, was in favor of a strong central government, as well as power for state governments.

PINCKNEY was the surname of two of South Carolina's delegates, who also bore the same Christian name: Charles Pinckney and Charles Cotesworth Pinckney. To further confuse, both their fathers were also named Charles.

Charles Cotesworth Pinckney who celebrated his forty-first birthday in 1787 had lived a full life and was only in mid-span of his days. By age twenty-three Charles Cotesworth had attended Westminster School, graduated from Christ Church College, Oxford, attended the Middle Temple in London, and had been admitted to the English bar.

Returning home to Charleston to practice law, he was elected to the Council of Safety, chaired a committee which drafted South Carolina's temporary government, and served in both houses of the legislature. While practicing law, Pinckney kept active in the militia and became a colonel in September 1776. He was captured in the fall of Charleston in 1778 and spent four years as a prisoner of war.

After the Convention he campaigned actively for ratification. President Washington offered him command of the army and later an associate justice position on the U.S. Supreme Court. Pinckney declined both positions. After declining to serve as either Secretary of State or War, he did finally accept the ambassadorship to France in 1796.

In 1804 and 1808 Charles Cotesworth Pinckney was the unsuccessful Federalist candidate for president. Pinckney was twice married. His first wife Sarah was a sister of Arthur Middleton, a signer of the Declaration of Independence. His second wife was Mary Stead.

Monday, June 25, 1787

It rained hard last night and this morning, then cleared and turned pleasant.

Convention

The Convention took up Resolution 4; this section

stated that members of second branch of the National Legislature were to be elected by state legislatures, be at least thirty years old, serve for a seven year term, receive a fixed stipend and be ineligible for other state or Federal office.

Charles Pinckney (SC) began the day with a speech stressing the unique equality among Americans which precluded a House of Lords. He wished to retain the state governments and favored election of the second house by the state legislatures. Mr. Gorham (MA) remarked that he inclined to a compromise on the rule of proportion (the number of Senators to be allowed each state).

After extensive debate, the Convention agreed to have the state legislatures elect senators and that they should be at least thirty years old. It defeated proposals that they serve seven, six or five year terms, leaving that question undecided.

Delegates

General Washington dined and drank tea at the Morris' and spent the evening in his room. Years later, Mrs. Mary White Morris would recall the General was the most thoughtful guest she ever entertained.

Robert Morris (PA) wrote to sons Robert and Thomas at their school in Leipzig, Germany. In a passage peculiar for its detachment, he discussed the Convention.

> *General Washington is now our guest having taken up his abode at my House during the time he is to remain in this City. He is President [at Morris' nomination] of a Convention of Delegates from the Thirteen States of America [of whom Morris was one] who have met here for the purpose of revising, amending or altering the Federal Government. There are Gentn. of great abilities employed in this Convention, many of whom were in the first Congress and several that were Conserned in forming the Articles of confederation, now about to be altered and amended. You my Children, ought to pray for a Successful issue to their [not our] Labours . . .*

The Convention—A Big Risk

THE Convention and its product were so successful that they have obscured the risks involved in holding the Convention in the first place. With all its faults at least there was a confederation government, and it was accepted, if not heeded and supported by the states and the people of the states. But the agita-

George Washington served as president of the Convention; he was nominated by his host Robert Morris who noted that this was an "assemblage of gentlemen of great ability."

tion for a Convention exposed the weakness of the existing government, and the calling of the Convention and the quality of the delegates raised expectations for a miraculous reformation which would solve all of the problems without disturbing any of the status quo. Had the Convention not succeeded in creating a new government, it might very well have succeeded in finishing off the old one. The letter from Secretary of Congress Charles Thomson to William Bingham illustrates this danger.

> *Dear Sir,*
> *On my arrival here I had the pleasure to find five States represented namely Massachusetts, New-York, New Jersey, Virginia and South Carolina and that the attendance of Pennsylvania and North Carolina would form a Congress. As I think of great importance to the honor and safety of the Confederacy that*

Congress should be in session and the form at least of government kept up in the present situation of affairs, and as the delegates for North Carolina are now in Philadelphia and as one of them assured me will return immediately as soon as they know their attendance is necessary to form a house I have written to them and entreat your attendance as speedily as possible. You cannot imagine what an alarm the secession of the Members from Congress at this crisis has spread through the eastern states. Were I to

hazard an Opinion it would be that the peace of the union and the happy termination of the Measures of the Convention depend on the Meeting and continuance of Congress and keeping up the form of government until the New plan is ready for Adoption. I have given similar information to Mr. Meredith and have written to you both in Confidence. If the President is returned I beg you will press him to come on immediately.

Tuesday, June 26, 1787

The day was clear and pleasant.

Convention

The Convention resumed its debate on the Senate's term of service. Gorham (MA), seconded by Wilson, moved for a six-year term for senators with one-third to go out of office every three years. General Pinckney (SC) preferred four, lest members become tied too closely to the capital city. Read (DE) moved nine years since he couldn't get a life term; Broom (DE) seconded. Madison favored nine years with a high minimum age. Sherman (CT) thought six years sufficient to insure steadiness and wisdom in the system. Hamilton (NY) favored at least nine years. Mr. Gerry (MA) "wished we could be united in our ideas. . . . All aim at the same end, but there are great differences as to the means." He favored four or five years. Eventually, the Convention agreed upon six-year terms, with senators being ineligible for other federal offices during their terms.

Delegates

General Washington had a family dinner with Governor Randolph, then went to Gray's Ferry with a party and had tea there.

After Washington left, Randolph wrote Acting Governor Beverly Randolph to announce George Wythe's resignation as a delegate. John Lansing wrote Hamilton's father-in-law, Phillip Schuyler, noting "The business of the Convention is going on very slowly and it is still in such a stage as to render the Result very dubious."

Printer and bookbinder Benjamin January wrote Dr. Franklin to apologize for an accident to some of Franklin's books which he was binding, and to offer to replace them.

Oliver Ellsworth wrote home. Later letters were less somber, so this one may reflect the effect of today's battle over representation (or a staunch small stater).

Mrs. Ellsworth
Our business is yet unfinished and it yet remains uncertain when I shall return home—I am sure I

The printing press used in Franklin's printing shop was similar to this. In 1787 the printing trades were flourishing in Philadelphia.

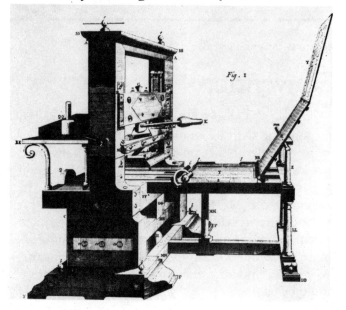

wish for the time for this city has no charm for me—I mix with company without enjoying it and am perfectly tired with flattery and forms.

To be very fashionable we must be very trifling and make and receive a thousand professions which everybody knows there is not truth in—Give me a little domestick circle where affection is natural and friendship sincere and I do not care who takes the rest.

I seldom write long letters to any body and I am sure I need not to you to convince you that I am with the truest and tenderest affection.

Yours Oliver Ellsworth

Love to the little ones. Chauncey is well through the small pox.

John Langdon turned forty-six today.

Philadelphia's Printing and Publishing Trade

BENJAMIN JANUARY, printer, in a letter to Benjamin Franklin belies the fact that Philadelphia's printing and publishing trade was flourishing in 1787. In the first half of the century, William and Andrew Bradford and Benjamin Franklin had raised the city's printing trade to its preeminent position in the colonies and had prepared the way for those firms active in the late eighteenth century.

At least nineteen Philadelphia firms had imprints dated 1787. Together they provided the city with five weekly, two semi-weekly, and most remarkably, one daily newspaper.

They also informed the citizens of all acts and laws, by-laws and ordinances, minutes, constitutions, proceedings, debates, rules and regulations. They offered moral tales, anecdotes, sermons, orations, epistles, and hymns. They printed gazettes, journals, advertisements, magazines, and almanacs. They published original essays in prose and verse, remarks, discourses, and addresses to the public. They entertained with collections of riddles, tragedies, and comic operas. And they educated with medical treatises, spelling books, histories, travelogs, and catalogs of books for sale.

A sampling of titles with 1787 Philadelphia imprints reveals great diversity. Heading the list are John Dunlap and David C. Claypoole's printings of the Constitution, including two working drafts for use by the members of the Convention, the first issue as agreed, and the first official edition. Their *Pennsylvania Packet* for September 19th is entirely given up to the new Constitution of the United States. T. Bradford printed the *Proceedings of the Federal Convention Held at Philadelphia,* and by the end of the year, Hall and Sellers printed the first four essays of "The Federalist" in their *Pennsylvania Gazette.*

Wednesday, June 27, 1787

Today was clear and warm.

Convention

According to Madison: "Mr. Rutledge (SC) moved to postpone the sixth Resolution defining the powers of Congs: in order to take up the 7 and 8 which involved the most fundamental points; the rules of sufferage in the two branches, which was agreed to nem. con." Mr. Luther Martin (MD) then took the floor, and held it for the entire day with a long, rambling and passionate speech, the point of which was that the general government was meant to represent state governments, not people, and that the Articles of Confederation should be retained.

Delegates

Dr. Johnson (CT) dined at Samuel Merideth's and purchased John Adam's *Defense of the Constitutions of the United States.*

Since he paid seven shillings and six pence for the book, it must have been the bound version advertized for sale by Hall & Sellers, J. Cruikshank, and Young and McCulloch at that price. The paperback version was six shillings.

The New Hampshire Senate concurred with the House in electing John Langdon, B. West, John Pickering and Nicholas Gilman as delegates to the Convention. John Pickering would become a federal judge and the first man to be impeached and convicted.

The Pennsylvania *Gazette* for June 29 reported that Scanetoyah, a Cherokee on his way to Congress in New York, had been introduced to Alexander Martin and a number of other delegates who had then taken him to the State House to meet General Washington today.

John Langdon (1741–1819)

JOHN LANGDON was born on a farm in Portsmouth, NH, on June 26, 1741 (or December, 1739 or 1740—accounts differ). He attended the local grammar school, served for a while in the office of merchant Daniel Rindge, and then went to sea. By 1774 he had become an active and prosperous shipowner, shipbuilder and merchant.

By 1775, he was the speaker of the New Hampshire legislature, and a delegate to the Continental Congress. Thereafter he was an agent for the Continent, purchasing military supplies, building ships (including the *America*) and at the same time continued in private business as a privateer owner and merchant. By 1784, he had started an active trade with the French West Indies, exporting barrel staves, fish and so forth and importing sugar, rum and cotton.

Associated as a continental agent with marine superintendent and financeer Robert Morris, he also acted as Morris' Portsmouth correspondent, and as agent for the Bank of North America. He was speaker of the New Hampshire House in the late 70s and 80s and of the state Senate in 1784, president of the state in 1785.

Langdon was married to Elizabeth Sherburne and was the father of a daughter, Elizabeth (Betsy). A son died in infancy.

Due to election delays at home, Langdon didn't take his seat in the Convention until July 23. He was

John Langdon played no important role in the Convention after he arrived in July.

moderately active in the debate. He seemed to have perceived the nature of federalism as envisioned in the Constitution, saying, on August 23, "As one of the people, . . . [I can] say, the National Government is mine, the State Government is mine—In transferring power from one to the other—I only take out my left hand what it cannot so well use, and put it into my right hand where it can be better used."

Thursday, June 28, 1787

The day was clear and pleasant.

Convention

Luther Martin (MD) finished the speech he had started yesterday, arguing that the general government should be formed for the states and therefore they should be represented equally. Lansing (NY), seconded by Dayton (NJ), moved to amend the Seventh Resolution to read, "the right of suffrage in the first

Franklin's proposal that the Convention open each day with prayer is probably the best known motion of the Convention. It was made at the end of a day of heated debate and was never put to the vote.

practice might rouse fears in the community. Williamson (NC) remarked that the Convention had no money to hire a chaplain. Randolph (VA) proposed a fourth of July sermon instead; Franklin seconded. The Convention then managed to adjourn without voting on the motion.

Delegates

General Washington dined with the Morrises in a large company, a company which the general noted was not appropriate since news arrived last night that Mr. Morris' bills had been protested (the equivalent of having checks bounce). He took tea with the Morrises and spent the evening in his room. William Blount (NC) wrote from Philadelphia to his brother in Washington, NC: "I am not a Liberty to say what is done or doing in Convention but I can say things are so much in Embryo that I could give you no Satisfactory account if I was ever so much at Liberty. It is generally supposed the Convention will continue to sit for two months at least."

Dr. Johnson (CT) dined with William and Ann Bingham, and had expenses of nine shillings.

Franklin Prayer Proposal

BENJAMIN FRANKLIN proposed what has become probably the best known motion of the Convention when he suggested that the sessions open with prayer. It is ironic that this was a motion which had nothing to do with the provisions of the proposed Constitution, and which was not voted on.

Some of the fame of this motion may derive from its incongruous source. Benjamin Franklin was not among the most devout or formally religious of the delegates. Some of it may derive from the timing—at the end of a day of heated, even ill-tempered, debate. Some of it probably derives from its susceptibility to improvement, such as the story that Hamilton argued against the motion because the delegates were competent to transact the business entrusted to them and did not need to call in foreign aid.

Once made, the motion was seconded by Roger Sherman, a devout Puritan. Hamilton and others objected—word that the Convention had called for prayer would leak out and alarm the public. However,

branch ought to be according to the rule established by the Confederation" one vote per state.

Williamson (NC) opposed the motion saying that if the states were equally sovereign now and parted with equal proportions of sovereignty, they would remain equally sovereign. Madison (VA) also opposed it—even Brearley (NJ) and Paterson (NJ) had agreed an equal vote was unjust to the larger states. Wilson (PA) chimed in that if the small state argument was followed, instead of London complaining because the rotten borough of Old Sarum had one vote, Old Sarum should complain because London had four. Sherman (CT) observed that it wasn't a question of natural rights, but one of how rights may be guarded in society. The question was postponed at the request of the Deputies of New York.

Franklin (PA) then suggested, in view of the small progress made and the different sentiments, that the Convention should be opened each day with prayer as the Congress had been. Sherman seconded. Hamilton (NY) and others opposed the motion because the it was a firm Presybterian minister who voiced the strongest argument. Hugh Williamson (NC) noted that the Convention had no funds and therefore couldn't offer honoraria for the services of the person offering the prayer.

Friday, June 29, 1787

Convention

Debate continued on the motion to have each state have an equal vote in the lower house, the motion was defeated: Connecticut, New York, New Jersey, Delaware aye, six no, Maryland divided, and it was agreed that each state would not have an equal vote in the lower house. Voting in the Senate was then taken up. Ellsworth (SC) moved for an equal vote for each state in the Senate, noting that "we are partly national, partly federal." He felt the small states needed protection from the large. Baldwin (GA) opposed the motion—he wanted vote in the Senate to be based on wealth.

Delegates

General Washington dined with Mr. Robert Morris (PA) and spent the evening there.

Nicholas Gilman (NH) took eight certificates of the liquidated debt amounting to 6,654 at 79 to 90 dollars at specie value to the continental loan officer for New Hampshire (who happened to be his brother Nathaniel) and received fifty-one certificates with a face value of 954 at 60 to 90 dollars in payment for interest due through December 31, 1784.

Joseph Jones wrote from Richmond to James Madison. Jones noted accounts that the Convention would continue into August and therefore "some of your uxorius members will become impatient for so long absence from home. How does the Dr. [McClurg] stand it—enjoy himself as usual in the society of his friends, or cast longing looks towards Richmond. Mrs. McClurg is, and looks well, and will I dare say on his return prove at least a full match for him. Mrs. Randolph and the children have I hope got up safe."

Nicholas Gilman arrived at the Convention on July 21 and later served on the Committee of Unfinished Parts.

Nicholas Gilman

NICHOLAS GILMAN, born in Exeter, New Hampshire, and educated in local schools, was commissioned a captain early in the Revolution. Elected a delegate to Congress in 1786, he was chosen with John Langdon to represent New Hampshire in the Convention. Arriving late, July 21, he did sign the Constitution and labored mightily for its ratification. There is no evidence that he ever spoke in the Convention.

Elected to the new House of Representatives in 1789 Gilman served until 1797. He was elected to the United States Senate in 1804 and retained his seat until his death in 1814. He seemed never to be popular with his fellow members of Congress. Gilman never married.

Saturday, June 30, 1787

It was a hot and partly cloudy day.

Convention

Brearley (NJ), seconded by Paterson (NJ), moved that the President write New Hampshire . . . "that the business depending before the Convention was of such a nature as to require the immediate attendance of the deputies of that state." This motion indicated that the small states wanted reinforcements. Rutledge (VA), King (MA) and Wilson (PA) opposed the motion, and it lost: New York and New Jersey aye, 5 no, Maryland divided, Pennsylvania, Delaware and Georgia "not on the floor."

Debate on Ellsworth's motion for an equal vote in the Senate resumed with increasing acrimony. Dr. Franklin proposed a compromise, a equal vote in the Senate for each state except on appropriations and tax bills—the vote on these to be proportioned to the money provided by each state. He was ignored. Debate continued, with neither side yielding.

Gunning Bedford (DE), always a hot head, then delivered perhaps the harshest speech of the debates thus far. Why not simply give Congress the power it needed? "The large states dare not dissolve the confederation. If they do, the small ones will find some foreign ally. . . ." Ellsworth (CT) said he looked to the states for preservation of his rights and for happiness. King (MA) then closed the day's debate by acknowledging that the states should be preserved and by reprimanding Bedford for courting relief from a foreign power.

Delegates

General Washington "Dined with a Club at Springsbury [a Penn family manor near Bush Hill]—consisting of several associated families of the City—the gentlemen of which meet every Saturday, accompanied by the females of the families every other Saturday. This was the ladies day." He also wrote Annis Boudinot Stockton to acknowledge her letter of May 26 with the poem enclosed, and dashed off a note to Lafayette to introduce Thomas Lee Shippen, son of Lafayette's old acquaintence Dr. William Shippen.

After the Convention adjourned, Dr. Johnson (CT) rode out to Mr. Hamilton's estate, Bush Hill. His daily expenses were eight shillings.

George Mason wrote Acting Governor Randolph, suggesting that Francis Corbin be appointed as a delegate in place of George Mason, who had resigned. He added that two or three days would determine whether or not the Convention could agree on a sound and effectual system. Mason was pessimistic.

Dining Out in Federal Philadelphia

THE EIGHTEENTH-CENTURY TAVERN is the common ancestor of the modern restaurant, hotel and bar. A successful urban institution like the

The Old London Coffeehouse at the corner of First and Market was frequented by merchants. Like the many other taverns in eighteenth-century Philadelphia, it provided the only alternative to domestic dining, an acceptable place for a gentleman to conduct business, and accommodations for travelers or visitors to the city.

City Tavern provided both natives and travelers with their only alternative to domestic dining. For a Philadelphia merchant or gentleman conducting business outside his office or home, a tavern's coffee rooms ran an acceptable line between privacy and the marketplace. For a traveler, its "ordinary" or common dining room was sufficiently well monitored by the tavern keeper to prevent his being jostled by an uncontrolled crowd. For both, the club supper or dining club was an attractive alternative to eating the evening meal at home or in rented quarters.

Informal and convivial, these meals were organized around the punch bowl. A relatively fixed number of diners attended, in the range of six to twenty. They met at regular intervals, shared a common menu and divided costs equally.

Such an arrangement was advantageous for diner and innkeeper alike. The members dined among congenial associates in familiar surroundings. The cost of meals was fixed beforehand and varied little. The innkeeper knew in advance the number and habits of the diners in his private dining rooms. He could even predict the amount and varieties of alcohol a particular group was likely to demand. And he was insured a gentlemanly clientele during the evening hours.

Papers and diaries of the delegates to the Convention leave little doubt that the club suppers at the City Tavern or elsewhere were frequent. George Read of Delaware wrote, "We . . . dine at the City Tavern where a few of us have established a table for each day in the week, save Saturday. . . . A dinner is ordered for the number, eight, and whatever is deficient of that number is to be paid for two shillings and sixpence a head, and each that attends pays only the expense of the day."

Sunday, July 1, 1787

The day was warm and overcast with occasional very light rain, and a mean temperature of 74°.

Convention

The Convention was in recess, enjoying a much needed respite from a week of heated argument. While the six "large" states (Massachusetts, Pennsylvania, Virginia, North Carolina, South Carolina and Georgia) had a majority, it is now obvious that the four "small" states (Connecticut, New York, New Jersey, Delaware) and perhaps Maryland might be so intransigent as to leave the Convention.

Delegates

General Washington dined and spent the evening "at home." He wrote to David Stuart on business, and his usual Sunday letter of instruction to George Augustine Washington at Mt. Vernon.

The letter included a touch of sarcasm very rare for Washington: "By the letter you sent me from Mr. Polk, he seems to understand the art of charging for his Plank, perfectly well. . . ."

Dr. Johnson attended an ordination service at St. Peter's Episcopal Church at Third and Pine Streets, then dined at Captain Barra's.

A written invitation from some of the delegates to Thomas McKean survives today:

The Gentlemen of the Convention at the Indian Queen [George Mason, Caleb Strong, Nathaniel Gorham, Charles Pinckney, Alexander Martin, Hugh Williamson] in 4th Street Present their compliments to the Honbl. Thomas McKean Esquire (Chief Justice of Pennsylvania) and should be glad of his company at Dinner Tomorrow at half past 3 o'clock.

Luther Martin wrote to Nicholas Low of New York demanding 20 guineas as his fee in a legal matter.

Oliver Ellsworth wrote his weekly letter to his wife Abigail.

Hugh Williamson

HUGH WILLIAMSON was a preacher who never preached, a doctor who rarely practiced, an anti-Catholic and an anti-Semite who kept his

bigotry out of his public service—he was among the more interesting and active delegates.

Born in West Nottingham, PA, to parents who were devout Presbyterians, he was educated at New London Crossroads school and the College of Philadelphia (BA 1757, MA 1760). After studying theology and being licensed as a Presbyterian minister, in 1762 he took up the study of medicine and at the same time joined the College of Philadelphia as a professor of mathematics. In 1764, he went abroad, studying medicine at Edinburgh and earning his MD from Utrecht. After a brief return to America, he went back to London in 1773, carrying the first word of the Boston Tea Party. In London, he worked with Franklin on some experiments in electricity, and later claimed to have procured the Hutchinson letters for Franklin.

Returning in 1776, he settled into a career as a merchant in Edenton, NC, and during the Revolution served as surgeon general of North Carolina. In 1782 he was elected to the North Carolina House and to the Continental Congress, serving through 1785. A bachelor in 1787, he may have already met a young New York lady, Maria Apthorpe, whom he married in January 1789 and by whom he had two children before she died soon after the birth of the second child.

In the Convention, Williamson led the North Carolina delegation, and served on five of the six eleven-member committees chosen. On the floor, he spoke briefly but frequently, and was generally constructive. His remarks seem to have led to decennial reapportionment of the House based on a census, to requiring each presidential elector to vote for more than one person and thereby lessening the advantage of candidates from large states, and to having presidential elections in which no candidate had a majority broken by the House voting by state.

On the broader issues, he was a nationalist, although he opposed giving the new government a veto of state laws, and proposed a three-man executive to represent each of the three regions within the nation. Within this context, he was alert to regional interests. He wished to retain freedom to impose special conditions on new states to be admitted, wished to require a two-thirds vote to pass navigation acts, and, though personally opposed to slavery, supported continuation of the slave trade because Georgia and South Carolina would leave the Union otherwise. He was a strong supporter of proportional representation in both houses of Congress, a reluctant supporter of the Connecticut Compromise, and insisted on House origination of money bills. He opposed limiting the electorate to freeholders, opposed long residency requirements for representatives and senators, but wanted to extend the years of citizenship required. He also fought to increase the presidential term to six or seven years. From July on, he pushed to increase the size of the House of Representatives. When the time came to sign, he did so with fewer reservations than many of his fellows.

Monday, July 2, 1787

After a foggy morning, the day turned clear and hot.

Convention

On the question for allowing each state one vote in the Senate: the vote was 5 aye, 5 no, Georgia divided. Maryland's no was made possible by Mr. Jenifer's absence, leaving Luther Martin to cast the state's vote. The Convention was deadlocked. The large states remained utterly convinced that giving Delaware the same voting power as Virginia was unfair. The small states were utterly convinced that giving Virginia ten votes to Delaware's one would ensure Delaware's destruction. Both sides were correct.

General Pinckney suggested referral to a committee. No one expected much from this, but something had to be done.

The proposal passed: 9 aye, New Jersey and Delaware no. An eleven-member committee was elected by ballot: Mr. Gerry (MA), Mr. Ellsworth (CN), Mr. Yates (NY), Mr. Paterson (NJ), Dr. Franklin (PA), Mr. Bedford (DE), Mr. Martin (MD), Mr. Mason (VA), Mr. Davie (NC), Mr. Rutledge (SC) and Mr. Baldwin (GA).

Delegates

General Washington joined Chief Justice McKean in dining with the members of the Convention staying at the Indian Queen tavern, took tea at Mr. Binghams,

The area behind the State House was a pleasant place for a stroll and it was here that General Washington walked after tea on July 2.

and then walked in the State House yard. Before the Convention session he sat ". . . for Mr. Pine who wanted to correct his portrait of me." (This portrait displayed in the 1986–87 "Miracle at Philadelphia" exhibit at Independence National Historical Park.)

William Paterson wrote to his wife of two years, Euphemia White Paterson:

My dear Affa,

The Burlington Court did not continue as long as I expected. I arrived here on Friday last, about 10:00 o'clock at night. This letter will be handed to you by the Govr. [Livingston] who will set out to-morrow. It is impossible to say when the Convention will rise; much remains to be done, and the work is full of labor and difficulty.

I am in hopes that your sisters have by this time been so kind as to take up their residence with you. It will be best for you all. My heart feels for them and you— the affliction is severe, but it is our duty to bow, and be resigned; my best respects to them. They will ever find in me a brother. My warmest love to my little girl and boy [by his first wife, who had died three days after the boy's birth] their happiness is near to my heart. I hope that Cornelia [7] is attentive to her books. . . . An uncultivated mind, who can bear.

*I am your's Affectionately
Wm. Paterson"*

The Connecticut Compromise Committee

OLIVER ELLSWORTH was chosen by the Convention as Connecticut's representative on this day's committee. Ellsworth was a very able and experienced man, having served in various local and state offices, but he had fought hard for an equal vote in the Senate and he could be stubborn (Aaron Burr once said "If Ellsworth had happened to spell the name of the Deity with two *D*'s, it would have taken the Senate three weeks to expunge the superfluous letter.") His colleague Roger Sherman was even more experienced and regarded by his contemporaries as a consummate committee politician. When the committee met, Ellsworth was ill and Sherman substituted.

The Convention made some unusual choices as it elected today's committee. Ellsworth may have been regarded by the Connecticut delegation as an error to be silently and tactfully corrected. The Pennsylvania delegation had several young, vigorous and articulate members, notably Gouverneur Morris and James Wilson. Why was Franklin, old and ill, selected instead?

The committee membership did not include the most active and impassioned advocates of proportional representation—King, G. Morris, Wilson, Madison, Williamson. However, one does find the most impassioned proponents of state equality—Ellsworth, Paterson, Gunning Bedford, Luther Martin.

It appears that a majority of the delegates had decided a concession to the small states was essential and had structured the committee to facilitate concession. In the one state in which the Convention could have made a better choice, the delegation had rectified the error.

Tuesday, July 3, 1787

Today was clear and hot, with a high of 90°.

Convention

The Convention was in recess but the Grand Committee met. Mr. Yates noted its activity in his notes:

The grand committee met. Mr. Gerry was chosen chairman. The committee proceeded to consider in what manner they should discharge the business with which they were entrusted. By the proceedings in the convention they were so equally divided on the important question of representation in the two branches, that the idea of a concilatory adjustment must have been in contemplation of the house in the appointment of this committee. But still how to effect this salutary purpose was the question. Many of the members, impressed with the utility of a general government, connected with it the indispensible necessity of a representation from the states according to their numbers and wealth; while others, equally tenacious of the rights of the states, would admit of no other representation but such as was strictly federal, or in other words, equality of suffrage. This brought on a discussion of the principles on which the house had divided, and a lengthy recapitulation of the arguments advanced in the house in support of these opposite propositions. As I had not openly explained my sentiments on any former occasion on this question, but constantly in giving my vote, showed my attachment to the national government on federal principles, I took this occasion to explain my motives.

These remarks gave rise to a motion of Dr. Franklin, which after some modification was agreed to, and made the basis of the following report of the committee.

The committee to whom was referred the eighth resolution, reported from the committee of the whole house, and so much of the seventh as had not been decided on, submit the following report:

That the subsequent propositions be recommended to the convention, on condition that both shall be generally adopted.

That in the first branch of the legislature, each of the states now in the union, be allowed one member for every 40,000 inhabitants, of the description reported in the seventh resolution of the committee of the whole house—That each state, not containing that number, shall be allowed one member.

That all bills for raising or apportioning money, and for fixing salaries of the officers of government of the United States, shall originate in the first branch of the legislature, and shall not be altered or amended by the second branch; and that no money shall be drawn from the public treasury, but in pursuance of appropriations to be originated in the first branch.

That in the second branch of the legislature, each state shall have an equal vote.

Delegates

After his morning ride, General Washington sat for Charles Wilson Peale, who was making a mezzotint of the General for sale to the public. The General dined at the Robert Morrises, drank tea at Samuel Powell's mansion on Third Street, and in the evening went with Powell to the Philadelphia Society for Promoting Agriculture meeting at Carpenters' Hall.

Alexander Hamilton, who had gone back to New York, wrote General Washington that he had been sampling informed public opinion, and found support for a strong central government.

Richard Dobbs Spaight wrote again to John Blount in North Carolina reminding Blount of his two earlier requests for an advance of salary, "The time which I expected to stay here is already elapsed, and as I did not provide for a longer stay, my cash is already expended. Judge then my situation should I receive no further supplies."

Richard Dobbs Spaight

RICHARD DOBBS SPAIGHT was one of two delegates to the Constitutional Convention who were later killed in a duel. Everyone should know that Alexander Hamilton was shot by Vice President Aaron Burr in 1804. Another delegate met the same fate two years earlier—Richard Dobbs Spaight of North Carolina.

Richard Dobbs Spaight did not speak often in the Convention, but was consistent in his attendance. He was responsible for the motion to give the President power to make interim appointments.

Spaight was born in North Carolina in 1758 and orphaned at the age of eight. His guardian sent him to Ireland one year later for his education, which included a degree from the University of Glasgow in Scotland. When he returned home in 1778, he joined the army and served as aide-de-camp to General Richard Caswell. His military career was undistinguished, but he found a new and more agreeable position in politics. He was elected to the North Carolina House of Commons in 1779, and held the same office for all but two years in the next ten. Spaight filled a vacant seat in Congress in 1783 and was reelected in 1784, but returned home in 1785 to his old state legislative seat.

As a delegate to the Constitutional Convention, he did not make any major contributions in the debates. He supported the seven-year term for senators and the president and agreed that the president should be elected by Congress. At the conclusion of the sessions, he signed the Constitution, and throughout the debates, he was a strong advocate for a strong central government. When Spaight returned to North Carolina, he worked hard for ratification. His state, however, rejected the new form of government until 1789. When North Carolina finally did ratify, Spaight ran unsuccessfully in a race for the Senate. During the 1790s, he served three terms as governor of his state and one term in Congress in 1798.

Spaight's untimely death came following a personal dispute with John Stanly, a political enemy. Spaight apparently provoked Stanly into challenging him for a duel in September 1802. Each man fired at the other four times, and on the fourth try Stanly hit Spaight on his right side. He died the next day.

Wednesday, July 4, 1787

Warm sunny weather helped to make the fourth of July quite a day in Philadelphia.

Convention

The Convention was in recess so the delegates could observe the anniversary of Independence. The observance must have had particular meaning for many of them. Seven had signed the Declaration, including two members, Franklin and Sherman, of the committee which wrote it. Washington had signed the treaty in which Great Britain acceded to it. One had commanded the army which won it. With the exception of William Houston (GA) and William Samuel Johnson (CT), all of the others had served in the army or on one or more of the committees, conventions, congresses and state legislatures which had directed the war effort.

Delegates

Dr. Johnson (CT) attended the celebration. General Washington visited Dr. Abraham Chovett's Anatomical Museum of wax human figures, and then attended an oration by "Mr. Mitchell," (actually, Mr. Campbell). He dined with the Pennsylvania Society of the Cincinnati at Epple's tavern, and drank tea at Mr. Powel's.

Pierce Butler's (SC) wife of sixteen years, Mary Middleton Butler, wrote from New York to son Thomas in London and included a telling comment for a Charleston, SC, lady to make on Philadelphia's summer climate:

> *Your Papa I left ten days since at Philadelphia. My health was so bad that I could not support the excessive heat of that Climate, and was obliged to come to a more temperate one. . . .*

Governor William Livingston (NJ) attended the July 4 celebration in Trenton, where he delivered a patriotic speech.

Celebrating the Holiday

JOHN ADAMS pleas for celebrating the anniversary of Independence on July 2nd. He felt that date was really the anniversary, for on that day Richard Henry Lee resolved that "these colonies are, and of right ought to be, free and independent states." Regardless of Adams' choice of days, his sentiment carried and included activities we still participate in today.

James Madison believed that the Fourth of July would be celebrated by succeeding generations. The view from the State House would show the sky filled with fireworks and the smoke of bonfires while the streets would be the scene of parades, shows, games, sports, and other noisy celebrations.

I am apt to believe that it will be celebrated, by succeeding Generations, as the great anniversary Festival. It ought to be commemorated, as the Day of Deliverance by solemn Acts of Devotion to God Almighty. It ought to be solemnized with Pomp and Parade, with Shews, Games, Sports, Guns, Bells, Bonfires and Illuminations from one end of this Continent to the other from this Time forward forever more.

James Madison said in the *Notes of Debates* he was keeping on Convention deliberations that the delegates would adjourn so that "such as chose to attend to the celebrations on the anniversary of Independence . . ." could do so.

President of the Convention George Washington chose to participate in one of Adams' suggested activities. He noted in his diary, "went to hear an Oration on the anniversary of Independence delivered by a Mr. Mitchell, a student of law—After which I dined with the State Society of the Cincinnati at Epplees Tavern . . ."

That group of Revolutionary war officers had much to share in the way of collective memories of the war effort . . . and many absent colleagues to toast.

Thursday, July 5, 1787

After a clear, warm morning the day became cloudy.

Convention

Chairman Elbridge Gerry (MA) reported from the

committee to find a compromise how many votes each state would have in Congress. The first house would have one representative for every 40,000 inhabitants and the exclusive right to originate all money bills, which were not to be amended by the second house; each state would have an equal vote in the second house.

What Gerry did not mention was that the compromise was proposed by Connecticut's Roger Sherman in committee. Sherman, an elder statesman and wily veteran of many political battles, had convinced his colleagues that this compromise was critical to the survival of the Convention.

Gorham (MA) asked for an explanation. Gerry replied that the Committee was of different minds, and agreed to the report "merely in order that some ground of accommodation might be proposed."

Wilson (PA) said that the committee had exceeded their powers. Martin (MD) wanted a vote on the entire report. Wilson wanted a vote by section. Debate continued, with the large state delegates opposed, and the small state delegates supportive.

Delegates

General Washington dined, drank tea and spent the evening at Mr. Morris', while Dr. Franklin, as President, attended a meeting of the Supreme Executive Council of Pennsylvania.

Nathan Dane wrote from Congress in New York to Gorham (MA) and King (MA). He had to make a short visit home and wanted to know if either of them would be able to attend Congress so Massachusetts would be represented in his absence.

Roger Sherman

Roger Sherman was very much responsible for the compromise reported today. Sherman, from Connecticut, was one of the more remarkable men of his generation. Born in 1721 in Newton, Massachusetts, and educated in the local school, Sherman moved to Connecticut in 1743. At various times he had been a farm worker, a shoemaker, a surveyor, an almanac publisher (he did all of the mathematical calculations required himself), Treasurer of Yale, an incumbent of nearly every town and state office except Governor, amateur theologian, the father of fifteen children (from two marriages) a delegate to the First and Second Continental Congress, a strong advocate of American independence, a member of the committee to draft the Declaration and a workhorse in every session of the Confederation Congress, except 1782, between 1775 and 1785.

His characteristics were as remarkable as his accomplishments.

Stiffness and Awkwardness itself. . . . Rigid as Starched Linen—Awkward as a junior Batchelor. . . . an old Puritan, as honest as an Angell. . . . as staunch as a blood Hound firm as a Rock in the Cause of American Independence. . . . The oddest shaped character I ever remember to have met with. . . . Awkward, unmeaning, and author of a book of sermons, unaccountably strange in his manner. . . . As cunning as the Devil. . . . if he suspects you are trying to take him in, you may as well catch an EEL by the tail. . . . that strange New England Cant which runs through his . . . speaking. . . . No Man has a better Heart or a clearer Head. . . . He is an able politician, and extremely artful in accomplishing any particular object.

Sherman came to the Convention to patch up the Articles of Confederation. Gradually, he came to accept the fact that a new government was needed. Once a new government became his object, he was effective, if not "extremely artful," in attaining it.

Roger Sherman was a valuable delegate due to his previous experience in government. He proposed the Connecticut Compromise and was known for his diligent work.

Friday, July 6, 1787

The day was a clear and very warm with a breeze from the north east.

Convention

Debate resumed on a proposal for one representative for every 40,000 people in the first house. Gouverneur Morris moved to send it to a committee to spell out the number for each state, leaving later Congresses to make adjustments. Wilson seconded. Gorham disagreed. He thought numbers of inhabitants the true guide, particularly since Virginia and Massachusetts were about to lose Kentucky and Maine, and other states would be divided. After debate, the Convention referred the matter to Gouverneur Morris, Gorham (MA), Rutledge (SC), Randolph (VA) and King (MA).

The compromise proposed for an equal vote in the second branch was taken up. Dr. Franklin observed that this question could not properly be put separately, since it was part of a package compromise. The Convention voted to postpone this issue.

The Convention went back to the proposal for originating money bills in the first house and voted to retain the provision: 5 aye, 3 no, 3 divided.

The question was raised as to whether a vote in which there were only 5 ayes out of 11 votes was an affirmative. By a vote of 9 aye, New York and Virginia no, the Convention said it was.

Delegates

Dr. Johnson dined with General Washington and both wrote in the evening. General Washington's diary entry read as follows: "Sat for Mr. Peale (Charles Willson, who was preparing a mezzotint of the General for sale to the public) in the morning. Attended Convention. Dined at the City Tavern with some members of convention and spent the evening at my lodgings." Dr. Johnson indicates that General Washington was the dinner host; a fact which the General would not have mentioned even in his diary.

Abraham Baldwin took time as he sat in the Convention to write his friend and brother-in-law Joel Barlow.

James Gordon wrote from Tobago to John Langdon in Portsmouth enclosing an account of the firm's disbursements for Langdon's ship *Danot*. Langdon's Portsmouth neighbor John Wentworth wrote him to ask that he check on the progress of the "suite brought for the Prize Lussanna by Mr. Doane at Philada," since Langdon is going there.

Abraham Baldwin

ABRAHAM BALDWIN was born in Guilford, CT, the son of a poorly educated blacksmith. His father, a strong believer in the necessity of education, removed his family to New Haven where Abraham

Abraham Baldwin served on three committees. He opposed Congress having power to limit the slave trade and supported giving representation in Congress on the basis of population.

was graduated from Yale in 1772. Abraham became a minister and tutored at Yale.

In 1779 he joined the Continental Army as a chaplain. Two years later he was appointed professor of divinity at Yale, but refusing this post Baldwin studied law and was admitted to the bar in 1783.

Moving to Georgia the following year, Baldwin involved himself in politics and education. While serving in the Georgia House of Assembly he wrote the charter for the state's first college. Franklin College became the centerpiece of the University of Georgia.

His accommodating nature led him to be regarded as the ablest of Georgia's delegates. Baldwin never married but lavished great attention on the needs of his brothers and sisters, virtually educating them all at his own expense following his father's death in 1787. His sister Ruth married Joel Barlow, a fellow Yale graduate, poet, diplomat, and historian. His half-brother Henry became an associate justice of the Supreme Court of the United States.

Saturday, July 7, 1787

The day was fair and very warm, with a median temperature of 75.5°.

Convention

A letter from William Rawle, Secretary to the Library Company of Philadelphia enclosing a resolution offering the use of the company's books to the delegates was read, and the thanks of the Convention voted.

The clause of the Connecticut Compromise providing each state an equal vote in the Senate branch was brought up. Gerry would rather agree to it than have no accommodation. Sherman thought it would give the government more vigor—the small states have more vigor in their governments than the large ones. Wilson was still opposed. On the question shall the words stand: 6 aye; Pennsylvania, Virginia and South Carolina no; Massachusetts and Georgia divided.

Gerry wanted to move on to enumerate and define the powers to be given the new government. Madison disagreed—it was impossible to decide what powers to give Congress until it was decided how many votes each state would have. Paterson said an equal vote in the Senate was essential to the small states; he was against the Connecticut Compromise as conceding too much to the large states as it was. G. Morris was against the report because it maintained the improper constitution of the second branch.

It had been said that the new government would be partly national, partly federal; that it ought in the first quality to protect individuals; in the second, the states. *But in what quality was it to protect the aggregate interests of the whole. Among the many provisions which had been urged, he had seen none for supporting the dignity and splendor of the American Empire.*

Sherman and Ellsworth moved to postpone a vote on the compromise as a whole until the committee to fix the initial representation in the first branch reported: passed, 6 aye; New York, Virginia, North Carolina, South Carolina and Georgia, no.

Delegates

General Washington dined at Springsbury with the club, and drank tea at Mr. Meredith's. Dr. Franklin paid Sebastion Sybert seven pounds fifteen shillings for hauling sand, loam, dirt, boards and lumber between May 14 and July 5. Apparently, Sybert hauled the material to Franklin Court to be used in landscaping.

Governor Caswell wrote from Newington, North Carolina, to John Gray Blount forwarding warrants for 120 pounds each for Mr. Spaight and Mr. Williamson, which Blount was to remit to them. He also enclosed a letter to be forwarded to them.

Thomas Blount wrote from London to John Gray Blount to report that Robert Morris' business associate, "Mr. Rucker, . . . about the beginning of May last, took French leave, as the saying is, and embarked for America, leaving his business in a very deranged state and no person to manage it. . . ."

Robert Yates

ROBERT YATES is probably better remembered for leaving the federal Convention in disgust after only six weeks than for any other thing he ever did, yet he had a long and honorable career.

Born in Schenectady to a family which was mostly Dutch, Yates received a classical education in New York City, read law under William Livinston, and was admitted to the bar in 1760 and settled in Albany. Married in 1765 to Jannetie Van Ness, by 1787 he was the father of four, the youngest of whom had just turned seven.

In 1771 Yates was an alderman and as the Revolution approached, he was active on many of the committees and congresses which bridged the gap between colony and state, serving with Gouverneur Morris in the convention which wrote the New York state constitution of 1777. He was then appointed to the New York Supreme Court, on which he sat until 1798. In 1786, he served on a commission to settle the boundary between New York and Massachusetts.

Chosen as a New York delegate to the Federal Convention because he would defend state power, he left the Convention July 10 or 11, and opposed ratification. While in the Convention he kept notes of the debate. These are less detailed than Madison's, but contain arguments that Madison didn't record. According to William Pierce, a Georgia delegate, "Mr. Yates is said to be an able Judge. He is a man of great legal abilities, but not distinguished as an Orator."

Sunday, July 8, 1787

It was very warm (79° in the morning) and cloudy as usual.

Convention

The Convention was in recess. Some of the delegates probably used part of the day to reveiw progress in the twenty-nine working days of the session thus far.

The Convention had reached very few final decisions—on this day, a pessimistic delegate could say the Convention hadn't even decided it could or would stay together long enough to propose any new government. Even an optimist could see that in working days they had decided only that they would recommend a new government instead of revising the existing one, and that the government would have three branches. So far, they had spent ten days deciding how to apportion votes in the two branches of the legislature and still hadn't finally decided.

Still, the collective mood should have improved over the low of the previous Sunday. Then there seemed to be a stalemate. Now, much as the large state advocates of proportional representation may have regreted it, there seemed to be enough votes to pass the compromise and give each state an equal vote in the Senate.

Delegates

About noon, General Washington rode out to Doctor George Logan's estate, Stenton, in Germantown, where he dined. He returned in time to drink tea at Robert Morris'. He also wrote his weekly letter of instruction and inquiry to George Augustine Washington at Mount Vernon. "How does your Pompkin Vines look? and what figure does the Pease, Potatoes, Carrots and Parsnips make? Does your Turnip come up well, and do they escape the Fly?"

Dr. Johnson (CT) visited Richard Peters at Belmont, overlooking the Schuylkill and General Mifflin.

He also wrote his son Charles to commiserate on losing the legal cases of Samuel and Abraham Judson, to advise on appeal (don't), and to inclose the latest edition of Carey's *American Museum*.

Hugh Williamson (NC) wrote James Iredell that the Convention might last until the middle of August. Williamson was afraid that Davie, also a friend of Iredell, would want to leave for home before the Convention was over.

A Long Hot Summer

RECENT BOOKS on the Constitution make a point of the weather—"the worst summer since 1750." Connecticut's William Samuel Johnson would have agreed; he frequently noted that the weather was "hot" or "very hot."

Philadelphia was hot and humid and miserable at times that summer, but local sources indicate there was also a lot of cool and comfortable weather. Indeed, the contemporary records suggest that 1787 was no worse than usual, and may have been a bit cooler than average.

The Belmont Mansion belonged to prominent Philadelphian Richard Peters. The cool of the country setting was welcome relief for delegates such as Dr. Johnson during the hot humid summer.

Sources of climatological data—diaries of Philadelphia brewer Thomas Morris and Philadelphia stable-keeper/farmer Jacob Hiltzheimer, Dr. Johnson's memorandum book, and the weather charts from *Columbian Magazine* (which chart the weather at Spring Mill, on the Schuylkill just north of Philadelphia)—agree that spring was unusually cool. Both Morris and Hiltzheimer needed to keep a fire burning as late as June 4. Beginning on June 10, Dr. Johnson reported six straight "hot" days; Morris says they were "warm" and records a temperature of 86° on the 15th; Hiltzheimer says the 11th and 12th were "warm" and Spring Mills reports readings ranging from 71° to 81°.

Thereafter, Dr. Johnson reports both hot and cool weather until July 2 when he notes the first of eleven consecutive days of hot weather. During this spell, Morris was out of town; Hiltzheimer has the 4th, 5th and 10th "clear and warm," the 9th "warm," and the other days "very warm." Temperature recorded at Spring Mills ranged between 74° on the seventh and 85° on the third. The longest stretch of hot weather seems to be those eight days in July.

Considering the fact that Philadelphians then and now expect their summers to be hot and muggy, the delegates of 1787 seem to have experienced nothing out of the ordinary during the Convention months.

Monday, July 9, 1787

After a night of heavy thunder but little rain, the day dawned sunny and hot (mean of 81° at Spring Mill).

Convention

Today, and for the rest of the week, the Convention wrestled with the thorny issue of how to choose representatives for Congress. Pennsylvanian Gouverneur Morris, as the chairman of the Committee of Five, presented a report recommending that the first house should consist of 56 members. In the committee's formula, Virginia, the largest state, would have nine representatives, and Rhode Island and Delaware, the smallest states, would have one. The legislature would regulate future representation based on wealth and population. One representative would be elected for every 40,000 inhabitants.

The delegates accepted the idea of proportional representation giving the legislature the power to regulate the number of representatives. But the section specifying the number of representatives from each state and limiting the total membership to only 56 was not satisfactory to many delegates. After a brief discussion, the matter was referred to a Committee of Eleven (made up of a member from each state present) for resolution.

Robert Morris was recognized as a strong nationalist, although he infrequently spoke on the floor of the Convention. He nominated Washington to lead the Convention and served as his host.

Delegates

In the morning, Washington posed for the popular local artist Charles Wilson Peale. In the evening, he

dined at the home of Pennsylvania delegate Robert Morris, his host and a leading Philadelphia merchant. Later he accompanied Mrs. Morris to the home of Dr. John Redman, a prominent physician, for tea. He also wrote a letter to Hector St. John De Crevecoeur, a Frenchman who had just arrived in this country. He thanked him for his offer to transmit letters to the Marquis de Lafayette, whom Washington called his "good and much esteemed friend."

Daniel Carroll of Maryland took his seat in the Convention today.

Wealth or Population?

WEALTH AND POPULATION was the main issue of the Convention. Every member agreed that both should be the basis for representation. Popu-lation was fairly simple to measure, but wealth was difficult to quantify. The slave and plantation economy of the South represented greater wealth than the small farm and commercial society of the North. Should slaves be counted as wealth or population? William Paterson of New Jersey suggested that slaves be counted as property rather than as part of the popula-tion. In a similar view, Rufus King of Massachusetts wanted the slave population counted in the apportion-ment for taxation. With a combination of both pro-posals, slaves could be counted as wealth and popula-tion. Yet, while population and taxation might be linked, the delegates could not decide a meaningful way to tie other types of wealth to representation. In other words, the delegates were not so much opposed to wealth as a determining factor; they simply could not devise a method to quantify it.

Tuesday, July 10, 1787

This was a warm and sunny day.

Convention

The delegates continued their discussion of represen-tation in the House, focusing on the number of con-gressmen that would be elected from each state. The Committee of Eleven, appointed the previous day, recommended increasing the number of representa-tives from 56 to 65. Several counter-proposals sug-gested different numbers, but each motion was de-feated. During the course of the debate, James Madison of Virginia moved that the number of repre-sentatives should be doubled. He argued that the majority of a simple quorum of 65 members was too small to represent and vote for all the inhabitants of the United States. Although several members agreed with Madison, the body voted 9 to 2 to leave the number of congressmen at 65 members.

Delegates

In a letter to Alexander Hamilton, who had returned to New York, George Washington expressed his frus-tration with the Convention's lack of progress and with those who hesitated to create a strong national government. "I almost despair of seeing a favourable issue to the proceedings of our Convention, and do therefore repent having had any agency in the busi-ness."

That evening he went to the Southwark Opera House just south of the city limits to attend a James Townley play, *High Life Below the Stairs*.

John Lansing

JOHN LANSING was large, handsome and digni-fied. Born and raised in Albany, Lansing studied law under Robert Yates, with whom he served in the 1787 Convention. No sooner had he passed his bar in 1775 than the Revolutionary War called him. He served as military secretary to General Phillip Schuyler in 1776 and 1777 and as a member of the New York Legislature and the Continental Congress during war-time. In 1781 he married Cornelia Ray, of New York City. The couple had two children, one of whom died in childhood. Within two weeks of this tragedy their baby daughter also died shortly after birth.

On May 6, 1787, the New York Legislature chose Alexander Hamilton, Robert Yates and John Lansing

The Assembly Room was where the delegates sat during long hours of frustration as the business of the Convention seemed to be making slow progress.

as delegates to the Federal Convention. Lansing arrived on June 2, but stayed only a month. Both Lansing and Yates protested the centralizing tendencies of the Convention. Lansing contended that the Convention lacked the authority to prepare a new general government. The states, furthermore, had not supported such an undertaking. On July 10 Lansing and Yates withdrew and submitted a joint letter to Governor George Clinton explaining their situation.

Lansing opposed ratification at the state convention in 1788, and continued to serve his state, most notably

as a chief justice of the state supreme court in 1798 and as chancellor of New York from 1801–1814.

On December 12, 1829, he left a New York hotel to mail a letter, and was never seen again. What happened to him remains an unsolved mystery.

Wednesday, July 11, 1787

This day was hot and partly cloudy.

Convention

The delegates agreed that a census would be taken every ten years to measure the population and determine representation in the House. But just how the census would be counted was not clear and the debate on the issue was lively. Many delegates had balked at a proposal to count slaves at a three-fifths ratio of the

The residence of Robert Morris on High Street where General Washington stayed had trees in the side yard, but not in front. Early fire companies banned trees in front of insured property because they were thought to be a hindrance to fire fighting.

actual population. South Carolinians Pierce Butler and General Charles Pinckney believed blacks should be counted equally with whites, which was voted down. Northerners, such as James Wilson of Pennsylvania, wondered if blacks should be considered as citizens—each would be counted in the census—or as property, which would mean that none were included. The Convention recessed without reaching a decision on how the census was to be implemented.

Delegates

John Langdon of Portsmouth, NH, was in such a hurry to leave for Philadelphia that his friend, Richard Champney, did not have an opportunity to ask him to purchase a flax cleaning machine. In a letter Champney expressed hope that Langdon could buy the equipment for about 30 pounds and have it delivered by September for the flax harvest. With the new machine, Portsmouth would not need to rely on Boston for

processing flax seed. Langdon purchased the machine and shipped it home.

William Paterson of New Jersey noted in a letter to his wife that during this week of intense debate Philadelphia was unbearably hot. In fact, he wrote that it was "the warmest place I have been in."

Fire Insurance Companies

FIRE INSURANCE COMPANIES formed in England shortly after the Great Fire of London in 1666 and were well established by the early eighteenth century. Not until 1752 when Benjamin Franklin and other prominent Philadelphians formed The Philadelphia Contributionship for the insurance of Houses from Loss by Fire, however, was fire insurance successfully launched in the New World. An earlier attempt in Charleston, South Carolina, failed after only four years when a large fire swept the city and bankrupted the company.

Franklin and his colleagues planned their new venture carefully, presumably patterning the company after the mutual system of insurance of the Amicable Contributionship of London. They drafted articles of agreement, which hung in the courthouse, and obtained favorable responses from 75 individuals. Within a few months the Philadelphia Contributionship began operation, its directors examining surveys, issuing policies and ordering fire marks—four clasped hands on wood—to be placed on insured structures. The company's success paved the way for other insurance ventures, but it wasn't until 1784 that its first competitor, The Mutual Assurance Company for Insuring Houses from Loss by Fire, formed. A decision by the membership of the Contributionship to ban trees in front of insured properties (no doubt fearing it hampered the efforts of fire fighters) caused a number of policyholders to break away and, together with other Philadelphians, form a new company which would accept trees in front of such properties as an additional risk. Not surprisingly they chose as their symbol a green tree which appeared on policies, the company's seal and its fire marks, resulting in the company's nickname, "The Green Tree." This too was a mutual company where no one individual achieved personal gain; it provided protection for all.

Residents of other states were, no doubt, aware of these ventures, and eventually followed suit. The earliest being The Mutual Assurance Company for Insuring Houses from Loss by Fire in New York in April of 1787.

These appeared to be the only fire insurance companies operating in this country prior to the Constitutional Convention. With the promise and later fulfillment of a new more effective system of government, however, and an improved economy, other companies formed, stocks as well as mutuals.

Only two of these early companies survive: The Philadelphia Contributionship and The Mutual Assurance Company. Both have prospered over the centuries and expanded their geographic areas of operation as well as their products. They remain today, as in the past, friendly competitors.

Thursday, July 12, 1787

The weather continued hot (mean of 77°), despite the clouds.

Convention

The delegates continued their discussion on the method for determining representation in the House, gradually moving toward a spirit of compromise. Gouverneur Morris of Pennsylvania argued that states and people should be taxed in proportion to the number of representatives in Congress. During the debate, Morris was convinced to change his motion to read that states and people should be taxed directly. The amended motion was adopted.

At the conclusion of today's discussion, the Convention voted to give the legislature the power to vary representation according to wealth and numbers of inhabitants. William Samuel Johnson probably expressed the feelings of many delegates when he stated that population could actually be one of the best measures of wealth. He also stated that the number of blacks should be included in any computation for representation, which would marry wealth and population together. A census would be taken six years after the adoption of the Constitution and, thereafter, every ten years. All free inhabitants and three-fifths of the slaves would be counted.

Delegates

George Washington dined at the Morris house and drank tea with Mrs. Anne Livingston. Mrs. Livingston was the daughter of Dr. William Shippen and the estranged wife of Henry Beekman Livingston, son of Judge Robert R. Livingston. The General had tea with Mrs. Livingston several times during the Convention.

Jacob Broom

JACOB BROOM was somewhat an anomaly among the delegates to the Convention. He never served in Congress nor did he participate in the new national government. Born in Wilmington, in 1752 he was the oldest son of a blacksmith and wealthy farmer. Jacob followed his father in farming. At 24 he began service in the city government in Wilmington which spanned several decades. Broom then served four years in the state legislature.

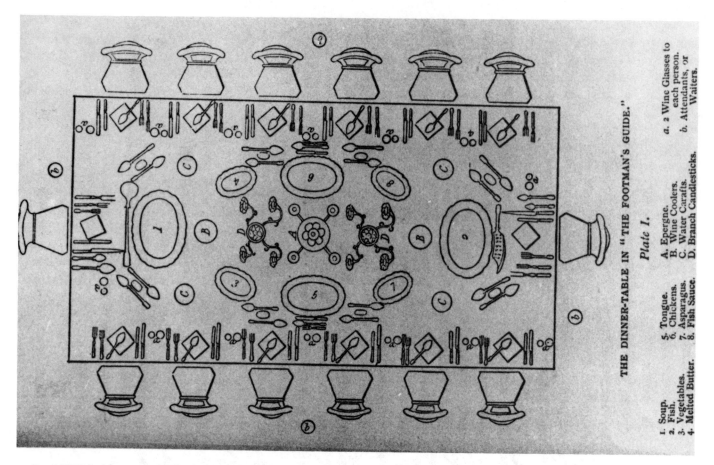

THE DINNER-TABLE IN "THE FOOTMAN'S GUIDE."

Plate I.

a. 2 Wine Glasses to each person.
b. Attendants, or Waiters.

A. Epergne.
B. Wine Coolers.
C. Water Carafts.
D. Branch Candlesticks.

5. Tongue.
6. Chickens.
7. Asparagus.
8. Fish Sauce.

1. Soup.
2. Fish.
3. Vegetables.
4. Melted Butter.

In 1790 he became Wilmington's first postmaster. He was active in banking, a cotton mill, and a machine shop.

Broom served as a trustee of Wilmington College and was active in Old Swede's Church. Jacob and his wife, Rachel, had eight children.

The proper setting at a dinner table in 1787 was a complicated affair. During that summer the hostesses of Philadelphia were busy entertaining the delegates.

Friday, July 13, 1787

The heat spell broke, giving Philadelphians a pleasant sunny day (mean 71°)—"but very dusty."

Convention

The delegates continued debating the report of July 2 recommending the Connecticut Compromise of proportional representation in the House and equal representation by state in the Senate. Old issues were rehashed and progress seemed slow.

Edmund Randolph of Virginia moved to drop wealth as a factor in fixing each state's representatives in Congress and use free population plus three-fifths of the slave population as a basis for representation. Gouverneur Morris of Pennsylvania opposed it saying that if slaves were people they should be fully represented and if they were property they should not be represented at all. Randolph's motion passed, 9–0–1.

Delegates

Massachussetts delegate Caleb Strong and Manasseh Cutler breakfasted at Massachussetts delegate Elbridge Gerry's rented house on Spruce Street. Later that afternoon Gerry accompanied Cutler to Franklin Court. Cutler was enthralled with Franklin the man, his library, and practical inventions. These inventions included: a large rocking chair equipped with a fan operated with a simple foot pedal, a long artificial arm and hand that took books from library shelves, and a letter-copying press designed to make a facsimile of written or printed documents.

During the conversation, Franklin produced a pickled two-headed snake in a vial. The doctor "was then a going to mention a humorous matter that had that day taken place in the Convention in consequence of his comparing the snake to America," Cutler wrote, "[but] he seemed to forget that everything in Convention matters was [to be held in strict confidence] which stopped him, and deprived me of the story he was going to tell."

Jonathan Dayton of New Jersey wrote William Livingston, governor of his state and the leader of his delegation, to vent his frustration at the lack of progress in the Convention. Yet he added that it would be improper to relate any specific information.

Northwest Ordinance Passes

NORTHWEST ORDINANCE was passed with little discussion and virtually no opposition by the United States in Congress Assembled. By this action Congress made a fundamental break with traditional European practices. Instead of acquiring new territories as colonies subject to the rule of a parent state, the United States decided that newly acquired areas could become full-fledged states with all privileges and responsibilities of the original thirteen.

Each would go through three phases of government. First, it would be ruled by a governor appointed by Congress; second, when the male population reached 5,000, the citizens could elect a legislature and send a delegate to Congress; and third, when there were 60,000 people, the territory could enter the Union as a state, completely equal to the original

Benjamin Franklin (here in a David Martin portrait) enthralled delegates with his library and practical inventions, and the curiosities he produced to enliven conversations.

thirteen. A bill of rights guaranteed each citizen freedom of speech, worship, and other basic liberties. As a final and important provision, the ordinance prohibited slavery.

Although the population requirements have changed, the process of admission established by the Northwest Ordinance continues today. Alaska and Hawaii were admitted as states in 1959.

Saturday, July 14, 1787

With a morning temperature at 61° and the high at 77°, diarist Christopher Marshall noted that Philadelphia had remarkably cool weather for the season.

Convention

Luther Martin of Maryland began the day's proceedings by asking the body to vote on the whole report of the July 2 Grand Committee, including the origination of money bills in the House and the important question of equality of votes for each state in the second branch or Senate. Much discussion ensued with the delegates from the smaller states favoring the equality of votes for the Senate and the larger states opposed. The discussion ended with neither a conclusion nor a vote.

Delegates

Delegates James Madison and George Mason of Virginia, Caleb Strong and Nathaniel Gorham of Massachusetts, Hugh Williamson of North Carolina, Charles Pinckney and John Rutledge of South Carolina and Alexander Hamilton of New York all dined together at the Indian Queen tavern on Fourth Street, south of Market. The tavern had several halls to accommodate such large private parties. These delegates presumably met this evening to try to hammer out their differences of opinion on the issue of equal votes in the Senate.

George Washington, after the Convention's adjournment, "Dined at Springsbury with the Club and went to the play in the afternoon." The play was Shakespeare's *The Tempest* adapted by John Dryden. Benjamin Franklin, as his state's governor, attended the Supreme Executive Council of Pennsylvania.

Bartram's Garden

BARTRAM'S GARDEN, home of America's first native-born botanist and the oldest surviving botanic garden in America, was visited by the Convention members on July 14 during a recess specifically for that purpose. When the great botanist John Bartram (1699–1777) died he left his house and botanic garden to his son John, Jr., who along with Bartram's other famous son William ran the garden as a commercial nursery. In 1783 they published a broadside of plants which became the first catalog of trees and shrubs in America. One of the visitors accompanying the members of the Convention was the Rev. Manasseh Cutler. The following description of the garden is Rev. Cutler's account of that famous visit.

We crossed the Schuylkill at what is called the lower ferry, over the floating bridge to Grays Tavern, and, in about two miles, came to Mr. Bartram's seat. We alighted from our carriages, and found (included in) our company . . . all members of the Convention. . . . Mr. Bartram lives in an ancient Fabric, built with stone, and very large, which was the seat of his father. His house is on an eminence fronting to the Schuylkill, and his garden is on the declivity of the hill between his house and the river. We found him, with another man, hoeing in his garden, in a short jacket and trowsers, and without shoes or stockings. He at first stared at us, and seemed to be somewhat embarassed at seeing so large and gay a company so early in the morning. Dr. Clarkson (who was among us) was the only person he knew, who introduced me to him, and informed him that I wished to converse with him on botanical subjects, and, as I lived in one of the Northern states, would probably inform him of trees and plants which he had not yet in his collection; that the other gentlemen wished for the pleasure of a walk in his garden. . . . This is a very ancient garden and the collection is large indeed, but is made principally from the Middle and Southern States. . . . There are in this garden some very large trees that are exotic, . . . He had the Pawpaw tree, or custard apple, . . . He has also a large number of aromatics, some of them trees, and some plants. One plant I thought to be equal to cinnamon. The Franklin tree is very curious. It has been found (by Bartram in 1765) only on one particular spot in Georgia. . . . From the house is a walk to the river, between two rows of large, lofty trees, all of different kinds, at the bottom of which is a summer-house on the bank, which here is a ledge of rocks, and so situated as to be convenient for fishing in the river, where a plenty of several kinds of fish may be

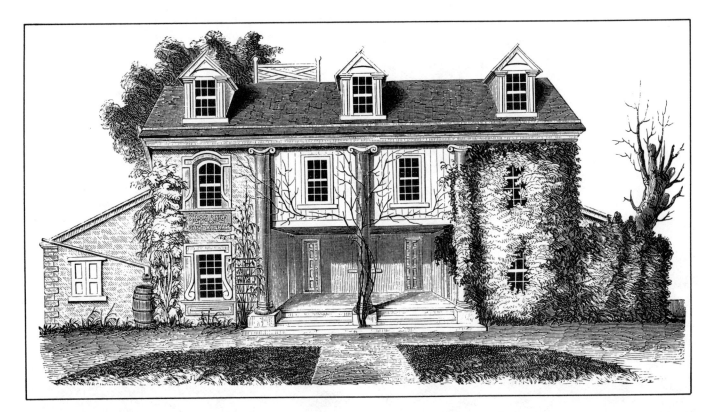

caught. Mr. Bartram showed us several natural curiousities in the place where he keeps his seeds; they were principally fossils. He appeared fond of exchanging a number of his trees and plants for those which are peculiar to the Northern states. . . .

About nine (A.M.) we took our leave of Mr. Bartram, who appeared to be well pleased with his visitors, and returned to Gray's tavern, where we breakfasted.

Bartram's House was at the site of the famous botanical garden of the botanist John Bartram. The gardens and commercial nursery were visited by the delegates during a Saturday morning recess called specifically for the purpose.

Bartram's Garden still occupies several acres on the west bank of the Schuylkill. It can be seen and enjoyed today as it was two hundred years ago.

Sunday, July 15, 1787

This was a cool July Sunday (mean of 64° at Spring Mill).

Convention

The preceding week no doubt had been draining and frustrating to many of the delegates. They had decided only a few minor issues and were on the verge of abandoning their efforts over representation in the Senate. The Saturday session ended with every indication that the large and small states would not reconcile their differences.

In the midst of this frustration, one can gain a better understanding of George Washington. With all of his responsibilities and honors, he considered himself a farmer, and like most planters, he did not want to be away from his fields during the growing season. Throughout the Convention, he wrote many letters to his nephew George Augustine Washington, advising him on proper farming techniques and asking for status reports. On this day the General advised his nephew to plant wheat in the corn ground as soon as possible. He wanted the cut oats sprinkled with lime

and the flax rotted in the same fields in which it grew. The General concluded by asking if George Augustine had "thinned the carrots which were too thick."

Mount Vernon, Washington's Virginia plantation, was always in his thoughts and many of his letters which advised proper farming techniques. Washington, with all his other responsibilities, considered himself a farmer.

Convention This Week

VEXING QUESTIONS still remained unanswered at the end of the week of July 9. Several details relating to representation in Congress were established. For example, the delegates had decided that the members of the first branch would be determined by a census every ten years. Other matters, such as tying direct taxes to the number of congressmen, counting three-fifths of "other persons" in the census, and dropping property as a measurement for representation were discussed at length and agreed to by many in principal. Yet the matter of representation in the second branch was still undecided and seemed not to have any possible resolution. Advocates from the large states—James Madison, Gouverneur Morris, and others—argued logically and with conviction that representation in the second branch should be determined by population. On the other side, delegates from the smaller states were absolutely intransigent in their position that all states should have equal representation in the Senate. No amount of logic or rhetoric could dissuade them from their position, and if the large state delegates persisted in demanding proportional representation, some small states were prepared to leave the Convention.

Even with the tension, there was opportunity for compromise. The report of the Grand Committee recommended a plan with proportional representation in the House and equal in the Senate. Delegates from the medium-size states, realizing that their constituents would never be large, understood that reconciliation would be essential for the Convention to continue.

Monday, July 16, 1787

After six days of 80°+ weather, today was a cooler 76° and overcast.

Convention

The Connecticut Compromise—votes in the first house based on population, an equal vote in the Senate, money bills to originate in the first house—passed by the narrowest of margins. Madison records this, the crucial vote of the Convention, as follows:

> *Mas. divided Mr. Gerry, Mr. Strong aye; Mr. King, Mr. Ghorum no, Cont. aye, New Jersey aye, Pena, no, Del. aye, Md. aye, Va, no, N.C, aye, Mr. Spaight no, S.C. no, Geo, no. Ayes—5; noes—4; divided 1."*
>
> *Gerry's very reluctant support for the compromise, Strong's vote for it, and the ayes of North Carolina's Davie, Martin and Williamson, may have kept the United States united.*

Delegates

General Washington drank tea with Mrs. Powell. Elizabeth Willing Powell was the sister of Thomas Willing, the aunt of Ann Willing Bingham, and a leader of Philadelphia society.

George Wythe wrote to acting Governor Randolph, resigning his seat in the Convention because his wife's health was, if anything, getting worse.

Nathan Dane reported from Congress to Rufus King, "We have been employed about several objects, the principal of which have been the government inclosed (Northwest Ordinance) and the Ohio purchase; the former you will see is completed, and the latter will probably be completed tomorrow."

By Guess-Apportioning Representatives

CONNECTICUT COMPROMISE provided that the Congress from time to time would reapportion the number of representatives among the states as

The Bush Hill Mansion was one of many lovely estates in the Philadelphia area. Leaders of society, such as the Powells and the Binghams, attended many festivities in such places.

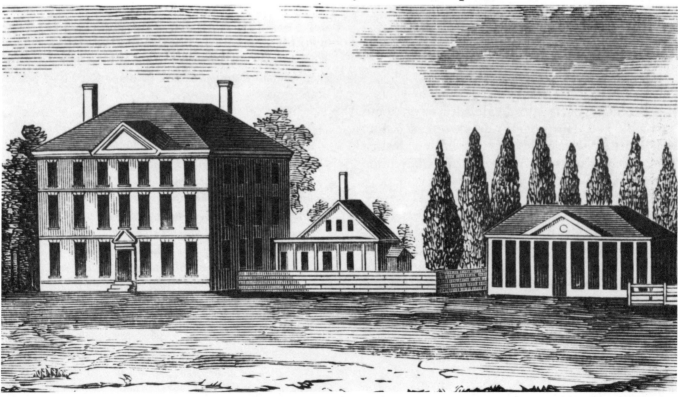

population changed. To get started, it allocated 65 representatives among the 13 states as recommended by a committee of 11 chaired by Rufus King. Since there had never been a census, this committee had to guess populations.

Their accuracy may be tested by assuming that the population of each state as a proportion of the nation's population did not change appreciably between 1787 and 1790 and second-guessing their guess by dividing the total 1790 population (3,564,715) by 65 (54,842), and then dividing each state's 1790 population by that figure.

State	1790 pop.	1790 pop. divided by 54,842	Rep. Assgd. in Const.	Error
NH	141,822	2.50	3	OK
MA	475,327	8.67	8	-1
RI	68,446	1.25	1	OK
CN	236,840	4.32	5	+1
Total		16.82	17	OK

NY	331,590	6.05	6	OK
NJ	179,570	3.27	4	+1
PA	432,876	7.89	8	OK
DE	55,541	1.01	1	OK
MD	278,514	5.08	6	+1
Mid-AT	1,278,091	23.31	25	+2
VA	699,264	12.75	10	-3
NC	387,846	7.07	5	-2
SC	206,235	3.76	5	+1
GA	70,842	1.29	3	+2
South	1,364,187	24.85	23	-2

Thus, the 1787 guess was reasonably accurate except for Virginia, North Carolina and Georgia. If the delegates considered Kentucky (68,725) and Tennessee (34,324) as so nearly separated that they shouldn't be considered in apportionment, the discrepancy is only −2 for Virginia and −1 for North Carolina, and the South as a whole would have been even.

Tuesday, July 17, 1787

The weather was very fair, with a WNW breeze.

Convention

A number of members from the large states met before the Convention opened to decide what to do about yesterday's vote. They couldn't decide on any action. Several small state delegates were present and saw that their interests were safe. As soon as the Convention convened, G. Morris moved to reconsider yesterday's decision, but was not seconded.

The Convention then took up the powers to be given the legislature, including the clause giving Congress a veto over state laws. The clause was defeated, MA, VA, and NC aye, 7 no. Luther Martin then proposed language that became the "supreme law of the land" clause, which was accepted without opposition.

Delegates

General Washington and Dr. Johnson both dined at "Houses." Afterwards Dr. Johnson went for a walk with Mr. Wilcocks and others and General Washington joined a party in an excursion to Grays Ferry to tea. William Paterson wrote to his wife of two years, Euphemia:

I expect to be with you on or about the first of next month, and hope I shall not be under the necessity of returning. The business is difficult; it unavoidably takes up much time; but think we shall eventually agree upon and adopt a system that will give strength and harmony to the Union, and render us a great and happy people. This is the wish of every good, and the interest of every wise man. I shall be in want of some hard money in order to clear me of this town, and, therefore, I request you to send me by the first good opportunity about 12 pounds. It is no end for me to draw upon the Jersey treasury, as it contains nothing but paper money, which few people will take: when tested by gold you must pay from 20 to 25 per cent, and the Pennsylva. paper is at present quite as bad, if not worse.

Elbridge Gerry turned 44.

The Congressional Veto

JAMES MADISON was perhaps the most thorough student of the history and theory of governments of his time and the one man most responsible for getting the Convention called and for providing a draft plan of a much strengthened federal government for it to work from. He certainly was one of the most effective advocates of its work once completed and was fighting hard to give the proposed Congress the power to review state laws and veto any that did not conform to federal policy. "The necessity of a general Government proceeds from the propensity of the States to pursue their particular interests in opposition to the general interest. This propensity will continue to disturb the system. Nothing short of a negative on their laws will control it."

The problem Madison stated was very real. His proposed solution would have been unworkable if it did not cause the defeat of the proposed plan.

At this point, Luther Martin stepped in. He was a defender of states rights, wanting, at most, only a few more absolutely essential powers to be vested in the Confederation Congress. He eventually left the Convention in disgust, and savagely opposed ratification of its work. But today, after Madison's veto of state laws was defeated, it was Martin who moved to include a provision "that the Legislature Acts of the United States made by virtue and in pursuance of the Articles of Union, and all treaties made and ratified under the authority of the United States shall be the supreme law of the respective States, as far as those acts or treaties shall relate to the said States, or their

James Madison on July 17 was outspoken in his desire to prohibit states from seeking their own good to the detriment of the majority, but his solution was not acceptable.

Citizens and inhabitants—and that the Judiciaries of the several States shall be bound thereby in their decisions, anything in the respective laws of the individual States to the contrary notwithstanding." This was adopted without opposition, sharpened and strengthened by the committe in style. This provision solved the problem Madison sought to address, and has proved one of the most distinctive and effective provisions in our system of government.

Wednesday, July 18, 1787

After a relatively cool morning, the day was clear and hot.

Convention

The Convention quickly agreed that the Executive should have a veto unless over-ridden by a two-thirds vote, and that a National Judiciary consisting of a

Supreme Tribunal should be established. Appointment of the judges by the Senate was hotly debated. Gorham preferred appointment by the Executive with the advice and consent of the Senate, as in Massachusetts. Wilson and Madison agreed. Luther Martin, Sherman, Mason, Randolph, and Bedford did not. Executive appointment lost: MA and PA aye, 6 no, NJ and GA absent. Executive appointment with Senate confirmation also lost and the Convention went on to other provisions.

Delegates

General Washington dined at Mr. James Milligan's on South Street. Milligan was a government auditor. The General drank tea at Mr. Merediths.

Dr. Johnson dined at Mrs. Wilson's and paid her bill for 30 shillings. Apparently finding City Tavern too expensive, he seems to have moved to a boarding house.

James Madison wrote his brother Ambrose about a land sale. He also wrote to Jefferson that the Convention was still sitting and about unrest in Philadelphia caused by a refusal to accept paper money and about crops; and to Edward Carrington to have the letter to Jefferson carried to Paris by John Paul Jones.

Dr. Franklin entertained Noah Webster at tea, and allowed him to take some extracts from Franklin's copy of the history of New Jersey.

Thomas Mifflin

THOMAS MIFFLIN was born and raised in Philadelphia, son of wealthy Quakers John and Elizabeth Mifflin. After attending Quaker grade school he graduated at sixteen from the College of Philadelphia—today's University of Pennsylvania. Mifflin then entered a countinghouse for four years until he visited Europe. When he returned he joined his brother in the mercantile business.

In 1772 Thomas Mifflin was elected to Pennsylvania's assembly where he served for four years. One of the youngest delegates to the First Continental Congress in 1774, Mifflin was a known radical. Elected to the Second Continental Congress, his political activity soon became secondary to army recruiting. In June 1775, he was appointed an aide de camp to General Washington and in August 1776 became quarter master general. After dissatisfaction developed over his administration the next year, Mifflin resigned, but was persuaded to stay on until March 1778 when a successor was appointed.

Mifflin was involved in the cabal to place General Horatio Gates in command of the Continental Army in George Washington's stead. When the plot was exposed, Mifflin disavowed all connection with the conspiracy. Washington was ordered to investigate and conduct court-martials if warranted. Such a tribunal was never called and Mifflin returned to state politics. From 1782 to 1784 he served in the Second Continental Congress, and from December 1783 to June 1784 he was president, the third president under the Articles of Confederation.

Mifflin strongly supported the new Constitution. He was elected president of Pennsylvania in 1788 and served as the state's chief executive until 1799. Due to an extravagant and lavish lifestyle, Thomas Mifflin died penniless and was buried at state expense. He was survived by his wife of thirty-three years, Sarah Morris.

Thomas Mifflin was in attendance for the entire Convention, but is recorded as only seconding a motion.

Thursday, July 19, 1787

The day was warm, humid and overcast, with light and variable winds and an afternoon shower.

Convention

The Convention proceeded to debate whether or not the Executive should be eligible for reelection. Gouverneur Morris, in a lengthy speech, noted the need to consider everything that related to the Executive in one view, ending with a motion to reconsider "the whole Constitution of the Executive." As Morris saw it, the Executive must be given vigor to pervade every part of the extensive Union and to guard the people against the legislature. How to balance the way he was elected, eligibility for reelection, authority to veto laws and the power given him so as to produce an independent executive but not a potential dictator took up the entire day, and several more days to come.

Delegates

General Washington dined at John Penn the Younger's and spent the evening in his lodgings. He wrote R.H. Lee concerning navigation of the Mississippi. It would be economically and politically preferable to improve navigation and bring Western goods to the East Coast, but the attitude of Western settlers made the point moot.

William Livingston (NJ) wrote from Elizabeth to son-in-law John Jay. A colleague has to leave the Convention so Livingston will have to "set out for that cool city and excellent fish market." Mrs. Livingston will send grandson Peter Jay home by a safe conveyance.

William Blount wrote from New York to Governor Caswell, reporting on events in Congress and in the Convention.

Hugh Williamson wrote to John Gray Blount of Washington, NC. Williamson told Blount that the delegation had asked the governor for another two months allowance. If he had received it, he was asked to please invest it in something, preferably pitch, on Williamson's account.

William Blount

WILLIAM BLOUNT was born in 1749 in Windsor, NC. Little information has survived about his early life. He received a solid education, but he did not attend college. His name surfaced during the Revolution as a paymaster for various units in North Carolina's militia. Then in 1780 he entered politics, which became his major interest.

Blount's two younger brothers, Thomas and John Gray Blount, became very successful merchants in North Carolina, selling tobacco in Europe. William was involved in the family business, and appeared to have been the political muscle in the various transactions. From the correspondence among the three brothers, it was apparent that the confederation government was not very helpful in promoting their business interests.

William Blount was a signer of the Constitution and left several letters written during the Convention.

William Blount had served in the North Carolina legislature since 1780, and was selected to represent his state in Congress in 1786. He was in Congress while the Constitutional Convention was in session, and in fact, spent more time in New York than in Philadelphia during the summer of 1787. Following the Convention he was a member of North Carolina's second ratifying convention in 1789 (the first convention did not ratify the document), then, when the Constitution was approved, he ran for the Senate. He was unsuccessful in his bid for office, and moved to Tennessee as the appointed governor of that territory. When Tennessee became a state in 1796, he was elected as one of the first U.S. senators, but his term was cut short by a scandal.

The source of Blount's problems seems to have been financial. He had overextended himself in land speculation and was desperate for money. He hatched a plot with Indians, frontiersmen, and the British fleet to forcibly take Florida and Louisiana from Spain and give jurisdiction to the British. President John Adams found out about the plot, turned the information over to Congress, and the Senate voted to expel him by a vote of 25 to 1 in July 1797. He returned to Tennessee and was elected to the state senate one year later, but he died in 1800. He was survived by his wife and six children.

Friday, July 20, 1787

Today was clear and pleasant, although there was an evening shower.

Convention

As today's session opened, the Convention, after some maneuvering, approved the proposal to elect the Executive by 25 electors apportioned among the states.

Next on the agenda was impeachment. Charles Pinckney (SC) and G. Morris (PA) moved to strike the provision. A lively debate followed. Those who opposed making the Executive subject to impeachment—Charles Pinckney, Governeur Morris, and Rufus King (MA)—argued that impeachment would lessen the Executive's independence; that he should not be given powers, the abuse of which would severely harm the public; and that a short term precluded the need for impeachment. Those who favored it—Davie (NC), Wilson (PA), Mason (VA), Franklin (PA), Madison (VA), Gerry (MA), Randolph (VA)—argued from a fear of power. As Madison put it, some provision must be made, . . . "for defending the Community against the incapacity, negligence or perfidity of the chief Magistrate."

Delegates

Dr. Johnson "Set out at 8 o'clock in the Mail Stage with Judge Sherman, we came in the evening to Brunswick." General Washington dined at home, drank tea at Mr. Clymers and wrote a note to Philadelphia blacksmith Jacob Rakestraw:

Sir:

Perceiving a Vessell advertized for Alexandria, you would oblige me much in hastening the Work you have under taken for me, that I may send it by her. I should like to have bird (in place of the Vain) with an olive branch in its Mouth. The bird need not be large (for I do not expect that it will traverse with the wind and therefore may receive the real shape of a bird, with spread wings), the point of the spire not to appear above the bird. If this, that is the bird thus describe, is in execution, likely to meet any difficulty, or to be attended with much expence, I should wish to be informed thereof previous to the undertaking of it. I am etc.

Alexander Hamilton, acting as a second to John Auldjo, who had been challenged by William Pierce to a duel, wrote Delaware Congressman Nathaniel Mitchell, Pierce's second. Mr. Auldjo was willing to consider an explanation to Mr. Pierce of the offending comments, if he was informed of what those comments were. Hamilton hoped that a duel could be avoided. Hamilton also wrote Pierce, either this day or a few days later, enclosing, apparently, an explanation from Mr. Auldjo, and urging Pierce to accept it.

Alexander Hamilton, Promise Partly Realized

ALEXANDER HAMILTON, on this his 30th [or 32nd] birthday, was beginning a brilliant career but one which somehow fell short of Hamilton's ability. Perhaps fellow delegate William Pierce's sketch catches both the promise and the weakness of this man: "Colo. Hamilton is deservedly celebrated for his talents. . . . To a clear and strong judgement he unites the ornaments of fancy, and whilst he is able, convincing, and engaging in his eloquence the Heart and Head sympathize in approving him. . . . He is about 33 years old, of small stature, and lean. His manners are tinctured with stiffness, and sometimes with a degree of vanity that is highly disagreeable."

Born in Nevis, Leeward Islands, Hamilton was early placed as a clerk with a merchant firm in Christianstandt, Virgin Islands. In 1772, he wrote a letter to a newspaper describing a hurricane which swept St. Croix Island. This display of precocious brilliance led a group of merchants to sponsor Hamilton's education. He was sent to the mainland and after several months at Francis Barber's grammar school at Elizabethtown, NJ [where he became acquainted with the family of William Livingston], in 1773 he entered King's College.

Graduating in 1776, Hamilton was commissioned as a captain in a New York artillery company. He soon came to Washington's attention, and joined Washington's staff as an aide. On December 12, 1780, he married Elizabeth Schuyler, daughter of General Phillip Schuyler. By 1787, the couple had three of the eight children which would eventually be born to them.

Alexander Hamilton tried to prevent a duel while acting as a second to John Auldjo, challenged to a duel by William Pierce.

Having established a reputation as a financial expert, Hamilton read law, joined the New York bar, and served as a member of Congress from New York, as receiver of Continental taxes, and as a member of the New York legislature and a delegate to the Annapolis Convention in 1786. In 1787 he was chosen, along with anti-Federalists John Lansing and Robert Yates to represent New York in the Federal Convention.

Hamilton did not play a major role in the Convention. While they were present, his two anti-Federalist colleagues outvoted him. When they left, New York's quorum went with them, and thereafter Hamilton attended only sporadically. His major contribution came in the fight for ratification.

Saturday, July 21, 1787

This day was again fair and hot.

Convention

Wilson moved to join the Supreme Court with the Executive in vetoing acts of Congress. Gorham, Gerry, Strong, L. Martin and Rutledge all opposed the motion; Ellsworth, Madison, Mason, G. Morris and of course Wilson defended it. Those who were opposed argued that the proposal violated the doctrine of separation of powers and that, as Luther Martin put it, "... as to the Constitutionality of laws, that point will come before the Judges in their proper official character." Those in favor argued that it was needed to balance the power of the Executive as against that of Congress, and that, while the judiciary would review unconstitutional laws, the veto would extend to constitutional but unwise laws. Wilson's proposal lost: CN, MD, VA aye; DE, NC, and SC no, PA and GA divided, NJ absent. The Committee of the Whole resolution giving the Executive a qualified veto was then approved without opposition.

Delegates

Dr. Johnson and Mr. Sherman left New Brunswick, NJ, at 5 A.M. and arrived in New York about noon. Dr. Johnson stayed with his daughter, Elizabeth VerPlank, and in the afternoon visited members of the Congress.

In a house on North Second Street, Oliver Ellsworth visited the merchant Josiah Gibbs who had numerous curiosities from his European travels, including part of an Egyptian mummy.

General Washington dined at Springsbury with the Cold Springs Club. In the evening, he attended James Thomas' play *Edward and Eleanora* at the Southwark theater.

Alexander Hamilton's unsigned letter attacking Governor George Clinton appeared in the New York *Daily Advertizer*. It charged that the governor "... has, in public company, without reserve, reprobated the appointment of the Convention, and predicted a mischievous issue of that measure." It then listed the governor's objections, and refuted them.

Oliver Ellsworth, in an unusually ebullient mood, wrote home.

A Humorous Letter

LIGHTER MOMENTS were also part of the founding fathers' experience. As evidence is the sometimes sarcastic and stubborn Oliver Ellsworth's letter to his wife on this day.

Dear Mrs. Ellsworth
I believe the older men grow the more uneasy they are [away] from their wives. Mr. Sherman and

Doctor Johnson are both run home for a short family visit. As I am a third younger than they are [Ellsworth was 42, Johnson 59, Sherman 66], I calculate to hold out a third longer, which will carry me to about the last of August [he left Philadelphia August 24].

I yesterday dined with Mrs. Gibbs [wife of Josiah Willard Gibbs, Merchant, 92 North Second Street] and Nancy Perry whose company was the more acceptable because they inquired so particularly about you and your little ones. I go to Mr. Gibbs the oftener for the sake of conserving with Billy, who since his return from Europe where he's spent five years traveling through different nations and examining everything curious, is to me a pleasing and profitable companion. Curiousity and the love of information you know has no bounds. My curiosity was gratified the other day by clasping the hand of a woman who died many hundred years ago. The ancient Egyptians had an art, which is now lost out of the world, of embalming their dead so as to preserve the bodies from putrefication many of which remain to this day. From one of these an arm has lately been cut off and brought to this city.

The hand is intact. The nails remain upon the fingers and the wrapping cloth upon the arm. The flesh, which I tried with my knife, cuts and looks much like smoked beef kept till it grows hard. This will be a good story to tell Dr. Stiles [president of Yale since 1777, a student of Arabic and Syriac and an orientalist], which is all the use I shall probably make of it. His avidity for food of this kind you know is strong enough to swallow the arm and body whole. No other reference to this object has been found. It is precisely the type of thing which would have fascinated Franklin, or Charles Willson Peale, or Benjamin Rush. It seems to have been owned privately and not available for public viewing].

This letter is so much lighter than what I commonly send you that I will not pursue it any further lest you should imagine I am growing light headed— and which for ought I know [will] be the case before we get through the business of the Convention.

Love to Nabby and the little boys and a smack to Fanny.

Oliv. Ellsworth

Sunday, July 22, 1787

After a warm and overcast morning, the weather cleared and grew hot with a temperature in the 80s.

Convention

The Convention was adjourned until Monday morning, following a week of solid accomplishment.

Delegates

Dr. Johnson recorded Mr. Sherman's punishment for sneaking home early. "Embarked [from New York] at 8 o'clock on Board Capt. Allen. Fair wind and agreeable Passage, tho Mr. Sherman Sea Sick, arrived at Newfield 5 o'clock. . . ." The Doctor arrived home in Stratford at 8, and found the family well.

General Washington got up early, and left Philadelphia with General Mifflin at 5 A.M. to ride to Spring Mill. The party dined at Mifflin's country seat before returning to the city. The General wrote Chevalier John Paul Jones a note asking him to deliver a small package to LaFayette, and to tender the General's best regards to the Count de Rochambeau, Marquise de Chastellu and others. Dr. Franklin also wrote Jones, promising to send the papers Jones needed to France in care of Jefferson, and asking Jones to give Jefferson Franklin's regards. Hugh Williamson wrote home to James Iredell.

After much labor, the Convention have nearly agreed on the principles and outlines of a system which we hope may fairly be called an amendment of the Federal Government. This system we expect will in three or four days be referred to small committee to be properly dressed; and if we like it when clothed and equipped, we shall submit it to Congress; and advise them to recommend it to the hospitable reception of the States. I expect that some time in September we may put the last hand to this work. And as Congress can have nothing to do with it put the question—pass or not pass—. I am in hopes that the subject may be matured in such time as to be laid before our Assembly at its next session.

Daniel Carroll observed his 57th birthday.

Vineyards and Bees

WEATHER was pleasant during the Sunday respite from the work of the Convention. The average temperature of 72° was a considerable improvement over a humid 96° high earlier in the month. At Spring Mills, thirteen miles northwest of Philadelphia, Peter Legaux meticulously recorded the day's statistics for his meteorological tables in the *Columbian Magazine.* Occasionally, his observations were also presented to the American Philosophical Society, which elected him to membership in 1789.

Legaux's routine was enlivened this morning when, according to his diary (still in family hands in 1898), "Gen. Washington, Gen. Mifflin and four others of the Convention did us the honor of paying us a visit in order to see our vineyard and bee house. In this they found great delight, asked a number of questions, and testified their highest approbation with my manner of managing bees."

George Washington's diary entry for July 22 reveals that he left Philadelphia at "5 o'clock A.M. Breakfasted at Genl. Mifflins. Rode up with him & others to the Spring Mills and returned to Genl. Mifflins for Dinner." Washington's route from Market Street took him out Ridge Road to the village called Falls of Schuylkill and the stone Mifflin mansion in today's East Falls neighborhood of Philadelphia. The house eventually became a beer garden and was pulled down in 1892 to make way for rows of houses.

After breakfast, the expedition continued northwest on the ridge climbing the hills of Manayunk and Roxborough to Barren Hill Road in newly designated Montgomery County. There, near the site of Lafayette's 1778 encounter with the British, they turned left and rode about a mile down to Spring Mill on the Schuylkill River.

Mount Joy, Peter Legaux's stone, gambrel-roofed house, stands today above Hector Street in Conshohocken. Terraces which exposed Legaux's vines to the sun and a stone-faced vault carved into one of the slopes can still be seen much as they were when Brissot, Rochefoucauld-Liancourt, Wansey and other travelers as well as the delegates from the Convention visited him.

Strolling by Friends Meeting on Front Street on a lovely day had little appeal for George Washington. He much preferred a ride in the country in pleasant weather.

Monday, July 23, 1787

After a warm night, the day dawned fair, with a light breeze from the west. The mean temperature was 75°.

Convention

Mr. John Langdon and Mr. Nicholas Gilman from NH took their seats. After considerable debate, with Williamson (NC), Gerry (MA), Wilson (PA), and Gorham (MA) involved, the Convention agreed to require oaths from state and federal officers to support the government. Gerry noted the key reason: "Hitherto the officers of the two Governments had considered them as distinct from, not as parts of, the General System and had in all cases of interference given a preference to the State Government. The proposed oaths will cure that error."

G. Morris and King moved that the Senate consists of members from each state, who should vote as individuals. G. Morris moved the number be three. Otherwise, a quorum would be fourteen, too small a number to trust. Gorham preferred two, otherwise with Kentucky, Vermont, Maine and Franklin [Tennessee] the Senate would become too big; Mason agreed. Williamson added that too many senators would burden the distant states. William, Houston (GA) and Spaight (NC) moved to reconsider appointment of the Executive by electors chosen by the state legislature, because of the expense of getting the electors from distant states like Georgia to the capital.

Gerry moved that the proceedings of the Convention be referred to a committee "to prepare and report a Constitution conformable thereto." General Pinckney announced his opposition to any committee report which did not give security against emancipation of slaves and taxes on exports. Committees of ten and seven were defeated; a committee of five was agreed upon.

Delegates

General Washington dined at Mr. Morris', then called upon Elizabeth Willing Powel in his carriage and escorted her to Governor Penn's country seat, Lansdowne, for tea. William Bingham would later purchase Lansdowne.

Mrs. Powel's nephew by marriage, Alexander Hamilton, was in New York City practicing law. He wrote to Thomas Mullett concerning Mr. Brailsford's suit against Mr. Wooldridge, recommending a settlement.

Dr. Johnson made no journal entry; presumably he was at home in Stratford catching up on family business which had been awaiting his return.

William Houstoun

WILLIAM HOUSTOUN, who was on this day so worried about the cost of sending electors to the capital, is one of the least known delegates. Yet, his was the first American name to become known to thousands of immigrants in the early 1900s—Houstoun Street in New York City's lower east side was named for him.

Born in 1757, William was the youngest of five children born to Sir Patrick and Lady Priscilla Dunbear Houstoun. Nothing is known about him prior to 1775, when he was a clerk in the law office of his brother John. In June of 1776 he sailed for London to study law at the Inner Temple, returning to Savannah sometime after 1780. While the timing is suspicious, and his brother Patrick and George were Tories, his brother John was a leading patriot and delegate to Congress in 1775. William seems to have returned in time to serve in the Georgia militia before the Revolution was over, since he received a bounty land grant from the state. He was admitted to the Georgia bar in 1782, and in 1783 took a seat in the legislature. In 1784–86 he served in Congress. While there, he met Mary Bayard, a niece of Governor William Livingston, and married her in 1788.

Houstoun presented his credentials as a delegate on June 1. On June 30 he voted against giving each state one vote in the Senate, resulting in a 5 for 5 against 1 divided tie instead of a 6 for 5 against win for the smaller states. He was a member of the committee which apportioned 65 members of the House among the 13 states. That Georgia got 2 more than it should have may be coincidence. Shortly after July 24, he left the Convention.

Fellow Georgia delegate William Pierce's description of him may be quite accurate. "He is a Gentleman

of Family, and was educated in England. As to his legal or political knowledge he has very little to boast of. . . . His Person is striking, but his mind very little improved with useful or elegant knowledge. He has none of the talents requisite for the Orator, but in public debate is confused and irregular. Mr. Houstoun

Lansdowne Mansion was the destination of General Washington and Elizabeth Powel as they journeyed in his carriage to Governor Penn's country seat.

is about 30 years of age, of an amiable and sweet temper, and of good and honorable principles."

Tuesday July 24, 1787

The day was very warm and humid.

Convention

The Convention again spent the day discussing how the President should be elected, and made no progress.

Delegates

General Washington dined at Mr. Morris' and drank

tea, "by appointment & particular invitation at Doctor Rush's." The General's emphasis that tea with Doctor Rush was by particular invitation probably reflects past problems. During the Revolution, Rush had written Washington an anonymous letter attacking Dr. William Shippen's administration of the Hospital Department and, when no action was forthcoming, had some hard words for the General. On the other hand, Mrs. Rush was the daughter of the General's old admirer, Annis Stockton, a fact which may have kept the occasion less than glacial.

A house intended for the president of the United States was constructed on Ninth Street in Philadelphia (1799 view). Under the presidency of John Adams it was decided that Philadelphia would not be the seat of the nation's capital. At the Convention the problem of the President's selection and term were one of the most complex issues.

The General also wrote his weekly letter to George Augustine Washington; his Sunday excursion had prevented him from getting a letter into Monday's mail.

William Gardiner wrote from New York to John Langdon. Gardiner was trying to help get Langdon's accounts with the Confederation settled. He seems not to have admired Nicholas Gilman, noting with apparent sarcasm: "Suppose Mr. Gilman reach'd Phila. nearly as soon as your Honor, he being a Stage passenger. Make no doubt his *consummate abilities* will contribute to bring mighty things to pass."

The Presidency, A Complex Problem

THE PRESIDENCY—how to fill it, how long a term, should a second term be allowed—was one of the most intractible issues faced by the Convention. Some idea of the complexity of the problem is conveyed by remarks made this day by Hugh Williamson—remarks which also reflect sectional issues.

Mr. Williamson was for going back to the original ground; to elect the Executive for 7 years and render him ineligible a 2d time. The proposed Electors would certainly not be men of the 1st nor even of the second grade in State. These would all prefer seat either in the Senate or the other branch of the Legislature. He did not like the Unity in the Executive. He had wished the executive power to be lodged in three men taken from three districts into which the States should be divided. As the Executive is to have a kind of veto on the laws, and there is an essential difference of interests between the N.& S. States, particularly in the carrying trade, the power will be dangerous, if the Executive is to be taken from part of the Union, to the part from which he is not taken. The case is different here from what it is in England; where there is a sameness of interest throughout the Kingdom. Another objectic agst. a single Magistrate is that he will be an elective King, and will feel the spirit on one. He will spare no pains to keep himself in for life, and will then lay a train for the success of his children. It was pretty certain he thought that we should at some time or other have a King; but he wished no precaution to be omitted that might postpone the event as long possible. Ineligibility a 2d. time appeared to him to be the best precaution. With this precaution he had no objection to longer term that 7 years. He would go as far as 10 or 12 years.

After a clear warm morning, an all-day rain set in.

Convention

Debate on methods of choosing the Executive continued. Ellsworth moved for choice by the legislature except when an incumbent was running, and then by electors appointed by state legislature. Gerry repeated his opposition, ". . . election by the National Legislature was radically and incurably wrong." Madison recited objections against every possible method, recommending popular election. Once again, no good method surfaced.

Finally, Gerry (MA) and Butler moved to refer Executive election to the Committee of Detail. Langdon (NH) agreed. Wilson "hoped that so important a branch of the system would not be committed until a general principle should be fixed by a vote of the House."

Delegates

General Washington wrote Phillip Marsteller to inquire about blankets for his negroes. John Jay wrote to Washington that he had delivered the letters to John Paul Jones and suggested that the Convention limit the role of foreigners in government and prohibit any foreigner from serving as Commander-in-Chief.

Dr. Franklin presided at a meeting of Pennsylvania's Supreme Executive Council.

Governor Randolph wrote to Colonel Daniel Shepherd, in Kentucky. He supposes Kentucky is anxious to learn the results of the Convention, but says delegates are bound by rule of secrecy. However, first principles have been agreed on and referred to a committee to prepare a Constitution "Our western friends, beyond the Allegheny, may be assured that we shall not be unmindful of their interests in our regulations."

William Pierce wrote from New York to William Short, in Paris, to report on his recent activities.

Robert Morris

ROBERT MORRIS was born near Liverpool, England, in 1734 and arrived in Maryland at age thirteen. Shortly afterwards he started working for the Willing mercantile house in Philadelphia. Rising rapidly in the firm, he was made a member at twenty years of age.

Morris was a delegate to the First Continental Congress in 1774 and in November 1775 he joined the Second Continental Congress. Although initially opposed to the Declaration of Independence, because he felt it premature, Morris nonetheless signed it in August.

Because of his extensive business experience, Morris turned his attention to gathering supplies and money to prosecute the War for Independence. His unremitting labor greatly aided the long struggle earning him the title "Financier of the Revolution." He simultane-

Robert Morris was one of the wealthiest men in America at the time of the Convention. He signed the Constitution although he seldom participated in the debates.

ously increased the fortunes of his company Willing and Morris. While a common practice of the day, it earned him criticism in some quarters—congressional committee investigation exonorated him. In 1781 Morris was chosen Superintendent of Finance. A loan from France made possible the establishment of America's first bank, the Bank of North America, in which Morris was a heavy subscriber.

Morris seldom participated in the Convention, but favored the new government proposed enough to sign the Constitution. At this time he was one of the wealthiest men in America.

In 1789 Morris was elected to the United States Senate. Unfortunately he became engaged heavily in land speculation. In 1798 he was arrested and held in debtor's prison. After three and a half years he was released to live on an annuity which Gouverneur Morris had established for his wife Mary. Mary, the sister of Bishop William White, was Robert's wife for thirty-seven years. She survived for another twenty-one years after Robert died in 1806. Three of their five sons and two daughters survived their father.

Morris was one of the triumvirate without whom the War for Independence could not have succeeded. Washington "the General," Franklin "the Diplomat," and Morris "the Financier" insured the success of the struggle.

Thursday, July 26, 1787

Today was rainy and cool—64° at Spring Mill.

Convention

In its rush to adjourn, the Convention continued to consider how to elect the Executive. Mason summarized the possible methods, the objections to each, and found he favored election by the national legislature. He moved for a seven-year term and ineligibility for re-election. Davie seconded, Franklin supported, and the motion passed: 7 aye, CT, PA and DE no, MA absent. G. Morris then attacked the whole proposal, but it passed: 6 aye, PA, DE, and MD no, VA divided (GW & DE no, JB & GM aye, ER absent).

Mason (VA) moved to have the Committee of Detail to report property ownership and years of residence requirements, as well as provisions to disqualify those in debt to the government. "It seemed improper that any man of merit should be subjected to disabilities in a Republic where merit was understood to form the great title to public trust, honors of rewards."

Madison, G. Morris and others opposed a property ownership requirement. Daniel Carroll and others opposed barring those who had unsettled accounts with the government. Finally the Convention referred to the Committee of Detail its proceedings, the Pinck- ney Plan and the Paterson Plan and adjourned until August 6.

Delegates

General Washington dined and drank tea at Mr. Morris' and "stayed within all the afternoon."

Dr. Franklin attended Pennsylvania's Supreme Executive Council meeting. Noted artist Benjamin West wrote Franklin from London that Mr. Jennings had arrived and West would be glad to help him. Mrs. West and their two sons are well. "Your Godson Benjamin is near six feet high." Twenty-odd years ago, Franklin, Bishop William White and Francis Hopkinson had helped Elizabeth Shewell run away to London to marry West.

Mr. Sherman was a pallbearer at the funeral of the Rev. Chauncey Whittlesey, pastor, First Society Church of New Haven. Hamilton wrote John Auldjo to announce that Major Peirce had agreed to drop his challenge, and the affair between them was at an end.

Abraham Baldwin wrote from Independence Hall to his brother-in-law Joel Barlow. He had hoped to travel to Connecticut with Sherman and Johnson, but dared not leave Georgia unrepresented. He would stay in Philadelphia as long as his money or credit lasts or until the work is finished.

Alexander Hamilton finally succeeded in getting Major Pierce to drop his challenge to a duel with John Auldjo, as he announces in a letter to Auldjo on this day.

Daniel Carroll

DANIEL CARROLL is one of the more obscure delegates, overshadowed by his cousin Charles, a signer of the Declaration of Independence and his brother John, the first Roman Catholic Bishop of North America. Born in Upper Marlboro, Maryland, to planter/merchant Daniel Carroll and Eleanor Darnell Carroll, Daniel had been educated at the Jesuit College of St. Omer in Flanders (most of the Carrolls, including Charles of Carrollton, Bishop John and most unusual, Daniel's mother, attended there). In about 1751, he married Elizabeth Carroll, a cousin of his and of Charles and they had a son and daughter. He was widowed in 1761 and never remarried.

A planter and businessman like his father, Carroll had been active in Maryland politics, serving on the Governor's Council from 1777–1781, in the state Senate beginning 1781, (president, in 1786), and as a delegate to the Congress in 1781–83. In the latter capacity he had signed the Articles of Confederation. Fellow delegate William Pierce seems to have been accurate in saying "Mr. Carroll is a man of large fortune, and influence in his State. He possesses plain good sense, and is in the full confidence of his Countrymen."

Carroll arrived at the Convention late (July 9). Thereafter, he appeared on the record with some frequency, but was not among the leaders. He defended guaranteeing each state a republican form of government and supported the electoral college concept, although he preferred popular election.

He opposed having the state pay members of Congress and supported letting the Senate amend money bills; he fought for requiring a two-thirds majority in the House and Senate for bills regulating trade and laying import duties, and supported a provision providing equal treatment for each state in trade regulation. He also fought, as Maryland's instructions and Constitution required, for requiring the consent of all thirteen states to ratify the Constitution, and supported every measure which tended to confirm federal ownership and control over the Northwest Territory.

Perhaps his most important role was that within the Maryland delegates, voting with Jennifer for most of the proposals for a stronger central government and thus offsetting the state's rights position of Martin, Mercer, and in part, McHenry. He also helped lead the pro-ratification forces in Maryland.

Friday, July 27, 1787

The day was very pleasant and cool, with a median temperature of 71°.

Convention

The Convention was in recess. The Committee on

Style began its work by assembling the proceedings of the Convention for the period June 19–June 23, the proceedings for July 24–26, the Paterson Plan and the Pinckney Plan.

Delegates

Dr. Johnson wrote from Stratford to the Rev. Samuel Peters in London, reporting that he has been in Philadelphia all summer at a convention of the states for strengthening the Union and vesting more ample power in the general government.

William Paterson, who had earlier been ready to leave the Convention if New Jersey was deprived of an equal vote, now wrote from Philadelphia to John Lansing:

> The Convention adjourned today to meet on Monday the 6th of next month, by which time it is expected, the Business will be departed. It is of moment that the Representation should be complete, and, I hope, that Mr. Yates and yourself will not fail to attend on the very day. The Comms. from New Hampshire arrived a few days ago; So that with a Representative from your state, all the States, except Rhode Island, will be on the Floor.
> "I hope to See you & Mr. Yates at New Brunswick on your way to Philada.

General Pinckney visited stablekeeper Jacob Hillzheimer to get a list of the best public houses on the road to Bethlehem, where he and Mrs. Pinckney were to visit for a few days.

John Rutledge

JOHN RUTLEDGE, who chaired the Committee of Detail, had been born either in Charleston or nearby Christ Church parish in September 1739. His mother, fifteen when he was born, must have been a remarkable woman. Widowed at 25, with seven children under ten, she nevertheless saw to John's education, including the study of law at England's Middle Temple.

Returning to Charleston in 1761, Rutledge was an immediate success in both his legal practice and provincial politics. Elected to the provincial assembly in 1762, in 1765 he represented South Carolina at the Stamp Act Congress and chaired its committee to draft a memorial and petition to the House of Lords. He served in both the First and Second Continental Congress, as a member of the provincial congress and the state's constitutional convention. Elected president of South Carolina in 1776, he resigned in 1778, and

was elected governor under a new constitution in 1779. From the British occupation of Charleston in the spring of 1780 until November 1781, he was the government of the state, a dictator commissioning partisan leaders such as Sumter, Pickins, and Marion, badgering Washington and Congress for assistance, working with Generals Gates and Greene, and keeping the cause alive in South Carolina.

Government restored, and ineligible for re-election, Rutledge was promptly elected to the state House of Representatives and then in 1784, as one of three chancellors. When the Convention opened, he had been married for 24 years to Elizabeth Grinki and had fathered nine children, of whom seven survived. Within the Convention, he was one of the more active members.

He favored a single executive, elected by the Senate. He wanted representation in both houses to be based on wealth, favored election of the House by the state legislature, favored lengthy residence and citizenship requirements for legislators, and moved that senators serve without pay. He reluctantly supported the Connecticut Compromise—"altho we could not do what we thought best in itself, we ought to do something." He opposed appointment of judges by the Executive and opposed joining the judiciary in the veto.

John Rutledge, of South Carolina, was anxious that the slave trade be protected. He was chairman of the Committee of Detail which produced the first version of the Constitution.

As one would expect, Rutledge was a zealous defender of slavery and the slave trade. However, he supported federal regulation of trade. "As we are laying the foundation for a great empire, we ought to take a permanent view of the subject, and not look at the present moment only." He wanted to protect public creditors, and to assume state debts, and moved

to substitute the language we now find in the Supremacy Clause. He opposed special provisions for appointing the treasurer of the United States—opposed Congressional veto of state laws, and opposed any provisions for suspending habeus corpus. Expressing impatience by mid-August, he remained a constructive member of the Convention until it adjourned.

Saturday, July 28, 1787

The day was cool, 70° and cloudy, with rain in the evening.

Convention

The Convention was in recess, as the Pennsylvania *Herald* for today noted:

The Federal Convention having resolved upon the measures necessary to discharge their important trust, adjourned till Monday week, in order to give a committee appointed for the purpose, time to arrange and systamize the materials which that honorable body had collected. The public curiously will soon be gratified; and it is hoped from the universal confidence reposed in this delegation, that the minds of the people throughout the United States are prepared to receive the respect, and to try with a fortitude and perserverance, the plan which will be offered to them by men distinguish for their wisdom.

Delegates

General Washington dined with the Cold Spring Club at Springsbury, drank tea there, and spent the evening at his lodgings.

James Madison wrote to James McClurg, who had returned to Richmond, to report on the proceedings since he left, and to urge his return. He also wrote to his father concerning the misbehavior of his slave Anthony, national affairs, and the weather.

Mercy Otis Warren, sister of the redoubtable James Otis, friend of John and Abigail Adams and Elbridge and Ann Gerry, poet, historian and political gadfly, wrote this day to Ann Gerry in New York.

James McClurg left the Convention in late July and is not recognized for any major contribution.

James McClurg

JAMES McCLURG was regarded by his peers as one of the finest physicians in the country. He received his undergraduate education at the College of William and Mary and his medical training and degree at the University of Edinburgh. For several years he remained in Europe to continue medical studies. While there he published a highly regarded article entitled "Experiments Upon the Human Bile," which established his reputation as a major medical scholar.

Following his studies in Europe, McClurg returned to Virginia to establish a practice in Williamsburg. He served as a physician during the Revolutionary War, then in 1779 he accepted a chair in anatomy and medicine at his alma mater. Four years later he left William and Mary and established a practice in Richmond, where he stayed for the rest of his life. McClurg continued to study as well as practice medicine, but did not publish any further observations. One medical biographer wrote that it was unfortunate that Mc-Clurg did not write about the nature and treatment of diseases related to the climate of Virginia.

McClurg's appointment to the Constitutional Convention was his first venture into politics. William Pierce of Georgia wrote "He attempted once or twice to speak, but with no great success." He advocated a life term for the president and a federal veto over state laws. Neither position was adopted, and McClurg left the Convention early to return to his medical practice.

Later McClurg served on the executive council in Virginia and as mayor of Richmond. He did not enjoy a long or distinguished political career, but is remembered as one of the nation's eminent early physicians. Not long before his death, he was honored in the first volume of the *Philadelphia Journal of Medical and Physical Sciences* (1820).

Sunday, July 29, 1787

The day was cool and cloudy after an early morning rain.

Convention

The Convention was in recess to give the Committee of Detail time to draft a Constitution.

Delegates

Dr. Johnson was at home in Stratford, Connecticut, for one of eight times he would be there this year. The longest of these stays at home had been thirteen days and together they totaled 62 days, or 17% of the year. No wonder his daughter complained of his absence.

Thomas Fitzsimons

THOMAS FITZSIMONS was born somewhere in Ireland in 1741 (at least four possible birthplaces are listed), came to America during his teens, and probably started working as a mechanic. His name is also problematic—contemporaries spelled it Fitzsimons or Fitzsimmons—but since he signed "Fitzsimons" on the Constitution, this has become the traditional spelling. Not all of his life, however, is obscure. He was a very devout and active member of the Catholic Church (He and Daniel Carroll were the only Catholic members of the Constitutional Convention.) He entered a mercantile business with his brother-in-law, George Meade, in 1762, and became a very successful merchant. During the Revolution, his company donated 5,000 pounds to the Army and he served on the Council of Safety and the Navy Board. He became a founder and trustee of the Bank of North America and a director of the Insurance Company of North America. He was associated with Robert Morris, invested heavily in various land enterprises, and as a result went into bankruptcy in 1805.

During the Convention, Fitzsimons spoke infrequently. He favored provisions that encouraged American shipping and commerce and opposed motions that taxed American manufactured goods before they were firmly established. Yet, while he was quiet on the floor, he seems to have been active behind the scenes. He arranged for Noah Webster to write an essay in support of the Constitution on September 15 and traced the progress of the Constitution through Congress by corresponding with Pennsylvania Congress-

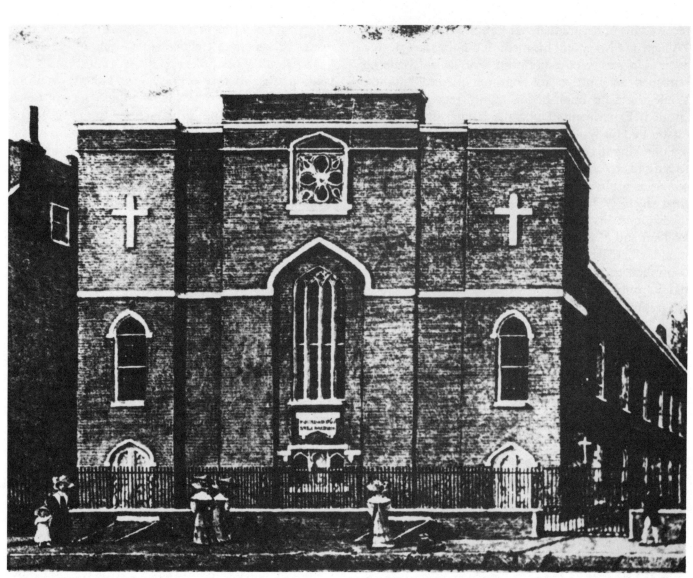

man William Bingham. He was, however, an outspoken advocate of the new government in the Pennsylvania Assembly, and along with fellow delegate George Clymer, he moved the Constitution very quickly through the Assembly and the ratification convention in Pennsylvania. He was elected a repre-

St. Mary's Church (here in 1830) is the burial place of Pennsylvania delegate Thomas Fitzsimons. He and Daniel Carroll were the only Catholic members of the Convention.

sentative to Congress in 1789 and was a strong supporter of Alexander Hamilton's financial program.

Monday, July 30, 1787

Today was uncommonly cool and overcast.

Convention

In recess.

Delegates

In company with Gouverneur Morris, and in Morris' phaeton pulled by the General's horses, General Washington went to Valley Forge to Mrs. Jane Moore's to fish for trout. Before leaving, he wrote a brief and unusually spritely note to Mrs. Elizabeth Powell:

General Washington presents his respectful compliments to Mrs. Powell, and would with great pleasure, have made one of a party for the School for Scandal *this evening; had not every-thing been arranged, and Mr. Govr, Morris and himself on the point of stepping into the Carriage for a fishing expedition at Jenny Moore's at which place Mr. & Mrs. Robt. Morris are to be tomorrow, to partake of the success, of Mr. Govr, Morris and himself this day. The Genl, can but regret that matters have turned out so unluckily, after waiting so long to receive a lesson in the* School for Scandal.

Benjamin Franklin presided as Pennsylvania's Supreme Executive Council met in their room on the second floor of the State House.

Madison drew a bill on Jaquelin Ambler in favor of Francis and John West of Philadelphia for $552 as an advance for one quarter's attendance on Congress.

Edmond Randolph endorsed it. William Blount wrote from New York to Thomas Blount in London, with a copy to John Gray Blount in Washington, NC.

George Washington

GEORGE WASHINGTON had steadfastly for several months refused to attend the Constitutional Convention. He listed numerous reasons for his decision: his health was poor, with rheumatism and other ailments; he needed to devote time to his farming activities, since he had left it to overseers for so long when he fought in the Revolution; he had retired from all political affairs and had no intention to reenter the arena; he was concerned that the Convention would not be considered legitimate by Congress: and he was concerned that he would offend his friends in the Society of Cincinnati. No doubt he could have thought of another dozen or so excuses as well.

James Madison had been pestering the General to attend, so much so in fact that he had not even responded to his letters. Washington, however, was beginning to consider the Convention in his summer plans when he heard from Henry Knox that Congress had sanctioned the Convention on February 21, 1787. Knox said (on March 19) that the General's prestige alone would give a legitimacy to the meeting that it might otherwise lack. Further, if he arrived in Philadelphia a little early, he could attend the Society of Cincinnati convention. All of his friends would be happy to see him and would understand why he was there. Humphreys wrote from Connecticut on March 24. He advised his former commander to avoid the Convention at all costs. It might turn out to be a disaster, and the general's reputation might be severely tarnished if he was associated with the meeting.

Before he received Humphreys' letter, though, Washington had already decided to take Knox's advice and attend the Convention. On March 28 he wrote to Edmund Randolph, governor of Virginia, and informed him that he would accompany his state's delegates to Philadelphia. That is, he would attend if his health held up.

George Washington, perhaps the most put-upon man of his generation, was about to be imposed upon again. At heart a farmer who wished only to be let alone to restore Mt. Vernon and the adjacent farms to

George Washington, in his position as president of the Convention, gave the meeting prestige. The power and responsibility given the President in the Constitution were influenced by the knowledge that he would be the first to serve in that office.

productivity and profit, he had given nine years to his country. Now he was asked to give another summer.

His presence in the proposed Convention would add nothing to its debates. He was neither a political theorist nor a student of the history of republican government, and he was known for keeping his eyes, ears and mind open and his mouth closed. But, if the Convention came up with a proposal for strengthening the federal government, that proposal would need all the credibility and all the support it could possibly get. For this, Washington's presence was essential.

Tuesday, July 31, 1787

The day was cloudy and so cool as to be like a fall day.

Convention

The Convention remained in recess while its Committee of Detail drafted a constitution for its further consideration.

Bishop William White, whose brother-in-law was a delegate and who as chaplain to the Continental Congress had met most of the delegates, wrote to Dr. Richard Price, in London:

> The Interest you take, Sir, in the civil Happiness of America will doubtless make you anxious to hear of the Event of the Convention now sitting for the Improvement of our federal Government. As they observe Secrecy in their Measures, I have cautiously avoided every thing which might look like a prying into their system. This much, however, I find, that Gentlemen among them whom I consider possessed of great and enlightened minds, entertain agreeable Prospects on the Occasion. It is now well known that they have settled the Principles of the Plan which they are to propose; as the Body has lately adjourned for a short Time, leaving a Committee to digest and arrange the Business.

Delegates

General Washington's diary entry describes his day, and indicates the relative interest he took in past events and present and future pursuits:

> Tuesday 31st. Whilst Mr. Morris was fishing I rid over the old Cantonment of the American [army] of the Winter 1777, & 8. Visited all the Works, wch. were in Ruins; and the Incampments in woods where the ground had not been cultivated.
>
> On my return back to Mrs. Moores, observing some Farmers at Work, and entering into Conversation with them, I received the following information with respect to the mode of cultivating Buck Wheat, and the application of the grain. Viz.—The usual time of sowing, is from the 10th. to the 20th. of July—on two plowings and as many harrowings at least—The grain to be harowed in. That it is considered as an uncertain Crop being subject to injury. by a hot sun whilst it is in blossom and quickly destroyed by frost, in Autumn—and that 25 bushls. is estimated as an average Crop to the Acre. That it is considered as an excellent food for horses, to puff and give them their first fat—Milch cattle, Sheep, and Hogs and also for fatting Beeves. To do which, 2 quarts of Buck Wheat Meal, & half a peck of Irish Potatoes at the commencement. (to be reduced as the appetite of the beasts decrease or in other words a they encrease in flesh) mixed and givn. 3 times a day is fully competent. That Buck wheat meal made into a wash is most excellent to lay on fat upon hogs but it must be hardened by feeding them sometime afterwards with Corn. And that this meal & Potatoes mixed is very good for Colts that are weaning. About 3 pecks of Seed is the usual allowance for an Acre.
>
> On my return to Mrs. Moores I found Mr. Robt. Morris & his lady there.

A Dignified Visitor in a Plain Suit of Black

HENRY WOODMAN, a Revolutionary War soldier, writing in 1850, recalled his father's charming remembrance of an encounter with General Washington at Valley Forge in the summer of 1787.

It was in the afternoon of the day, and [he] observed an elderly person of a very dignified appearance, dressed in a plain suit of black, on horseback, accompanied by a black waiter, ride to a place in the road opposite to him, where he alighted from his horse and came into the field to him, and shaking hands cordially with him, told him he had called to make some inquiry of him, concerning the owners and occupants of the different places about there, and also in regard to the system of farming practices in that part of the country, the kinds of grain and vegetables raised, the time of sowing and planting, the best method of tilling the ground, the quantity raised, and numerous other things relative to farming and agriculture, and asking after some families in the neighborhood. As answers were given he noted them down in a memorandum book.

General Washington, ever the sturdy farmer, was frequently more interested in agricultural topics than in matters of strategy or politics.

My father informed him that he was unable to give as correct information as he could wish, as he had not been brought up to the farming business, and was not a native of that part of the country, having settled there since the war, that he came from North Carolina, where he resided previous to the Revolution, that he had been in the army and was one of the number encamped there during the war. This gave a new turn to the conversation. The stranger informed him that he had also been in the army and encamped there, and was expecting in a few months to leave the city of Philadelphia, with not prospect of ever returning. He had taken a journey to visit the place, view the old encampment ground, which had been the scene of so much suffering and distress, and see how far the inhabitants were recovering from the disasters they had experienced, and the losses they had sustained from that event, adding that his name was George Washington.

The General, a reluctant delegate at first, honestly believed this was to be his last call to public service.

Upon receiving this information, my father told him that his costume and appearance were so altered that he did not recognize him, or he would have paid more respect to his old Commander and the Chief Magistrate of the Union. He replied that to see the people happy and satisfied, and the desolate fields recovering from the disasters they had experienced, and particularly to meet with any old companion of his in arms and suffering now peacefully engaged in the most useful of all employments, afforded him more real satisfaction than all the servile homage that could be paid to his person or station. He then asked his name, noted it in his memorandum book, and said that pressing engagements rendered it necessary for him to return to the city that night, or he would visit some of his former friends at their houses. Then taking him by the hand bade him an affectionate farewell.

Martha Washington understood that her husband George was done with public life after the Treaty of Paris (1783) and was going to spend his retirement repairing his finances and managing his long neglected plantation. Friends encouraged him to preside over the Convention.

Wednesday, August 1, 1787

Today was cloudy and cool, 66° at Spring Mill.

Convention

The Convention remained in recess while the Committee of Detail prepared a draft constitution. Lord Buckingham wrote today from London to Sir John Temple in New York:

> *As to America, we do not know what to make of her convention sitting in opposition to Congress, and yet tacitly approved: In her present state no power can treat with her and although our government will cherish every spark which may kindle old affection, yet the act of giving effect to the treaty of peace (standing by itself) be considered either as a reparation for the many flagrant breaches of that treaty on the part of America, or a competent security in future. . . .*

Delegates

Dr. Johnson (CT) set out from Stratford in the stage to New York with his son-in-law Daniel Crommelin VerPlank.

General Washington returned to Philadelphia after 11 A.M. when the rain stopped; later he dined at Mr. Morris' (PA). He had gone trout fishing but mentioned nothing about the number of fish caught—in anyone else this would indicate poor luck but no such inference can be drawn from General Washington's silence.

Dr. Franklin attended the meeting of Pennsylvania's Supreme Executive Council.

Pierce Butler (SC) wrote from New York to Weedon Butler in London:

> *My last letter from Carolina woud inform You of my intended visit to Philadelphia—As I declined the Honor my fellow Citizens offered me of the Chief Magistracy, I coud not refuse the last Appointment of acting as One of their Commissioners to the Convention to be held at Philadelphia—No doubt You have heard of the purpose of the meeting—to form a Stronger Constitution on strictly Federal Principles, for the Government. of the whole—I hope We may succeed—Our Country expect much of Us—We have satt every day since the 25th of May till last Saturday when We adjourned for one week—having placed my Family here, Philadelphia not being so healthy, I contrived the opportunity of visiting them—I go back to Philada on Sunday: and shall return home the first week in November. . . .*
>
> *The Political State of things in America prevents me for the present, from gratifying the first wish of my heart. I hope the day is not far distant when Our Government will shew stronger features of permanence. . . .*

Richard Bassett opposed the federal veto of state laws. He attended all sessions except for the first week in August.

The Rev. James Madison, president of the College of William and Mary, wrote from Williamsburg to his cousin James about Philadelphia.

Richard Bassett

BORN on this date at Bohemia Ferry, MD, Richard Bassett's family was deserted by the father, a tavernkeeper. Richard was adopted by a relative, Peter Lawson. During the Revolution he served in a Delaware cavalry unit as a captain. In the decade following 1776 he served in both houses of the Delaware legislature and was a member of that state's constitutional convention.

Bassett was a delegate to the Annapolis Convention, the second step on the road to a new federal form of government. He was, with fellow delegate Gunning Bedford, active in Delaware's ratification convention. On December 7, 1787, Delaware ratified the new constitution winning for herself the honor of being the first state.

Bassett participated in the new government serving as a senator from Delaware. In 1793 he was chief justice of the Court of Common Pleas and from 1799 to 1801 was governor. President Adams appointed Bassett a federal judge on March 3, 1801. Despite President Jefferson's ire, Bassett was confirmed to the U.S. Circuit Court but the position was legislated out of existence. Bassett was a close friend of Methodist Bishop Asbury and donated half of the cost of building the first church in Dover.

Thursday, August 2, 1787

Today was clear and much warmer than yesterday—the median temperature rose to 75°.

Convention

The five-member Committee of Detail continued working on a draft constitution for the further consideration of the Convention. The Convention remained adjourned while the committee worked.

Delegates

General Washington dined, drank tea, and spent the evening at Mr. Morris' home. Dr. Johnson (CT) arrived in New York early, and stayed with his daughter and son-in-law, the VerPlanks.

James Madison wrote to John Pendleton in Richmond, enclosing his bill for 165 pounds 12 shillings for attending Congress from July 20, 1787, to October 20, 1787, at $6 per day. Madison had forgotten to deduct 14 pounds already advanced him but would take it off next quarter's bill.

Deputy Secretary of Congress Roger Alden had seen Mr. Sherman and Dr. Johnson (his father-in-law) during their stop in New York on the way to Connecticut. Alden wrote Governor Trumbell this report:

The convention has adjourned till next Monday. A committee of five remain consisting of Mr. Gorham, Mr. Ellsworth, Mr. Wilson, Mr. Randolph and Mr. Rutledge. Mr. Sherman and Dr. Johnson have returned to Connecticut. I passed an evening at Stratford [Dr. Johnson's home town] but neither there nor here can I learn anything to communicate.

Oliver Ellsworth

OLIVER ELLSWORTH was born and brought up on a farm in Windsor, Connecticut. Ellsworth was forty-two, married to Abigail Wolcott, and the father of four or five children as the Convention opened. He attended Yale, parting from that institution (apparently at its request) at the end of his sophomore year, and graduated from Princeton in 1766 in a class with Luther Martin.

He taught school while reading law and was admitted to the bar in 1771; he married in 1772 and supported his family by farm work until his law practice grew. He served in many important political capacities: a colonial legislator in 1773, state's attorney for Hartford County in 1777, a member of the Governor's Council in 1780 and as a Superior Court judge in 1785. He had represented the state in the

Continental Congress from 1777 through 1783. He was an habitual snuff user, and supposedly consumed the most of any delegate in the Convention.

Within the Convention, Ellsworth was a staunch supporter of an equal voice in Congress for each state, and for the Connecticut Compromise once it was reached. Thereafter, he steered a middle course—not as strongly nationalistic as Madison and Morris but not a defender of state's rights; not as strong a defender of classic Republicanism as Gerry or Mason, but nevertheless a spokesman for frequent elections, no property qualifications for voters, and minimal requirements of citizenship and residence for holding office.

While in Philadelphia, he wrote home each week to "Mrs. Ellsworth" [in 1783, when he was in Congress, she had been "Dear Nabby"]. As a reward for staying in Philadelphia during the last two weeks in July while his colleagues were at home, he got to leave the Convention for home three weeks early.

According to fellow-delegate Pierce, Ellsworth was "a Gentleman of a clear, deep and copius understanding, eloquent, and connected in public debate; and always attentive to his duty . . . much respected for his integrity and venerated for his abilities." He seems to have been both an admirable and a thoroughly likable man.

Oliver Ellsworth helped other delegates clarify the issues. He was a member of the Committee of Detail which formulated the initial version of the Constitution.

Friday, August 3, 1787

The day was warm and pleasant, 77° at Spring Mill.

Convention

The Convention continued in recess. The Committee of Detail (probably)sent its draft constitution to Mr. Claypoole to be printed.

Delegates

General Washington accompanied Robert and Mary Morris, and Gouverneur Morris (PA) on a fishing trip to Trenton. The party stayed with Colonel Samuel Ogden at the Trenton Ironworks; Ogden's wife was G. Morris' younger sister.

Richard Champney wrote from Portsmouth, NH, to John Langdon (NH). He thanked Langdon for his attention in buying a flax seed cleaning machine, and asked him to ship it in the first vessel bound for Portsmouth, Boston or Newburyport. Champney wanted it by September, the time for cleaning the flax seed.

Jefferson wrote two separate letters from Paris to Edmund Randolph, Governor of Virginia. In the personal letter he expressed the hope that the Convention would enable Congress to pay its debts, commented on two incipient European wars, and offered to buy books, fashions, wines, and so forth for Randolph and his family. In the official letter, he discussed the weapons Virginia had purchased in France.

Gone Fishing: The Convention Takes A Break!

ADJOURNMENT of the Constitutional Convention between July 27th and August 5th, 1787, provided an opportunity for the delegates to escape "the foul airs" of a hot city and a demanding social schedule. Taking full advantage of this reprieve on July 30th, George Washington recorded the first of four fishing trips he was to take during his brief recess. That Monday, with fellow delegate and good friend Gouverneur Morris, he went "to one Jane Moore's in the vicinity of Valley Forge to get trout." They fished again August 3rd and 4th: "In company with Mr. Robt. Morris and his Lady, and Mr. Gouvr. Morris I went up to Trenton to another Fishing party. . . ."

In a city bounded by two rivers, fishing was a common Philadelphia activity. Fisheries lined the shores of the Delaware, and banks of the Schuylkill provided sites for a number of social angling clubs.

Indeed, the first fishing club in America, the Schuylkill Fishing Company, was founded in Philadelphia in 1732.

Provided with few clues as to the methods he used, we must assume that "The Father of Our Country" often fished with worms, as did his contemporaries. If this image of George Washington is less than heroic, there is one facet of his person that remains untarnished even in his pursuit of piscatory pleasure. Completing his diary entry for the August 3rd outing to Trenton, he wrote: ". . . In the Evening fished, not very successfully."

Fishing was a popular activity on the Schuylkill River. There were numerous social fishing clubs along the banks. George Washington recorded several fishing trips during the summer.

Saturday, August 4, 1787

The day was clear and hot, 83° at Spring Mill.

Convention

Letters to the editor designed to keep interest in the Convention alive and to pave the way for approval of its product continued. This day, "An American" wrote in the Massachusetts *Centinal*:

The Convention, I am told, have unanimously agreed on a system for the future government of the United States—which will speedily be laid before the several legislatures for their acceptance and ratification.—What this system is, is not as yet, known but to the framers of it—that it will be a system founded on justice and equity—in which the rights of the citizens, and of the rulers, will be properly balanced, considering the characters who have formed it, none can doubt:—That consistent with these, it may be energetic none can but wish.

Occasion, therefore, now presents itself, in which that good sense of the people can produce the most desirable events—for the people will NOW determine, whether a Nation possessing every advantage which nature can bestow to make it Great, and to which nothing is wanting but to improve those advantages, to make it such, shall be so, or not. But, my respected fellow citizens, can we have a reasonable doubt—Are we to behold a new thing under the sun?—Will the nature of things be reversed?—NO—the EXPERIENCE we have had, answers the queries in the Negative, and bids us anticipate the wished-for event of its meeting the approbation of all ranks of citizens—those excepted, who are, and ever will be, enemies to the prosperity of our infant empire.—Against such it behooves us to be on the guards—Be assured they will artfully cast stumbling—blocks in your way to national happiness and honour, and under the mask of patriotism, will endeavor to work your political destruction—That such are among us is certain—But, I trust your penetration will discover their designs—however thick their cloak—however specious their hypocrisy.

That this country may long remain under the guardianship of him who raisethup, and putteth down nations, is the fervent prayer of, AN AMERICAN.

Delegates

Dr. Johnson (CT) left Amboy, NJ, in the stage at 4:30 A.M. and arrived at Bordentown at noon. At Bordentown he boarded a packet boat headed down the Delaware to Philadelphia. The boat was delayed by head winds and, after dining on Newbold Island, at 11 P.M. he landed at Burlington, NJ. His expenses for the day were 3:15:0 proclamation money of New Jersey.

General Washington caught some perch in the Delaware River at Trenton, dined at General Philemon Dickinson's [John's brother] on the Jersey side a little above Trenton, and returned to Colonel Ogdon's in the evening.

Dr. Franklin and James Madison were visited by Noah Webster.

James McHenry

JAMES McHENRY was born in County Antrim, Ireland, in 1753 and educated in Dublin. At seventeen, he emigrated to Philadelphia. In the following year he convinced his family to join him. His father and brother established an importing business in Baltimore. James studied medicine in Philadelphia under Doctor Benjamin Rush.

He joined the Continental Army in 1775 as a surgeon. Captured at Fort Washington in 1776, he was paroled in time to join the Army at Valley Forge as a surgeon of the Flying Hospital [the eighteenth century M. A. S. H.]. On May 15, 1778, he was appointed secretary to General Washington and thereby abandoned medicine. Resigning from the army in 1781 to accept a seat in the Maryland Senate, McHenry served five years. Three of those years he was also a delegate in Congress.

McHenry missed much of the Convention. Arriving on May 28, he was called away by his brother's illness three days later. He did not return until August 6 and remained until the Convention concluded on September 17. As a member of Maryland's ratifying convention, McHenry campaigned ardently for adoption of the new constitution. After a term in Maryland's

Assembly (1788–1791) he again served five years in the Maryland Senate (1791–96).

In January 1796, President Washington appointed James McHenry Secretary of War. President Adams carried McHenry over into his administration. He served until May 1800 when the president forced him to resign; Adams believed that McHenry was conspiring against him.

In retirement, McHenry was joined by his wife Margaret at their suburban Baltimore estate. He died sixteen years later. Two children survived him.

Fort McHenry in Baltimore harbor, which figured in the War of 1812 and whose bombardment inspired our national anthem, was named by James McHenry while he was Secretary of War.

James McHenry was concerned with Maryland's interest in commerce and sought to get the state's delegates to agree on what was best for that state's interest.

Sunday, August 5, 1787

The day was very warm, 82° in the city, and fair.

Convention

The Convention remained in recess. All sorts of rumors concerning its work passed up and down the thirteen states. For example, James Warren wrote from Milton, MA, to his old friend Elbridge Gerry:

We hear that you have brought the great Business of the Convention nearly to a Conclusion. I wish it may be a happy one. We are told it will make us happy if it be not our own faults; but every Curiosity is raised to know the result in detail, every pen is held ready for Action & perhaps it will be as thoroughly scanned out doors. as it had been in Convention. . . .

As Warren was writing Gerry, Lafayette wrote to James Madison from Paris with a somewhat different view:

I am Very Anxious to Hear of the Convention. The fame of the United States Requires that Some thing be immediately done. It is Still More Important to their happiness.

Delegates

General Washington had an early dinner at Colonel Ogden's, after which he returned to Philadelphia with Gouverneur Morris (PA) and Robert Morris (PA), arriving about 9 P.M.

James McClurg (VA) wrote from Richmond to James Madison.

I am much obliged to you for your communication

of the proceedings of the Convention since I left them; for I feel that anxiety about the result, which its importance must give to every honest citizen. If I thought that my return could contribute in the smallest degree to its improvement, nothing should keep me away.

Dr. Johnson (CT) awoke in Burlington, NJ, to find that he could not get a passage to Philadelphia. His expenses for the day came to 12 shillings.

Elbridge Gerry turned 43 today.

Elbridge Gerry was active in debate but refused to sign the Constitution and opposed ratification. He was concerned about the "excesses of democracy" and was chairman of the Connecticut Compromise Committee.

Elbridge Gerry

ELBRIDGE GERRY, the son of a prosperous Marblehead merchant, graduated from Harvard in 1762, and promptly joined the family firm. (The firm did much of its trade in Spain through the Gadoqui family, one of whom, Don Diego, was in 1787 the Spanish ambassador to the United States). In 1772 Marblehead sent him to the Massachusetts House of Delegates.

An ardent defender of colonial rights, Gerry soon became a protégé of Sam Adams. On April 18, 1775, he escaped the British troops on their way to Concord by fleeing into a nearby field in his nightshirt. Chosen to represent Massachusetts in the Congress, he signed

both the Declaration of Independence and the Articles of Confederation.

On January 12, 1786, Gerry married 20-year-old Ann Thompson of New York. She and their infant daughter Catherine joined him in Philadelphia in June, but returned to New York at the July recess, and remained there.

Gerry was a republican in the eighteenth century sense. As such, he distrusted power and those who wielded it, feared standing armies, believed that successful republican government required a virtuous and eternally suspicious electorate which would elect virtuous and unselfish and devoted leaders (like Gerry), and that not even virtuous leaders could be trusted very long with any real power.

Gerry was by nature far more prone to criticize a proposal than to originate one. Thus, personality reinforced philosophy to assure that Gerry's major contribution would be to see that any power granted in the Constitution had been carefully considered. Also, however reluctant his support and vote for the Connecticut Compromise, it was vital in resolving the fight over representation. Nevertheless, Gerry refused to sign the Constitution. His opposition encouraged Massachusetts antifederalists to wage a tough ratification battle.

Monday, August 6, 1787

Convention

The Convention reconvened after its ten day recess, and Mr. John Francis Mercer, of Maryland, took his seat. Mr. Rutledge delivered the report of the Committee of Detail, and a printed copy was handed each delegate. The Convention then adjourned that the members might study the report.

The Committee of Detail printed report presented this day consisted of a preamble and twenty-three articles covering seven large pages with a wide margin to the left of the text for the members to make notes on. Of the twenty-three articles, two were introductions, seven dealt with Congress and its powers, one covered the Executive, one the Judiciary, three provided for interstate comity, and seven covered such miscellaneous topics as the admission of new states, amendment, ratification, and setting up the new government.

With this document, the provisions and phrases familiar to students of the completed Constitution begin to appear: a bicameral legislature composed of a House of Representatives and a Senate, an Executive called the President, an independent judiciary, a list of powers granted the legislature, including the authority "to make all laws that shall be necessary and proper for carrying into execution the foregoing powers," and ratification by conventions in the states.

There were other provisions which would be changed and deleted in the month ahead: money bills to originate in the House and not to be altered or amended by the Senate; the Congress to establish property qualifications for its members; senators and representatives to be paid by the states; no navigation acts except by a two-thirds vote in each house; treaties to be made and ambassadors and judges appointed by the Senate; the President elected by the Congress, and so on.

But, if much remained to be done, much had been accomplished. Perhaps it was a comparison with early July that led Davie to plan an early departure, confident that the work was moving to a satisfactory conclusion.

Delegates

Dr. Johnson embarked at Burlington at 9 A.M. in the rain; the boat ran aground on an island just north of Philadelphia, and he finally reached the city at 7 P.M. He dined at Wilson's and spent the evening at Mr. Lewis'.

General Washington dined at Mr. Robert Morris' and took tea at Samuel Meredith's. Dr. Franklin met with the Supreme Executive Council of Pennsylvania.

Hamilton wrote from New York to someone in Philadelphia to introduce a Mr. Israel, who was going there to settle his father's claim against the estate of Bernard Levi.

W.R. Davie wrote James Iredell in North Carolina, again praising John Adams' *Defense of the Constitution,* and announcing his departure from Philadelphia for North Carolina on Monday the 13th.

The Maryland delegates, Carroll, Jenifer, McHenry, Luther Martin and Mercer, met at Carroll's lodgings to form a state position on today's committee report. McHenry, acting as chairman, suggested moving to postpone the report to consider again an amendment to the Articles of Confederation. Carroll, Jenifer, and Mercer, who agreed on very little else, agreed that the articles couldn't be amended to meet requirements at the national level. Except for Martin, who was leaving for New York for a week, the delegation agreed to meet tomorrow, and McHenry prepared propositions for discussion.

John Francis Mercer spent less than two weeks at the Convention because he disliked the proposed plan and decided that the Constitution could not be ratified.

John Francis Mercer

JOHN FRANCIS MERCER, scion of a fine family of Virginia, was a Maryland delegate to the Convention. John Francis, one of nineteen children, was the fifth child of John Mercer and his wife Ann Roy. His father's first wife was George Mason's aunt; when Mason's mother died, the Mercers became his guardians.

Just after graduating from William and Mary College, Mercer enlisted as a lieutenant in the 3rd Virginia Regiment early in 1776. Two years later he was an aide to General Charles Lee. When General Lee (no relation to the Virginia Lees), was court-martialed after the Battle of Monmouth, Mercer resigned from the army.

Returning to William and Mary, John Francis studied law under the tutelege of Governor Thomas Jefferson. Afterwards he rejoined the army with Mercer's cavalry unit and aided General Lafayete in the Virginia campaign and was present at the surrender at Yorktown.

In 1782 and again in 1785–86 Mercer sat in the Virginia House of Delegates. In 1785 he married Sophia Sprigg and moved to Ann Arundel County, Maryland, to the estate, Cedar Park, that Sophie had inherited.

In the Convention Mercer opposed the strengthening of the central government and left before the Constitution was adopted. In the Maryland ratification convention he continued his opposition. Mercer served two terms in Maryland's House of Delegates and part of two terms in the United States House of Representatives.

In 1800 he began another term in the Maryland House and then served two terms as governor. In 1803 he returned to the Maryland House for four years. He was survived by his daughter Margaret, an educator and anti-slavery crusader.

Tuesday, August 7, 1787

The day was clear, warm and humid after a morning fog.

Convention

"The Report of the Committee of Detail was taken up," a motion to refer it to a Committee of the Whole defeated, (6 no, DE, MD, and VA aye), and the first two articles approved. The Convention then moved on to Article III—

> The legislative power shall be vested in a Congress, to consist of two separate and distinct bodies of men, a House of Representatives and a Senate; each of which shall in all cases have a negative on the other. The Legislature shall meet on the first Monday in December every year.

After debate the article was amended and approved. Next came Article IV, section 1:

> The members of the House of Representatives shall be chosen every second year, by the people of the several States comprehended within this Union. The qualifications of the electors shall be the same, from time to time, as those of the electors in the several States, of the most numerous branch of their own legislature.

Gouverneur Morris' (PA) motion to require voters to own property was defeated, although Madison supported it.

Delegates

General Washington dined and spent the evening with the Morrises (PA). He also dropped a note to his friend and factor Col. Clement Biddle to ask him to procure and send to Mount Vernon:

> *A Wimble [auger] bit-compleat. Pickled Walnut and India Mangoes none were sent before. Thompsons Seasons, and Gutheries Geography and the art of Speaking. Some Pamphlets which have been sent to me since I came to Town; and Books purchased for my amusement whilst in it, I now send to be packed up, and sent round.*
>
> *The Top of the Cupulo (from Mr. Rakestraw). The Venetian blind from Mr. Davis. A hogshed of Plaister of Paris, and a coog with two or three fowls, from Mr Barge; and the Chair. I mean shall take the opportunity afforded by the Dolphin of going to Mount Vernon, and I pray you to recommend them to the particular care of the Captn. I have bought one and mean to buy another, piece of fine linnen which I shall send to you.*

Dr. Johnson (CT) dined at Wilson's, his boarding house; his expenses totaled 10 shillings and 6 pence.

Qualifications for Voting

PREVENTION FROM VOTING due to lack of property, has not been experienced by any citizen of the United States for a long time. It has been over 100 years since a man would legally be prevented from voting because of his race. It has been nearly sixty years since a woman could be denied the vote.

This background may obscure just how enlighted (and astute) the Convention was on this day 200 years ago when it refused to require voters to own property, and instead provided that anyone could vote in federal elections who could vote for a representative to his own state legislature.

Any proposition subscribed to by Gouveneur Morris, John Dickinson and James Madison could be defended. Madison's notes tell us that Dickinson spoke out in favor of:

vesting the right of sufferage in the freeholders [property owners] of the Country. He considered them as the best guardians of liberty; and the restriction of the right to them as a necessary defense against the dangerous influence of those multitudes without property & without principle, with which our Country like all others, will in time abound.

As Madison viewed the subject;

in its merits alone, the freeholders of the Country

Benjamin Franklin's print shop on Market Street was one of many at a time when publishing flourished in Philadelphia. In their letters and diaries, many of the delegates noted pamphlets and books purchased.

would be the safest depositories of Republican liberty. . . . [In England] the greatest part [of Parliament] are chosen by the Cities & boroughs, in many of which the qualifications of suffrage is as low as it is in any one of the U.S. and it was in the boroughs & Cities rather than the Counties, that bribery most prevailed, . . ."

However, it was the philosophy of Dr. Franklin ("It is of great consequence that we should not depress the virtue and public spirit of our common people; . . .") and the hard common sense of John Rutledge (". . . restraining the right of suffrage to the freeholders [is] . . . very unadvised . . . It would create division among the people and make enemies of all those who should be excluded.") which prevailed. Consequently, although many blacks had to await the XIV Amendment in 1870 for ostensible recognition of their right to vote in federal elections, others who lived in northern states had that right recognized much earlier. So, too, with women. Women residents in Wyoming could vote years before passage of the XXX Amendment in 1920. The delegates to the Convention left voting rights up to each state.

Wednesday, August 8, 1787

The day was very hot and humid.

Convention

Debate resumed on having the lower house elected by citizens eligible to vote for the most numerous house of their state legislature. Mercer (MD) grumbled about the whole plan, Gorham (MA) defended the lack of property requirement for voters, and the section passed without opposition.

The delegates then turned to Article IV, Section 2 of the plan proposed by the Committee of Detail. This section proposed that members of the House be at least twenty-five years old, a citizen for three years, and at the time of election be a resident of the state in which they are chosen. The section was amended and approved.

The delegates then considered the remaining sections of Article IV. They spent considerable time on Section 4:

As the proportions of numbers in (the) different states will alter from time to time; as some of the States may hereafter be divided; as others may be enlarged by addition of territory; as two or more States may be united; as new States will be erected within the limits of the United States, the Legislature shall, in each of these cases, regulate the number of inhabitants, according to the provisions herein after made, at the rate of one for every forty thousand.

King (MA) immediately attacked including slaves in determining the basis for representation—"The importation of slaves could not be prohibited—exports could not be taxed. Is this reasonable?"

Madison objected to making one for every 40,000 inhabitants a rule; with population growth that number of representatives would be too large. Gorham didn't think that a problem because it was improbable that "this vast country including the Western territory will 150 years hence remain one nation." Sherman and Madison moved, and the Convention agreed, to insert "not to exceed" before "1 for every 40,000."

G. Morris then moved to insert "free" before "inhabitants," supporting the motion with a vehement attack on slavery. Dayton (NJ) seconded to get his position on the record. The motion lost.

Delegates

General Washington dined at City Tavern and re-

mained there till nearly 10 o'clock. Dr. Johnson (CT) dined at Dr. Rush's and bought four shillings and six pence worth of snuff.

Robert Morris (PA) wrote his New York partner, William Constable, to introduce Mr. John Richard "who I sent on to New York for the purpose of settling the Accounts of Willing, Morris & Compy. with the Treasury Board, . . ."

Massachusetts Congressman Doctor Samuel Holten wrote Gorham (MA) that he was leaving Congress in a few days, and Massachusetts would not be represented. The election of officers for the Northwest Territory was coming up. Holton favored Arthur St. Clair for governor and recommended ". . . to your particular notice my friend . . ." Major Winthrop Sergeant for secretary.

7551 Congresspersons

SIZE OF THE HOUSE OF REPRESENTATIVES was a problem for the Convention. As "representative" implies, House members were to rep-

resent a broad cross section of America—farmers, manufacturers, merchants, craftsmen, laborers, planters, iron makers, and a great variety of lesser interests. To insure reasonably complete representation, there should be a large number of representatives. However, if there were too many, the House would be terribly inefficient. Also, the country was going to grow and fill up the vast areas between the Appalachians and the Mississippi. The country might have 20,000,000 people some day—and these folks should be represented.

Many delegates would have liked to at least set a ratio of one representative for a specific number of people. The delegates determined that the first House of Representatives should have 65 members, that every ten years a census would determine the proportion of the total number each state would have, but Congress would determine the size of the House.

Future generations should not be tied to a fixed rule. The only limitation was that there could be no more than one representative for every 30,000 people.

After the first census, Congress provided 105 members of the House for 3,615,930 people, or one representative for every 34,438 people. As the years passed, both population and the House grew, until in 1910 the population stood at 91,972,266, and there were 435 members of the House (1:211,430). Today, 435 members represent 226,545,805 of us (1:520,795).

A House of 435 is probably too large for maximum efficiency. Congress could pass a law to reduce it to 200 or 250. On the other hand, Congress could increase the number of representatives to the 7551 authorized by the Constitution.

Thursday, August 9, 1787

Today was clear and warm until afternoon, then showers and an evening thunder storm moved in.

Convention

Article V, Section 1, came under consideration.

> The Senate of the United States shall be chosen by the Legislatures of the several States. Each Legislature shall chose two members. Vacancies may be supplied by the Executive until the next meeting of the Legislature. Each member shall have one vote.

Wilson (PA) objectd to having the governors fill vacancies. Randolph (VA), Ellsworth (CT), and Williamson (NC) urged its necessity, and the motion to strike it out lost.

Randolph wished to postpone the vote on "each member shall have one vote" pending reconsideration of the money bill provision. Strong (MA) agreed; Read (DE) explained that he had voted against House origination because he thought the large states didn't regard it as important; if they did, he would change his vote. While this debate was out of order, the chair let it continue, with Wilson, Ellsworth and Madison opposing House origination and Franklin, Mason (VA) and Williamson urging that a deal is a deal. All of Section 1 except the last sentence was then approved.

The delegates then turned to Article V, Section 3 (Senators to be at least 30 years of age; citizens for four years, and a resident of the state for which he shall be chosen). G. Morris (PA) wanted 14 years citizenship; his motion touched off a lively debate and was defeated. Thirteen years lost, and then ten. After more debate, the delegates agreed on nine years.

Delegates

William Blount (NC) wrote from Philadelphia to his brother in Washington, NC. On his way from New York he had stopped to inspect Robert Morris' iron works near Trenton (Morrisville, PA). Blount had paid particular attention to the nail works, and suggested that the Blounts might profitably use some of their slaves in a similar enterprise.

Forty-three-year-old Elbridge Gerry (MA) wrote to his wife of a year and a half, twenty-one-year-old Ann Thompson Gerry.

> *I arrived here, my dearest wife, about an hour ago (at 8 PM) with Colo. Hamilton, whom I met at the Hook. We escaped a heavy Thunder Gust, which gave us chase about an hour before we reached the city. We had a cool ride, free from Dust and I am not fatigued. How is my dearest girl, her little Pet [infant daughter Catherine], and family Friends. An answer to such questions as these is more interesting to me than all the delusive prospects of pleasure or Happiness from other Quarters. When I went to bed last evening, I began to reproach myself and have continued to do so ever since, for leaving behind my little comforter, in the absence of my lovely Friend. I mean her portrait. How happened it to escape your memory as well as mine . . .*

George Clymer

GEORGE CLYMER, born in 1739, was orphaned when he was barely a year old. He was raised by his uncle, William Coleman, a very prosperous Philadelphia merchant and at a fairly young age entered his uncle's business as a clerk. Fortune further shined on the young man when he married Elizabeth Meredith, the daughter of Reese Meredith, his uncle's partner. With his connections and natural ability as a merchant, Clymer rose through the ranks of the company until he became a partner and finally the owner.

Clymer became a captain of Pennsylvania volunteer soldiers in 1773 and was appointed a delegate from his state to the Second Continental Congress to replace a representative who had refused to sign the Declaration of Independence. Clymer signed the document, and because of his strong stand on independence, became a target of the enemy. As the British army was making its way to Philadelphia in 1777, the forces made a detour to destroy Clymer's property and terrorize his family.

From the Constitutional Convention and the subsequent fight for ratification in Pennsylvania, we have a sense of Clymer as a politician. He was not an active

George Clymer had no major role in the Convention, but attended regularly.

debater. He was content to let others speak who shared his viewpoint. But he was quite skillful at working behind the scenes to accomplish his goals. He cleverly maneuvered the Pennsylvania Assembly into calling for a state ratifying convention by not allowing the opposition forces the chance to coalesce their arguments. In fact, without Clymer's activities, ratification would have been a difficult proposition in Pennsylvania.

Following ratification, Clymer served one term in Congress, was an excise tax collector, and sat on a commission that negotiated with the Cherokee and Creek Indian tribes. He retired from public life in 1796, but remained active in the Philadelphia Bank, the Pennsylvania Academy of Fine Arts, and the Philadelphia Society for Promoting Agriculture. He died in 1813 at his suburban estate, Summerseat.

Friday, August 10, 1787

After last night's storm, the day was humid and showery, with a mean temperature of 77°.

Convention

Article VI, Section 2, giving Congress authority to establish property qualifications for the members of each house, was taken up. Mr. Charles Pinckney (SC) observed that the Committee of Detail had been instructed to write specific property qualifications into the Constitution. Instead, they permitted the Congress to determine the issue. Therefore, the first Congress will meet without such qualifications (Pinckney's concern was that if the Congressmen were rich they would make them high and if poor, they would make them very low. He thought the president, congressmen and judges should own property—he should think 100,000 pounds for the president, half that for judges and half again for legislators. However, he moved only that the president, the judges and legislators be required to swear that they possessed unencumbered property worth a certain amount. Rutledge (SC) seconded, observing that the committee hadn't reported a figure because they couldn't agree on one.

Ellsworth observed that a figure which would be high in the North would be low for the South; he suggested that they leave it to Congress. Franklin didn't like the whole idea: "If honesty was often the companion of wealth, and if poverty was exposed to peculiar temptation, it was not less true that the possession of property increased the desire of more property—some of the greatest rogues he was ever acquainted with, were the richest rogues." Madison

agreed. Pinckney's motion was rejected without a vote, and eventually the section was defeated.

The Convention then agreed to reconsider requiring seven years' citizenship for service in the House instead of three years, and plowed through Section 3 (size of quorums in each house). Section 4 (each house shall be the judge of the elections, returns and qualifications of its members), Section 5 (immunities of members), and Section 6 (each house to determine its rules) were handled with ease. They were debating Section 7, specifying that journals be kept, when the hour of adjournment arrived.

Delegates

Dr. Johnson again dined at his boarding house. He spent thirteen shillings and six pence for shoes, three shillings and nine pence for a knife (which judging from the thickness of lines in his diary he did not use to keep his quill pens sharp) and five shillings for a comb.

General Washington dined and drank tea at Mr. Bingham's and spent the evening at his lodging.

Elbridge Gerry (MA), as he did at least every second or third day, wrote his "lovely girl" Ann Thompson Gerry. He had called on Mrs. Carney for the articles left in the closet. He had called on Mrs. Bond, and been assured that Philadelphia in August was unhealthy for infants and it was best that Mrs. Gerry and the baby stay in New York. The president (probably Washington, but possibly Franklin), Major Butler (SC) Colonel Langdon (NH), Governor Rutledge

(SC) and others had inquired about her.

Edmund Randolph turned 34 today.

Edmund Randolph

EDMUND RANDOLPH, as Governor of Virginia, had played a major part in getting the Constitutional Convention called, and in persuading General Washington to attend it.

Born in Williamsburg to a prominent family (his father had been King's Attorney for Virginia, his uncle Peyton had been King's Attorney, member of the House of Burgesses, and president of the First and Second Continental Congress) and educated at the College of William and Mary, he had long known all of Virginia's leaders.

In 1775, he served briefly as one of Washington's aides, in 1776 he was a member of the Virginia Convention, and later, clerk of the house, state attorney general, and delegate to the Continental Congress. He succeeded Patrick Henry as governor in 1786, and attended the Annapolis Convention. Married in 1776 to Elizabeth Nicholas, he was the father of Peyton, Susan and Lucy at the time of the Convention. The birth of the latter postponed his wife's journey to Philadelphia; his family joined him here in mid-June.

While Madison must be given much of the credit for preparing the Virginia Plan, Randolph also worked on it, and it was Randolph who introduced the plan and thereby determined the course the Convention would follow. He spoke frequently and effectively, and introduced the language which, with editing, became Article VII, and introduced ratification by nine states.

At the end, the loose definition of the powers given Congress (and especially the necessary and proper clause), the power given the President to pardon even treason, the role of the Senate as a court of impeachment, the relatively small number of representatives,

Edmund Jennings Randolph, as head of the Virginia delegation, presented the Virginia Plan. He refused to sign the Constitution because he opposed the Connecticut Compromise.

the lack of controls of a standing army in time of peace caused Randolph to fear for liberty. He wanted amendments and changes proposed in the state conventions to be referred to a second Constitutional Convention. In the end, Randolph declined to sign. His support of the document in the Virginia ratifying convention, however, would be significant in that state's decision to ratify.

Saturday, August 11, 1787

Convention

The Convention Considered Article VI, Section 7 Today:

The House of Representatives, and the Senate,

when it shall be acting in a legislative capacity, shall keep a Journal of their proceedings, and shall, from time to time, publish them: and the yeas and nays of the members of each House, on any question, shall [,] at the desire of one-fifth part of the members present, be entered on the journal.

Sect. 8. Neither House, without the consent of the other, shall adjourn for more than three days, nor to any other place than that at which the two Houses are sitting. But this regulation shall not extend to the Senate, when it shall exercise the powers mentioned in the article 1.

King and Madison noted that this section authorized the two houses to adjourn to a new place. They thought too frequent moves had hurt the Confederation Congress, and that a law should be required to move it (Less that four months earlier, King had successfully fought off a group led by Madison which was trying to move Congress from New York to Philadelphia.) G. Morris made a motion to that effect. Spaight feared this would forever fix New York as the capital. Gerry, Williamson and Carroll agreed. The delegates disagreed with King and Madison, but did agree to delete the last sentence.

Randolph then moved to reconsider Article IV, Section 5 requiring money bills to originate in the House. Williamson seconded, Charles Pinckney opposed, and after discussion the motion to reconsider was approved, 9 aye, MD no, SC divided. This would be on the agenda next Monday.

Delegates

General Washington dined with the club at Springsbury and returned to the city after 10 P.M.

George Mason drew a bill of exchange on Acting Governor Beverly Randolph for 100 pounds, (Virginia currency) in favor of Thomas Fitzsimons for cash Fitzsimons had advanced to help Mason pay his expenses.

William Blount wrote John Grey Blount in Washington to expand on yesterday's letter about making nails.

A journal must be kept of the proceedings of the House and Senate when acting in a legislative capacity was the subject of Article VI, Section 7. In the eighteenth century writing materials were an inkwell and quill. One part of the inkwell contained sand for blotting the wet ink and preventing it from smearing.

William Blount, Entrepeneur

WILLIAM BLOUNT was not a literary stylist, but his letter of this day is so evocative of American society and the American economy in 1787 as to be worth reprinting.

Philadelphia, August 11th 1787

I yesterday wrote and forwarded by post to you a letter on the Subject of making Nails and the Advantages of employing Negroes at that Business but this will probably reach you sooner than that by post and as I have got some futher Information I will now [re] peat in part and add what I have since acquired. Nail Rod is to be had any quantity of Mr. Haselhurst who has the Selling of all that is slit at Morris's Works near Trenton at 33 pounds per Ton that is for 2240 lb put up generally in what the Workmen called Faggots of 56 lb each.-Stewart & Barr a few days past purchased of a Nailer here 3 Casks of 10d. 3 d, 20d and 3 of 30d. Nails at the average price of 9 pence. per lb. They say that the Task of a Journey man is per day 12 lb 10d. 16 lb of 20d & 18 lb of 30d. hence the average is 15 1/3 lb per day.-Gentlemen from Massachusetts of the first Information [say that Offenders] against the Public who are to be punished with Labour are generally chained and sat to making Nails whether they ever had a Hammer in hand before or not and that they generally will make good Nails some in a week and others in a Month. I saw Morris Nail Factory at his work at Trenton and I readily believed what had been said by the Gentlemen from Massachusetts and Yesterday I went to see a Nail Factory in this City in which there were four boys at Work, the younger of which was about 12 years of Age, he was making 4d. Nails [.] he made them fast and well[.] he had been at it about six Months another about 14 Years of Age who had been

at it seven Months was making 10d. Nails a Sample of which is inclosed [.] his Task was 10 lb per day but often made 14lb and the Owner paid him for Surplusage 4lb the other two were equally as good-The Master Nailer at this Work told me that 12lb 10d was the Task of a Journeyman but that a good Hand could easily make 20lb. and more or less in proportion of other Nails as they were greater or less. he adds that every faggot that is every 56 lb will make 48 lb of Nails. but if the Workman is good it will make 50 lb of Nails [he said that New Castle] Coal is the best but that Virginia Coal is nearly as good and that which is generally used here: Charr Coal that is your Wood Coal is not Coal. At every fire four Nailers Work [.] each bellows has two Handles one on each Side and each Nailer blows occassionally, the Bellows are very small compared to such as our Smith's use, each Nailer has a block and anvil to himself, the anvil is very small the face not much bigger than that of our Wedges used in Malling Rails, the only additional Tools are a small Hammer, [and a key to head the nails?] in and a [?] fixed in a block on which the Nail Rod is cut.-

It has appeared to me that this Business of Nail making is a Business better calculated than any others for the Employment of Negroes and that it is among the most profitable of Businesses, your man Pollypus and my man Will I suppose would readily make as good Nails as any body and I have four boys the greater part of which you Know I talked of making Coopers [barrel makers] who I suppose would as readily learn as the White boys I have seen here and if you should think it profitable to go largely into it I should suppose many white boys might be had prenticed [to us?] for seven years or more as their age might happens to be when bound by the Court-If Nails should be made more than would vend in Carolina they are an Article that would bear an Exportation from thence as well as from here-Addressed: John Gray Blount esquire

---

Sunday, August 12, 1787

Today was clear and pleasant, with a median temperature of 79°.

Convention

The Convention was enjoying its customary Sunday

recess. In the week since its twelve-day recess, the Convention had received, studied and worked on the draft constitution prepared by the Committee of Detail and had blocked an effort to refer the draft to a Committee of the Whole. Agreement had been reached upon the Preamble, and on a government of supreme legislative, executive and judicial power. The delegates had also gone almost all the way through the Articles pertaining to the composition, election, and privileges of the legislature. While much remained to be done, the more optimistic members were planning on a mid-September end.

Delegates

Dr. Johnson (CT) dined with the noted Quaker attorney William Lewis at the mansion overlooking the Schuylkill, now called Woodford. Lewis' varied career included an anti-slavery activist, and his counsel for the petitioners to unseat Albert Gallatin from the Senate and for John Fries in the latter's treason trial.

General Washington also dined in what is now Fairmount Park with Mr. William Hamilton at the latter's Bush Hill seat—and spent the evening "at home" writing letters.

James Madison wrote home to his father in Virginia as follows:

"HOND. SIR

I wrote to you lately inclosing a few Newspapers. I now send a few more, not because they are interesting but because they may supply the want of intelligence that might be more so. The Convention reassembled at the time my last mentioned that they had adjourned to. It is not possible yet to determine the period to which the Session will be spun out. It must be some weeks from this date at least, and possibly may be computed by months. Eleven States are on the ground, and have generally been so, since the second or third week of the Session. Rhode Island is one of the absent States. She has never yet appointed deputies. N.H. till of late was the other. That State is now represented. But just before the arrival of her deputies, those of N. York left us. We have till within a few days had very cool weather. It is now pleasant, after a fine rain. Our accts. from Virga. give us but an imperfect idea of the prospects with you. In particular places the drouth we hear has been dreadful. Genl. Washington's neighborhood is among the most suffering of them. I wish to know how your Neighbourhood is off. But my cheif anxiety is to hear that your health is reestablished. The hope that his may procure me that information is the principal motive for writing it, having as you will readily see, not been led to it by any thing worth commun[i]cating. With my love to my mother & the rest of the family I remain Dear Sir Yr. Affe. Son"

Richard Dobbs Spaight wrote to James Iredell in North Carolina that the Convention had agreed upon the outlines of a plan of government, referred it to a small committee, and the committee had reported. He hoped to complete the business by September 1st or 15th.

Robert Morris' (PA) protested bills have finally been paid.

Gerry (MA) and Butler (SC) called on Mrs. Cadwallader in the evening.

Pierce Butler

PIERCE BUTLER was born in County Carlow, Ireland, the third son of the fifth Baronet

Pierce Butler was instrumental in proposing that proceedings of the Convention be kept secret. He fought to protect slavery and thought wealth as well as population should determine a House member representation among the states.

Cloughran. Butler had had a commission as major, His Majesty's 22nd Regiment, purchased for him at age 11. In his teens he had served against the French in Canada, and after transfer to the 29th Regiment, returned to America in 1765.

On January 10, 1771, he married Mary Middleton, of the South Carolina Middletons (the cousin of Mrs. Charles Cotesworth Pinckney), and an heiress of a large estate. By 1787 they had five children. A sixth had burned to death at age 2.

By 1776 Butler had entered public service in South Carolina as a justice of the peace. Beginning in 1778, he was regularly elected to the state legislature. He also served as the state's adjutant general, working closely with Governor John Rutledge. While Butler escaped the capture of Charleston, his plantations and his family were captured, and his family had spent much of 1782 in Philadelphia. His wife accompanied him to Philadelphia for the Convention but found the climate unbearable and had gone on to New York.

Butler was an active member of the Convention from the beginning when he made the motion that the Convention maintain secrecy. One of the few members with no prior experience at the national level, he nevertheless supported the basic concepts advanced by Madison and the Virginia Plan while seeking adjustments to safeguard the interests of South Carolina. He favored a single executive, proportional representation in both houses of the legislature based on relative wealth, favored federal control of the militia and favored longer terms for the Executive and Congress. He opposed giving Congress the power to veto state laws, saw no need for inferior federal courts. He feared taking too much power from the states, and wanted senators to be dependent on the state legislators. He opposed giving Congress power to emit bills of credit, wanted very long residency requirements before immigrants became eligible for federal office, but opposed proposals limiting the right to vote. He wanted the seat of the federal government fixed [at some place other than New York City] by the Constitution. He tried to get slaves counted one for one in determining representation, and introduced what became the fugitive slave clause. While he opposed federal regulation of trade, he approved and stood by the north/south compromise on this issue and the slave trade. Finally he supported ratification by nine states and by conventions instead of state legislatures.

Monday, August 13, 1787

Today was again clear and warm.

Convention

The *Pennsylvania Hearld* for August 15 reported that today's session lasted until 5 P.M., "when, it is said, a decision took place upon the most important question that has been agitated since the meeting of this assembly." Madison's notes did not confirm this.

The session began by reconsidering the requirement that House members be seven years a citizen. Wilson (PA) and Randolph (VA) moved for four years, Williamson (NC) moved to require nine, Hamilton (NY) and Madison (VA) moved to require only residence and citizenship, letting Congress determine the length, and Gerry (MA) and Butler (SC) [himself an immigrant] opposed admitting foreigners to Congress in any case. Wilson's motion was supported by only Connecticut, Maryland, and Virginia. G. Morris moved to except anyone who was a citizen; Mercer (MD) seconded, Rutledge (VA), Sherman (CT), Gorham (MA), C. Pinckney (SC), Mason (VA), and Baldwin (GA) opposed the motion; Madison supported it, and it lost.

At this point, Carroll (MD) moved to reduce the citizenship requirement for House to five years. The motion lost.

Wilson next tried to reduce the requirement for senators from nine to seven years, and lost.

Randolph then moved to reinstate the requirement that money bills originate in the House. Mason supported him, as did Gerry, and Dickinson (DE); Wilson, G. Morris and Rutledge opposed. Carroll and McHenry (MD) pointed out the difficulty of defining money bills and the violent disputes this had caused between Maryland's senate and house. The provision lost.

Delegates

General Washington dined at Mr. Morris' and drank tea with Mrs. Bache at Dr. Franklin's. Mrs. Bache was Franklin's daughter Sarah. Dr. Johnson (CT) dined at his boarding house, took a walk, and paid 22/5 for washing.

John Dickinson was absent from the Convention in late June and early July, but was active as a delegate the rest of the time. He advocated the federal system

Gerry wrote his old friend James Warren:

It is out of my power in return for the information you have given me to inform you of our proceedings in convention, but I think they will be complete a month or six weeks, perhaps sooner. Whenever they shall be matured I sincerely hope they will be such as you and I

and promoted the idea that only men of superior talent should be Senators.

can approve, and then they will not be engrafted with principles of mutability, corruption or despotism, principles which some, you and I know, would not dislike to find in our national constitution. I wish you had accepted a seat in Congress, for the next year will be important.

Gerry spent the evening with the Robert Morrises.

John Dickinson

JOHN DICKINSON was one of the elder statesmen at the Constitutional Convention. Fellow delegate William Pierce of Georgia wrote that he was anxious to hear Dickinson speak for he was "considered one of the most important characters in the United States." His fame came from his articles and pamphlets published before the Revolution entitled *Letters from a Farmer in Pennsylvania to the Inhabitants of the British Colonies*. In these brilliant essays, circulated in the colonies and Europe, Dickinson discussed the evils of the British system in America. He believed a reconciliation was possible. Force could be used by the colonies to solve their problems, but only as a last resort.

Dickinson's approach to change always was cautious. He argued to maintain the proprietary government of the Penn family in Pennsylvania, although this position was not popular at the time. Later, as a member of the Continental Congress, he refused to sign the Declaration of Independence, believing that conciliation still was a viable option.

Following the Revolutionary War, Dickinson remained active in Delaware and Pennsylvania politics. He represented Delaware at the Annapolis Convention of 1786 and presided over the meeting. Thus he was a logical selection as a delegate to the Constitutional Convention. At the Convention, Dickinson was not a major figure, yet, his contributions were significant. He suggested the basic formula for the Great Compromise on June 2; he favored a national judiciary that was superior to state courts; he insisted that federal salaries be paid from the national treasury; and he recommended that the Senate be elected by state legislatures, and the House of Representatives by the people. His most memorable quote during the Convention came on August 13—"Experience must be our only guide. Reason may mislead us."

John Dickinson was born to a well-to-do family in Talbot County, MD, in 1732. When he was eight, the family moved to an estate near Dover, DE. He received the best education available—private tutoring when he was young and legal training in the office of John Moland in Philadelphia and the Middle Temple in England. He married Mary Norris in 1770 and had two daughters that survived infancy. Sarah was 16 in 1787 and Maria had just turned 5. Dickinson lived until 1808, but the Constitutional Convention was one of his last political activities.

Tuesday, August 14, 1787

Today was very warm, with temperatures in the high 80s.

Convention

The Convention took up Article VI Section 9:

> The members of each House shall be ineligible to, and incapable of holding any office under the authority of the United States, during the time for which they shall respectively be elected: and the members of the Senate shall be ineligible to, and incapable of holding any such office for one year afterwards

Charles Pinckney (SC) argued that this provision was degrading, since election indicated that incumbents had the trust of the people, and inconvenient, since it would keep the fittest men out of office. He moved to postpone and instead consider ineligibility to any U.S. office for which they were paid, with exceptance of a paid office vacating their congressional seat. Mifflin (PA) seconded. Mason (VA) vehemently opposed the new motion, as did Gerry, Williamson (NC), Sherman (CT), and Ellsworth (CT). Mercer (MD) strongly supported Pinckney—Wilson (PA) and G. Morris also (PA) supported the motion. It lost.

Morris then moved to except military offices from

the prohibition. Broom (DE) seconded and Randolph (VA) supported before Butler (SC) and Charles Pinckney proposed a postponement.

Article VI, Section 10—members of Congress to be paid by the states—was taken up. Ellsworth said he had changed his mind, and moved that this should be paid out of the federal treasury an allowance not to exceed a certain amount. G. Morris, Langdon (NH), Madison, Mason, Broom, Sherman, Carroll (MD) and Dickinson (DE) supported Ellsworth; Butler and Luther Martin (MD) defended payment by the state; Gerry saw arguments on both sides. Ellsworth's motion passed. Ellsworth proposed fixing the salary at $5 per day, Strong suggested $4. After Ellsworth's mo-

Much of the correspondence of the delegates to their wives was concerned with the health of the families, which was not an exaggerated concern in an eighteenth-century summer. Many delegates were no doubt made increasingly aware of their absence from their families when they saw the mothers and children of Philadelphia in the area of the State House.

tion for $5 lost, the Convention agreed to let Congress determine its own pay by law.

Delegates

Elbridge Gerry again wrote his wife; he opened by worrying about her health:

> *I am very Anxious for the health of my dearest Girl & her lovely infant in consequence of her letter of the 12th recd. this day, let me intreat you upon the receipt hereof, to ride every Day with the Baby, until you are both recovered. The morning before the Heat comes on is the best Time: . . .*

He then chides her for suggesting he would have thought her vain had she reminded him to take the miniature portrait of her when he left for Philadelphia. He then went on to discuss social gossip and family business.

Henry Knox wrote Washington. He had not written before because he feared that the business of the Convention might leak and the leak be ascribed to Washington. However, the business was now at the point where he could write. While he wished the new government were stronger, he supported it as the best attainable [Knox seems to have been much better informed about what the Convention was doing than the rule of secrecy permitted—probably by King, possibly by Gorham, certainly not by Washington]. If Gerry's concern for the health of his baby daughter seems overblown, consider one of Knox's concluding paragraphs,

> *Mrs. Knox and myself recently sustained the severe affliction of losing our youngest child of most eleven months old, who died on the 11th instant of a disease incident to children cutting their teeth in the summer season. This is the third time that Mrs. Knox has had her tenderest affections lacerated by the rigid hand of death*

Of Knox's twelve children, only three survived their parents.

Jefferson also wrote the General. While most of a long letter was devoted to European politics, the opening paragraph discussed the statue of Washington that Jefferson had arranged for Houdon to cast.

> *I was happy to find . . .-that the modern dress for your statue would meet you approbation. I found it strongly the sentiment of [Benjamin] West, [John Singleton] Copeley, [John] Trumbul and [Mather] Brown in London, after which it would be ridiculous to add that it is my own*

Who Pays Congress?

PAY FOR CONGRESS members is difficult for us today to conceive being paid by the states. It is equally difficult to understand the depth of concern about whether or not members of Congress should be eligible for other federal offices. Yet, the decisions on these issues, insignificant as they may now seem, may have altered the nation's history.

Members of the Confederation Congress were paid by their state, as were members of the Convention. The rates differed from state to state. The ability and willingness of the states to pay their delegates at all varied considerably. New Hampshire, whose legislature made sure it was paid on time, couldn't find funds to pay its delegates in 1787, and was not represented in Congress. The opportunity to reward or punish representatives by raising or lowering their pay was obvious, as was the tendency to make the national legislature dependent upon state government. Thus the change.

The English Whig writers and political leaders with whom Americans of the late eighteenth century were familiar had decried Parliament's practice of creating new government positions with which to award members who voted as the ministry wished. Many of the delegates had seen the ministry or royal and proprietary governors reward support with appointments to office. All were well aware that the national legislature might fall to the temptation of creating offices for popular members to take over.

Conversely, the delegates were aware of what a strict rule against members of Congress taking other federal office meant. If Gouverneur Morris wanted military offices excepted, it was because, as a member of Congress when it voted to form a continental army, George Washington would have been ineligible to take command had a strict rule been enforced. In the civilian arena, Benjamin Franklin would have been ineligible to serve as minister to France, and John Adams to serve as minister to Holland and as peace commissioner.

Wednesday, August 15, 1787

The day was warm but pleasant; the evening brought a thunderstorm.

Convention

After some preliminary discussion, Caleb Strong of

Massachusetts moved that tax bills and appropriations should originate in the House, leaving the Senate free to amend. George Mason of Virginia seconded the motion and a fight was on. Nathaniel Gorham of Massachusetts urged passage; Gouverneur Morris of Pennsylvania opposed. Hugh Williamson of North Carolina favored the motion, but thought the issue might be placed in a better perspective if it were postponed until the Senate's other powers were more carefully defined. John Rutledge of South Carolina seconded Williamson's motion; the Convention voted postponement by a vote of 6 to 5.

Next the delegates considered the executive vote power and the authority of Congress to override with a two-thirds vote in each house. James Madison moved that both the Executive and Supreme Court should have veto power, with a two-thirds vote of each House to override if either branch vetoed a law. James Wilson of Pennsylvania seconded the motion. James Francis Mercer of Maryland approved, but in part because he "disapproved of the doctrine that the Judges as expositors of the Constitution should have authority to declare a law void." On the other side, Charles Pinckney of South Carolina opposed the mo-

tion, and Elbridge Gerry of Massachusetts pointed out that a similar motion had already been rejected. Shortly, this motion also was voted down.

Gouverneur Morris expressed his regrets that the motion was defeated. He favored an absolute veto power by either the executive or judicial branches, which he thought would act as a strong barrier against legislative instability. John Dickinson of Delaware agreed with Mercer that the judiciary should not have a veto power. Roger Sherman of Connecticut distrusted the power of a one-man executive over the many in Congress. Daniel Carroll of Maryland wanted the issue postponed until the executive branch was better defined. Gorham, Rutledge and Ellsworth, growing impatient, opposed postponement. The motion to postpone lost. Then Williamson moved to require a three-fourths vote to override a veto. This motion passed.

George Washington had a big responsibility presiding over the debates of the Convention. The Doctrine of Judicial Review was debated on many occasions but is not spelled out in the Constitution.

The veto power remained as the principal topic for the remainder of the day. Madison was concerned that Congress would pass "joint resolutions" to avoid a veto since it would not fall under the definition of a "bill." His concern was not shared by many members. But the body concluded its business today by voting to allow ten days rather than seven for the Executive to return a bill.

Delegates

Many of the delegates had been in Philadelphia for three months or more and one senses from today's debates that some were growing impatient. Ellsworth, Gorham, and Rutledge the gentlemen who argued against postponement, had at least twenty-five children among them, including several under ten. It may not be coincidence that they were the first to express impatience with the rate of progress. From this day on, impatience to get home increased daily.

General Washington spent the evening "at home" and wrote Marquis de LaFayette. He promised details of the Convention when it ended early next month, congratulated LaFayette on his work in the French Assembly, and discussed European affairs. He was pleased that LaFayette was seeking toleration in religious matters, and took the opportunity to express his own philosophy. "Being no bigot myself to any mode of worship," he wrote, "I am disposed to indulge the professors of Christianity in the church, that road to Heaven, which to them shall seem the most direct plainest easiest and least liable to exception."

Madison wrote his fellow Virginia delegate to Congress, William Grayson, asking him to support the appointment of Major George Turner to a position in the Northwest Territory's government.

Roger Sherman (CT) wrote Henry Gibbs to order chinaware for his wife. He hoped the Convention would adjourn by the end of August concluding: "letters directed to me at New Haven are not free from postage, but if directed to me here as member of the Convention they are free." In 1787 the recipient paid the postage.

Judicial Review

DOCTRINE OF JUDICIAL REVIEW of laws is not spelled out in the Constitution. Rather, the doctrine was formulated by Chief Justice John Marshall in the landmark case of *Marbury v. Madison* in 1803, in which a law passed by Congress was declared unconstitutional. Yet, while judicial review is not embodied in the Constitution, the delegates did discuss the issue on several occasions.

Mercer and Dickinson argued that judges should not have the power to declare a law unconstitutional. After all, as few as three judges (a majority of the five needed to determine a case) can overturn a law passed by as many as 535 representatives and senators elected by and responsible to their constituents. Further, there is no opportunity of appeal from such a decision. Throughout the Convention, delegates had stated that the Judiciary would have and use the power of judiciary review. This assumption had the tacit acceptance of majority of the members. And at least two of the delegates, John Blair and David Brearley, already had practiced judiciary review as state justices in Virginia and New Jersey. They had weighed state laws against their states' constitutions and decided that they were enforceable.

Finally, the idea of judicial review was inherent in the idea of a written immutable constitution separate from, and above, statute law. Without the judicial check, the legislative branch instead would have functioned like the British Parliament which determined the British Constitution by the laws it passed.

Thursday, August 16, 1787

Today was sunny, cool and pleasant.

Convention

The Convention devoted the day to Article VII dealing with the powers to be given Congress, starting with Section 1 giving Congress power "to lay and collect taxes, duties, imposts and excises." L. Martin (MD) wanted to know if "duties" and "imposts" weren't the same thing. Wilson said they weren't. Mason (VA) urged a ban on taxing exports, and proposed an amendment to that end.

Morris (PA) considered such a ban inadmissable. He contended that it would not in some cases be equitable to tax imports without taxing exports; and that taxes on exports would be often the most easy and proper of the two." Madison agreed, and gave several additional arguments in favor of export taxes. Wilson agreed. Williamson (NC), Gerry (MA), Mercer (MD), Sherman (CT) and Carroll (MD) all favored the ban. It was then postponed until Article VII, Section 4 was considered. The motion on the power to tax passed.

The powers to coin money, regulate foreign coin and fix the standard of weights and measures passed without debate. A motion to add "and post roads" to the power to establish post offices was passed. Also passed with no debate was a clause which has played a vital part in the expansion of congressional authority in the twentieth century: to regulate commerce with foreign nations and among the several states.

Next came "to borrow money and emit bills on the credit of the United States." This motion touched nerves. Morris moved to strike the "emit bills" part—if the U.S. had good credit, bills wouldn't be needed; if it didn't, bills would be unjust and useless. Butler (SC) seconded. Gorham (MA), Ellsworth (CT), Wilson, Langdon (NH), and Read (DEL) supported Morris; Madison suggested prohibiting acts making bills a legal tender. Mason and Randolph hated paper money, but felt Congress needed this power, the former observing "that the late war could not have been carried on, had such a prohibition existed." Mercer defended both the original wording and paper money. The move to strike passed.

Delegates

Dr. Johnson (CT) dined with Pollack (perhaps Oliver Pollock, trader, planter and financier who, as a resident of New Orleans, had helped fund and supply George Rogers Clark's expedition against the British in the Illinois Country). He also paid Robert Edge Pine an initial six guineas for the portrait of himself now owned by Columbia University.

General Washington also dined at Pollock's, and spent the evening in his room. Both he and Dr. Johnson usually noted only their dinner host, so it is not unusual that neither noted the other's presence at the dinner.

Dr. Franklin's sister, Jane Mecom, wrote to him from Boston today. She was pleased with his description of his new building, and "that God has blesd. you in that Respect is mater of thankfulness . . ."

The New York Abolition Society met, agreed to appoint a committee to petition the Convention, appointed society president John Jay, White Matlack and Nathaniel Lawrence to write it, and adjourned.

Benjamin Franklin

BENJAMIN FRANKLIN, the tenth son of a Boston soap and candlemaker, was born in 1706. He was the eldest signer of both the Constitution and the Declaration of Independence.

At seventeen this apprentice printer arrived in Philadelphia. A year later he began a two-year stay in London to sharpen his printer's skills. In 1730 he published *The Pennsylvania Gazette*. When he retired nineteen years later he had interests in five more newspapers. Retirement drew Franklin into politics. He served fourteen years in the Pennsylvania Assembly and represented the state at the Albany Congress in 1754—the first attempt to unify the colonies. In 1753 he was named deputy postmaster general of North America. From 1757 to 1775 he represented Pennsylvania and other colonies in London. Stripped of his offices in 1755 and sent home in shame, Franklin was received as a hero and elected to the Second Continental Congress. That body sent him to Paris in the fall of 1776 as its first ambassador to France. There he negotiated recognition by France and secured munitions, money, and troops to aid the revolutionary cause. Franklin, with fellow commissioners Adams and John Jay, negotiated the Treaty of Paris in 1783 which ended the war.

An early and ardent advocate of American Independence, he had encountered Dickinson and such other moderates as James Wilson. As supporter of the radical state constitution of 1776, he had earned the suspicion of men such as Robert Morris, Gouverneur Morris, George Clymer and Thomas Fitzsimons. As a diplomat, he had acquired the distrust of Arthur Lee, the other Stratford Lees, and such Lee allies as Sherman and Gerry.

Time had undoubtedly softened the memory of old political antagonists, but not to the extent that they had become uncritical admirers. The omission of Franklin from the original list of Pennsylvania delegates may have been as much in hope as in fear that his health would prevent his attendance, and several of his fellow delegates may have cringed whenever he rose to speak. But his presence in the Convention was deemed as critical to its success as was General Washington's.

In 1787, at 81 Franklin was suffering from gout and kidney stones. Age and infirmities had slowed him down. As a delegate to the Federal Convention, however, he attended all but one or two of its daily four-hour or longer sessions.

Benjamin Franklin's attendance at the Convention gave it prestige albeit he was 81 and had several infirmities. He made the motion based on the Con-

That year he also directed construction of three new rental properties along Market Street and a print shop behind them, all incorporating innovative fire resistant features. As president of the American Philosophical Society, he attended meetings and conducted the business; and as president of the Pennsylvania Society for

necticut Compromise, opposed property qualification for voters, and made the speech on September 17 encouraging ratification.

Promoting the Abolition of Slavery with the Society . . . for the Advancement of Political Enquiriese, he attended meetings and conducted the business of these organizations.

As America's noted scientist, he introduced and promoted the discoveries and inventions of other Americans, such as Thomas Paine's iron bridge.

He also kept up a correspondence with his many friends here and abroad. That with his many female friends in particular remained spritely.

Franklin had entered into a common-law marriage with Deborah Read in 1730. This was necessary as Deborah had been married but her first husband had disappeared, precluding a divorce. They had two children: Francis died in infancy and daughter Sarah married Richard Bache and bore the Franklins' beloved grandson, Benjamin Franklin Bache.

Franklin had one illegitimate son, William, who grew up in the family and went on to become the royal governor of New Jersey. William remained loyal to the king in the Revolution, causing an irreconcilable break with his father. Possibly in an effort to soften this emotional blow, Franklin raised William's illegitimate son, William Temple Franklin, who in 1787 was an unsuccessful candidate for secretary to the Constitutional Convention.

Friday, August 17, 1787

After a cool and cloudy morning, rain set in.

Convention

Debate on the powers to be given Congress continued. "To appoint a Treasurer by ballot" came on and was approved, although George Read (DE) wanted to let the president appoint the treasurer.

The powers to constitute inferior courts and to make rules as to captures on land and water sailed through. That "to declare the law and punishment of piracies and felonies committed on the high seas" did not. After a series of motions and remarks made by Madison (VA), Mason (VA), Morris (PA), Randolph (VA), Wilson (PA), Dickinson (DE), and Mercer (MD), and a brief lecture on felony in the common law from Madison, the clause was changed to "define and punish piracies . . ." and approved.

"To subdue a rebellion in any state on the application of its legislature" also occasioned debate. Charles Pinckney (SC), Morris and Langdon (NH) wanted to drop the need to have the approval of the Legislature, and were opposed by L. Martin, Mercer and Gerry (MA). Ellsworth (CT) supported an amendment to allow the governor to request federal intervention if the legislature was not in session. Finally, the proposal lost.

"To make war" was then debated, amended and passed.

Delegates

General Washington dined and drank tea with Samuel and Elizabeth Powel. Ann Bingham was Mrs. Powel's niece, and their homes stood side by side on Third Street below Walnut.

Elbridge Gerry wrote his wife Ann. He had been at City Tavern yesterday evening when Mr. King arrived with her letter and the four other letters enclosed with it. He expressed sympathy for Mrs. Knox (whose youngest child had recently died), and warned Mrs. Gerry "to guard against the coolness and dampness of mornings and evenings, and also of the house when washed. . . ." Before moving on to discuss social events, he noted that "Some members of the Convention are very impatient but I do not think it will rise before three weeks."

George Read

GEORGE READ is very little known for a man who signed both the Declaration of Independence and the Constitution. He was fifty-three when the Convention opened and had been married for thirty-four years to Gertrude Ross Till Read. He had four sons and a daughter.

Read wrote and helped pass the Delaware law appointing delegates to the Convention; it included a

clause forbidding the state's delegates to approve anything which would deprive Delaware of an equal vote.
He went to Philadelphia on May 3 and stayed there
until September 18 to keep an eye on any plans by the
large states to change the "one state one vote" provision of the Articles of Confederation.

Read's concern was state taxes, not federal power.
Delaware had a heavy war debt and no vacant land to
sell to pay it off. Read wanted an equal vote so
Delaware could protect itself if states like Virginia and
Georgia, which did have vast areas of ungranted lands,
tried to ignore the small states and use the money from
selling land to pay only their own state debts.

Otherwise, he was an extreme nationalist. He suggested abolishing the states, favored a federal veto of
state laws, supported Hamilton's plan for a very
strong central government, favored appointment of
the Senate by the Executive for life terms, and supported an absolute veto by the president over congressional legislation. While Dickinson and Bedford were
more frequent speakers, Read led his state's delegation.

*George Read, as a member of the Delaware delega-
tion, was concerned that small states received equal
votes. Toward the end of the Convention, he became a
nationalist.*

Saturday, August 18, 1787

Today was cool, airy and pleasant.

Convention

As usual, the Convention met at 11 A.M. and proceeded to business. Madison (VA) proposed nine
additional powers to be given Congress; Charles
Pinckney (SC) suggested eleven more—a few of which
were similar to powers proposed by Madison. Mason
(VA) noted that federal regulation of the militia
should be considered. Gerry (MA) . . . "thought some
provision ought to be made in favor of public Securities, and something concerning letters of marque, . . ."
He proposed that these subjects should also go to a
committee. All of these were referred to the Committee of Detail elected in July to consider and report.

Rutledge (SC), seconded by King (MA) and
Charles Pinckney, proposed a committee to consider
assuming state debts. The committee was elected—
Livingston (NJ) (chair), Langdon (NH), King (MA),
Sherman (CT), Clymer (PA), Dickinson (DE),
McHenry (MD), Mason (VA), Williamson (NC),
General C.C. Pinckney (SC) and Baldwin (GA).
Rutledge then ". . . remarked on the length of the
session, the probably impatience of the public and the
extreme anxiety of many members of the Convention
to bring the business to an end;" moved to meet
precisely at 10 A.M. and adjourned precisely at 4 P.M.

Ellsworth observed the need for a council to advise the president. After remarks by C. Pinckney, Gerry and Dickinson, the discussion was postponed.

Then the delegates took up the power "to raise armies." Gorham moved to insert "and support" and the motion and the amended clause were approved.

The remainder of the day was spent on the militia clause.

Delegates

Dr. Johnson (CT) dined at his boarding house, then took a walk. He seems to have passed a bookstore on his route, since he notes spending thirty-six shillings for books, etc.

Washington dined at Chief Justice (of Pennsylvania) Thomas McKean's and spent the afternoon and evening at his lodgings.

Control of the Militia

STANDING ARMIES during times of peace, and to what extent the federal government should control the state militias were among the most hotly debated issues in the Convention. The eventual decision—no curbs on a standing army in times of peace and the federal government to provide for organizing, arming and disciplining the militia but the states to appoint officers and train the militia—was one reason Elbridge Gerry would oppose ratification.

All of the delegates knew that the world was a dangerous place, and an army would from time to time be needed. All of them also were aware that a large standing army was always dangerous, and usually fatal to a republic. So, they sought an army efficient enough to defend the country, but not so efficient as to take it over.

Strolling on the city streets was a common pastime. On August 18 Dr. Johnson notes that he took a walk after dining at his boarding house. This scene is in front of the Lutheran Church on Fifth Street.

One technique was to vest command of the militia (we call them the National Guard today) in the governors of the states unless they had actually been called into federal service. One result was that in every peace time year between 1789 and 1946, the forty-eight governors collectively had command of a larger army than did the President of the United States. Thus, even had a President or a commanding general thought about seizing power, he couldn't because he didn't control even half of the nation's armed services.

Sunday, August 19, 1787

Today was clear and pleasant.

Convention

Twelve weeks had elapsed since the delegates began their work. The twelfth week had seen the departure of Davie (NC) because he wanted to get back to his own business and family. Paterson (NJ) had departed on August 1 and by the end of the month so had Strong (MA). Ellsworth (CT) and Martin (NC) would also leave. They were the first of the delegates to openly demonstrate expressions of impatience at the rate of the Convention's progress.

If impatience at the progress of the Convention since May 25 seems warranted, the progress over discussion of the Committee of Detail's report was not. In the past two weeks, the Convention had worked through the composition of, qualification for, and method of election to the legislature as well as procedural requirements; it was well along in determining the powers to be granted to Congress. Some impatience may have resulted from the thoroughness with which the Convention was reviewing and re-working the report of the Committee of Detail.

Delegates

General Washington noted in his diary that he:

In company with [former Mayor of Philadelphia Samuel] Powel rode up to White Marsh. Traversed my old incampment and contemplated on the dangers which threatened the American Army at that place. Dined at German town. Visited Mr. Blair McClenegan. Drank tea at Mr. Peter's [Belmont Mansion] and returned to Philadelphia in the evening.

He also wrote his old friend General Knox:

My dear Sir:
By slow, I wish I could add and sure, movements, the business of the Convention progresses; but to say when it will end, or what will be the result, is more than I can venture to do; and therefore I shall hazard no opinion thereon. If however, some good does not proceed from the Session, the defects cannot, with propriety, be charged to the hurry with which the business has been conducted: Yet, many things may be forgot, some of them not well digested, and others become a mere nullity. Notwithstanding which I wish a disposition may be found in Congress, the several States Legislatures, and the community at large to adopt the Government which may be agreed on in Convention; because I am fully persuaded it is the best that can be obtained at the present moment, under such diversity of ideas as prevail.
I should have had great pleasure in a visit to New York during the adjournment of the Convention; but not foreseeing the precise period at which it would take place, or the length of it; I had previously thereto, put my carriage into the hands of a workman to repair, and had not the means of going. I condole very sincerely with Mrs. Knox and yourself on your late misfortune; but am sure, however severe the trial, each of you have fortitude enough to meet it. Nature, no doubt, must feel severely before calm resignation will over come it.
I offer my best respects to Mrs. Knox, and every good wish for the family, with great regard and unfeigned Affectn. I am etc.

Sites Visited by General Washington

COUNTRY AROUND PHILADELPHIA abounded in sites General Washington would well remember from his revolutionary days. The road he followed from Mt. Vernon through Baltimore, Wilmington and Chester passed within a few miles of Brandywine, where he had been defeated by Howe in September of 1777. Germantown, another defeat he suffered in October 1777, was within ten miles of Philadelphia. Six or eight miles to the north lay Whitemarsh, where his army had been in camp from November 2 to December 11, 1777. Also there was his winter camp at Valley Forge, some 15 miles west of Germantown, and Trenton, across the Delaware some thirty miles away, where his army had won a crucial victory in December 1776.

In today's diary entry, Washington specifically mentioned that Whitemarsh was an old encampment and that while there, he "contemplated on the dangers which threatened the American Army at that place."

An earlier visit to Valley Forge elicited a similar diary entry.

Today, he also rode along Germantown Avenue as he had during the battle there, and visited a house which had played a large part in his defeat. But there is nothing in his diary or letters to indicate that there had been a battle there. Earlier, he mentioned riding through Trenton, which meant that he rode over that battlefield (since there had been fighting on most of the village streets) without any indication that he had ever heard of that area. If he visited Brandywine Battlefield, he made no mention of it.

Perhaps it is only coincidence that he specifically recalled two of his encampments but not the three major battles. And if it is not a coincidence, one wonders why he consciously avoided reference to the battle scenes.

The coach in which Washington rode as President was a marked contrast to the man in simple attire who visited the Revolutionary War battle sites on his horse during the summer of 1787.

Monday, August 20, 1787

It rained hard all day.

Convention

Charles Pinckney (SC) submitted a number of propositions for consideration and reference to the Committee of Detail. Gouverneur Morris (PA), seconded by Mr. Pinckney, submitted a proposal for a Council of States, composed of the Chief Justice, and the secretaries of Domestic Affairs, Commerce and Finance, Foreign Affairs, War, Marine [Navy] and a Secretary of the Council of State.

The power to call forth the militia was postponed pending determination of the power to regulate it.

"And to make all laws necessary and proper for carrying into execution the foregoing powers . . ." was taken up. The very broad grant of power to the federal government was approved without opposition.

Article VII, Section 2, dealing with treason was then considered. Two issues of the debate concerned how broad the definition should be and whether or not treason against the individual states should be included. The debates showed a thorough knowledge of British statute law on the subject. The section was substantially amended and agreed to.

Ellsworth (CT) then moved to require a census within three years of adoption instead of six years. It was approved. Gerry (MA) moved that, until the census was taken, direct taxes should be apportioned as was the number of representatives. Langdon (NY) and Carroll (MD) opposed. At that point it was 4 P.M. and adjournment was called.

Delegates

William Blount (NC) wrote from Philadelphia to Governor Caswell to report that John Ashe had arrived in New York, that he [Blount] would join him when the Convention forwarded its proposals to Congress, and to assure Caswell that "it will be such a Form of Government as I believe will be readily adopted by the several states. . . ."

Hamilton, back in New York, wrote to Rufus King (MA) at the Convention and Jeremiah Wadsworth in Connecticut. He informed King that he had written the other New York delegates, Lansing and Yates, and offered to return to the Convention if either of them

would go. He asked King to write if substantial changes were made to the plan and to notify him when the Convention was about to end. His letter to Wadsworth asked Wadsworth to track down the source of the "sending for a king" report.

John Miller wrote Franklin asking for a state job. William MacIntosh, a British expatriate, wrote the doctor from Avignon, France, to enclose some thoughts on an appropriate government for the United States.

Philadelphia's Jewish Community

CHARLES PINCKNEY introduced a proposition today that would be incorporated in the finished document: No religious test or qualification shall ever be annexed to any oath of office under the authority of the U.S." Since the Convention was secret, nobody knew this. On September 7, Jonas Phillips, a prominent member of Philadelphia's Jewish community, wrote General Washington. Phillips noted that Pennsylvania office holders were required to acknowledge the Divine inspiration of both the Old and New Testaments, thus disqualifying Jews (and others) from office. He noted Jewish support of the Revolution, and asked the Convention to alter the required oath.

While his position to Washington did not so indicate, Jonas Phillips was president of the Congregation Mikveh Israel. A few Jews born in Holland were living on the Delaware before Penn arrived. Others trickled in to the tolerant Quaker colony in the 1700s. By 1738 the Penn family had granted land at Ninth and Spruce to Nathan Levy to be held in trust as "a burial place for the interment of Hebrews." In 1743 Levy organized a Sephardic congregation, Mikveh Israel, and in 1782, with the help of contributions from Benjamin Franklin, Charles Biddle and David Rittenhouse and other Phialdelphians the congregation built a synagogue in Cherry Alley between Third and Fourth Streets. Among its members had been Haym Soloman, Revolutionary financier.

The Jewish community also participated in 1787 in the newly formed abolition society. The society first was organized in Philadelphia in 1774, but the American Revolution interrupted its work. The enlarged

Benjamin Franklin had an amiable appearance and it is no wonder that people asked him for advice and employment. He was generous in his contributions and supported the Jewish congregation and the Abolition Society.

society in 1787 elected Benjamin Franklin as its president and Benjamin Rush its secretary. A few Jewish members of the community—especially Solomon Bush, but also David Nassy, Samuel Hays and Samuel and Solomon Alexander—worked in the society, specifically with manumission.

In the spring of 1788 it was determined that the finances of the Mikveh Israel congregation were dire. An appeal in the form of subscriptions on pledges was made to the community at large. The list of contributors included the leading men of the city—Benjamin Franklin, Alderman Hilary Baker, Pennsylvania Attorney-General William Bradford, Thomas McKean (signer of the Declaration of Independence), David Rittenhouse, Thomas Fitzsimmons (leading Catholic layman and a drafter of the Constitution of the United States), William Rush, a man named Biddle and one named Ingersoll.

Tuesday, August 21, 1787

Today was cloudy—warm, 79° and humid.

Convention

Governor Livingston (NJ) reported from the committee on State Debts and the Militia, recommending that the national legislature have power to pay the debts incurred by Congress and by the states during the late war, and the power to make laws for organizing—arming and disciplining the militia—reserving to the states the appointment of officers. Gerry (MA) opposed just giving the power to pay debts; he wanted the obligation to pay them recognized. Ellsworth (CT) moved to table the report; the motion carried.

After discussion on apportioning direct taxes, the Convention took up Article VII, Section 4:

No tax or duty shall be laid by the Legislature on articles exported from any State; nor on the migration or importation of such persons as the several States shall think proper to admit; nor shall such migration or importation be prohibited.

Langdon wished to give the federal government the power to tax exports. He was supported by Morris (PA), Dickinson (DE), Madison (VA), Wilson (PA), Fitzsimmons (PA) and Clymer, and opposed by Ellsworth, Williamson (NC), Butler (SC), Sherman (CT), Gerry (MA) and Mason (VA). The opponents won.

Luther Martin (MD) now moved to permit a tax on importation of slaves because the two-third provision was an encouragement to such imports, because slaves weakened a part of the Union which the remainder was bound to defend, and because "it was inconsistent with the principles of the revolution and dishonorable to the American character to have such a feature in the Constitution." Rutledge (SC) and Charles Pinckney (SC) defended the clause as it stood; Ellsworth was for leaving it alone, and the Convention adjourned.

Delegates

Elbridge Gerry wrote his "dearest Girl," wife Ann, on local gossip, family business (Ann's father had asked him to consult Hamilton and Dr. Johnson on a legal matter, and he had done so), and on his relationship with her and with his fellow delegates. On the former, he noted: ". . . I do not expect a long life (he died in 1814 at the age of 72), my constitution appears not to be formed for it, and such as it is, constant attention of one kind or any pray on it; but if anything makes life in the least desireable it is you, my dearest Girl, and our lovely offspring. Detached from your comforts, life to me would be a source of evils."

Later in the letter he gives the first indication of real dissatisfaction with the plan.

"I am as sick of being here as you can conceive, most of the Time I am at home or in convention. . . . We meet now at ten and sit till four but entre nous I do not expect to give my voice to the measure."

David Brearly wrote from Philadelphia to fellow New Jersey delegate William Paterson: "Cannot you come down and assist us—we have many reasons for desiring this; our duty, in the manner we now sit, is quite hard for three, but a much stronger reason is, that we actually stand in need of your abilities."

John Fitch wrote Dr. Johnson to thank him for visiting his steamboat yesterday in company with several other delegates. Francis Childs wrote from New York to Dr. Franklin to apologize for not making the payment due Franklin at the end of August and to order more type from Franklin's type foundry.

The Convention and Slavery

AMERICANS OF 1787 were no more willing to act on "We hold these truths to be self-evident

Dolly Madison married her husband James after the Convention where slavery was an issue that was not dealt with in the Constitution. Her husband was a

slaveholder all of his life, and in later years, while married to Dolly, was active in the American Colonization Society, which tried to resettle slaves in Africa.

that all men are created equal, . . ." than are most Americans today. Consequently, slavery was not dealt with in the Constitution and remained an issue to be resolved in an exceptionally bloody war.

The Convention should be judged in context on this issue. Some facts with which it had to deal with were these:

1. Slavery was being abolished by state action. Massachusetts courts had held the state constitution of 1780 aboloished slavery. Pennsylvania, Connecticut, Rhode Island, New York and New Jersey had passed laws for gradual abolition; Maryland had outlawed the slave trade and North Carolina levied a prohibition tax on imported slaves.

2. Slavery was a marginal, if not unprofitable institution, in Maryland and Virginia.

3. While abolition societies were getting started, public support had not developed to the point that the northern states would go to war to abolish slavery. It never did, even in 1860.

4. The Articles of Confederation gave the government no power whatsover over slavery or; the slave trade.

5. South Carolina and Georgia would not ratify a constitution which immediately stopped the slave trade. In North Carolina and Virginia such a provision would increase opposition to ratification. Since Rhode Island and New York would probably not ratify, losing Georgia and South Carolina would doom the Convention's effort.

At the very least, the Convention provided the new government the authority to cut off slave imports after 1808, and provided a Union which men would fight to preserve.

Wednesday, August 22, 1787

Today was clear and pleasant.

Convention

Pressure was building in the debates to resolve two controversial issues—the future of the nation's slave trade and navigation regulations. Article VII, Section 4, tied these two elements of the nation's economy together by setting taxes on all imports except slaves. Debate continued on Luther Martin's (MD) move to modify the article and section to include a tax on imported slaves. Slavery, its proponents argued, was not only contrary to the principles of the Revolution, but a real threat to the Union. Slaves, Col. Mason of Virginia argued, made every master a "petty tyrant" and they brought the "judgement of Heaven on a Country."

"If slavery be wrong," countered Pinckney of South Carolina, "it is justified by the example of all the world." Besides, South Carolina and Georgia could not "do without slaves."

As debate continued the range of opinions on slavery in America took more definition. John Dickinson (DE) was adamantly opposed to the Constitution's authorization of the slave trade in the states. Mr. King (MA) "thought the subject should be considered in political light only." If two slave states took exception to import duties on slaves, the northern and middle states would see it as unfair. Sherman (CT), who opened today's debate with a plea for compromise for the sake of the larger government scheme, felt it was "better to let the S. States import slaves than to part with them." Governor Randolph of Virginia disagreed; better to lose two slave states and keep the union which mostly favored restrictions on slavery.

Ellsworth (CT) interjected an ominous note: "This widening of opinions has a threatening aspect." If the delegates did not take the plan as it now stood, he feared the slave-owning states might "fly into a variety of shapes & directions, and most probably into several confederations and not without bloodshed."

The Convention promptly formed a committee to consider these Article 7 clauses again. Those delegates appointed—Langdon (NH), King (MA), Johnson (CT), Livingston (NJ), Clymer (PA), Dickinson (DE), L. Martin (MD), Madison (VA), Williamson (NC), C. Pinckney (SC) and Baldwin (GA)—were to hammer out a compromise to save the Constitution.

Delegates

Dr. Johnson (CT) dined at his boarding house and visited John Fitch's steamboat.

General Washington dined with the Morrises at the Hills and visited at Mr. Powel's in the afternoon. He also dropped a note asking Clement Biddle if he knew of a responsible person who would contract to buy herring, and if so, the number of barrels.

The Arch Street docks were busy with the activities of trade and transportation. The Slavery Compromise permitted the importation of slaves for another

James McClurg (VA) wrote from Richmond Madison to thank Madison for his letter. McClurg hoped to hear that the veto of state laws had been put back in the Constitution, and relayed the news of a riot in "Green-bryar" and the various attacks on John Adams' "Defence of the Constitutions of Government."

The Slavery Compromise

SLAVE TRADE until at least 1808 was one action of the Convention difficult for us to understand and accept. But in 1787 this clause of the Constitution allowed for a critical compromise on the hotly debated matter of federal regulation of navigation. Northern states tended to favor central regulation of commerce as a means to assure a steady national treasurey while distributing the trade more evenly among the major ports. Southern states, on the other hand, had less commerce, more agriculture, and a history of slavery

twenty years in exchange for federal control of foreign trade.

as a means to that lifestyle. They, therefore, tended not to favor regulation of commerce and particularly resisted any effort to restrict the importation of slaves.

The committee appointed in today's session faced the pressing problem of finding a compromise that would satisfy both factions. The Constitution's very future was at stake. The delegates from the eleven represented states (New York's quorum had gone home and Rhode Island never sent delegates) accepted this challenge after the Convention had been underway for close to three months. They realized that some among the delegates were willing to risk the future of the union on the matter of slavery. But they also knew such stalwart anti-slavery men as Virginia's Edmund Randolph and pro-slavery men as South Carolina's General Pinckney were seeking a middle ground.

Gouverneur Morris, formerly of New York but at the Convention a delegate from Pennsylvania, presented the issue of the committee squarely as wishing "the whole subject to be committed including the clauses relating to taxes on exports & to a navigation act." These things, he so wisely predicted, "may form a bargain among the Northern and Southern States." And so they did. As proposed by the committee and accepted as part of the Constitution's Article 1, Section 9, slaves would be imported into this country for another twenty years. In exchange as provided in Section 10, the nation got a navigation clause that provided federal control of foreign trade.

Thursday, August 23, 1787

Today was clear, warm, and reasonably pleasant.

Convention

The Convention considered giving Congress the power: "to make laws for organizing, arming & disciplining the Militia, and for governing such parts of them as may be employed in that service of the U.S. reserving to the States respectively, the appointment of the officers, and authority of training the militia according to the discipline prescribed."

Sherman (CT) moved to strike the last clause as unnecessary; the states already had it. Ellsworth (CT) disagreed. He also feared that "disciplining" was so broad as to include all power over the militia. King (MA) explained the committee's intent, and Sherman withdrew his motion.

Gerry (MA) was almost hysterical in his opposition. To give Congress such power reduced the states to drill sergeants. He would rather see the citizens of Massachusetts disarmed than subjected to the central government. (One wonders if he remembered this speech in 1812. In that year, Governor Caleb Strong of Massachusetts refused a request from the administration in which Gerry was about to become vice president to place a part of the state militia in federal service.) After much more debate, the proposal was accepted.

At Charles Pinckney's urging, a prohibition on government officers accepting foreign titles and gifts was passed.

Article VIII, which contained a very important provision (that the acts of Congress made in pursuance of the Constitution and all treaties made under the authority of the United States shall be to supreme law of the several states) was passed without debate.

Article IX, Section 1, giving the Senate power to make treaties and appoint ambassadors and judges, was taken up. Morris (PA) opposed having the Senate appoint officers; "it was too numerous, subject to cabal and devoid of responsibility." Besides, if the Senate were to try judges on impeachment, it certainly shouldn't be able to fill the very vacancies created by impeachment. Wilson agreed. The article was postponed.

Delegates

Dr. Johnson dined at his boarding house and went for a walk. General Washington dined, drank tea and spent the evening at the Morris'. Dr. Franklin met with the state's Supreme Executive Council.

James McHenry wrote to his wife of three years, Margaret Allison Caldwell:

my dear Peggy
   It is altogether uncertain when the convention will rise, but it is likely to be about three weeks hence.

William Paterson wrote from New Brunswick to Oliver Ellsworth. The letter bypassed Ellsworth as he left Philadelphia today for home.

Charles Pinckney

CHARLES PINCKNEY (not to be confused with his second cousin Charles Coatsworth Pinckney) was one of the youngest, and perhaps most arrogant, members of the Convention. He came from an aristocratic South Carolina family, read law and was admitted to the bar in Charleston, and, at the tender of age of 21, was elected to the South Carolina House of Representatives. He served as an officer during the

Revolution, and was held as a prisoner of war while the British occupied Charleston. From late 1784 to early 1787 Pinckney represented South Carolina in the Confederation Congress.

So, although Pinckney was quite young when he came to Philadelphia as a delegate, he had spent much of his life in politics. We know from the records of the delegates that Pinckney made a number of speeches during the Convention. He was quite perceptive and persuasive, often encouraging others to adopt his point of view.

There was, however, some controversy about Pinckney's participation in the Convention. First of all, he did not try to hide his youth; William Pierce of Georgia wrote that Pinckney was in his twenties. It is known that Pinckney offered some sort of plan for government early in the Convention, referred to as the Pinckney Draught. Although historians are not quite sure of the details embodied in this plan, they generally agree that it was not seriously considered by the Convention. For his part, Pinckney later perpetrated the myth that his plan was the basis of the finished Constitution.

Following the Convention, Pinckney was a strong advocate for ratification in South Carolina. He served several terms as that state's governor, and in 1798 became a United States senator. Between the Convention and his appointment to the Senate, Pinckney shifted from staunch member of the Federalist party to an equally strong Republican position. As a record of his transformation, Pinckney was chosen as Minister of Spain in 1801, a position he held until 1806. Following his diplomatic post, Pinckney returned to Charleston where he managed his business affairs and stayed involved in state politics. He died in 1824.

Charles Pinckney was one of the youngest delegates and considered very able. He was the first to suggest prohibiting religious qualifications and was against any proposal that controlled slavery. He supported a strong central government.

Friday, August 24, 1787

Today was clear and very warm—at least 85° or more.

Convention

Governor Livingston (NJ) reported that the Committee on the Slave Trade recommended the importation of such persons as the states care to import should not be prohibited prior to 1800, but that a tax might be placed on such imports, and navigation acts might be passed by a majority of those present. The Convention decided to delay a discussion of the report.

Article IX, Sections 2 and 3, a complicated procedure for resolving disputes between states (which had been lifted verbatum from the Articles of Confederation), was taken up. Rutledge (SC) noted that the provision of a judiciary made it unnecessary and moved to strike it. Johnson (CT) seconded; Sherman (CT), Wilson (PA) and Dayton (NJ) concurred. Williamson and Gorham were uncertain, but the Convention voted to strike the provision.

The delegates moved on to Article X dealing with the Executive.

Four methods for electing the president were considered and each was defeated. The least acceptable were direct election by the people and election by a joint ballot of the House and Senate. Election by the legislature with each state having one vote and election by electors chosen by the people were narrowly defeated. The delegates would have to return to this

The port of Philadelphia on the Delaware River was a busy place. It was here that the first steamboat constructed by John Fitch, was tested.

difficult question.

Article X, Section 2, on executive powers was taken up, and several amendments were passed. It was then "ordered, unanimously that the rule respecting adjournment at 4 o'clock be repealed, & that in future the house assemble at 10 o'clock & adjourn at 3 o'clock."

Delegates

General Washington dined at the Morris'. Walter Minto, Scottish-born mathematician and principal of Erasmus Hall, wrote to Washington, enclosing a "small Tract on the Theory of Planets."

Dr. Franklin attended Pennsylvania's Supreme Executive Council meeting at the State House. John Smith, administrator of the estate of Robert Smith, deceased, wrote to Franklin asking him to settle his account with the estate, and in the meantime advance the estate 130 pounds to discharge its debts. Smith had built Franklin's house.

Another Philadelphia First

A STEAMBOAT, the first successful one in North America was tested, not in New York, but in Philadelphia in August of 1787. The boat was the product of John Fitch, a silversmith, watchmaker, surveyor, and admiral of the Delaware. He developed the boat with the help of Henry Voigt, a Philadelphia watchmaker, who had a shop on Second Street between Race and Vine Streets. The spectators at the landing would have looked out on America's busiest port. Ships loading wheat, cattle, ship bread, and lumber for the West Indies would have lined the docks. Had a spectator arrived early enough, he would have seen a fleet of farm boats bring Jersey produce to the markets on Market Street.

Philadelphia was also a leading shipbuilding area. Looking upriver from Market Street, one could see three shipyards: the Wharton and Humphries Yard, the Penrose Yard, and the William West Yard.

For Fitch's test, a mile had been measured off along Front Street. The boat resembled a canoe with six paddles on each side. The engine took up a third of the space in the canoe. Fitch and Voight fired up the engine which built up pressure, the paddle turned and the boat moved upriver against the tide. It was described as looking like a long-legged waterbug. Everything was fine except for the speed. It did not go over three miles per hour. At that rate, the average stagecoach which galloped along the riverside road would beat the boat to Bristol, PA, by a full hour. Later that year, Fitch improved his boat. He offered excursions to Bristol and Burlington over the next two summers, traveling 2,000 miles in all and reaching speeds of eight miles an hour.

Saturday, August 25, 1787

The day was cool and pleasant with a moderate breeze.

Convention

The clause requiring the new government to pay the old government's debt was reconsidered. Mason (VA) objected to the obligatory "shall" in "shall fulfill the engagements and discharge the debts." The argument was that the creditors should be left as they were. There was a distinction between original holders and those who purchased obligations fraudulently. Langdon (NH) wished to do no more than leave creditors in status quo. Gerry (MA) had no interest in the question, owning only enough securities that the interest would pay his taxes (actually, he was the largest holder of public securities among the delegates—at least $50,000 worth).

He would observe, however, that as the public had received the value of the literal [face] amount, they ought too pay that value to some body . . . As to Stock—jobbers he saw no reason for the censures thrown on them—They keep up the value of the paper. Without them there would be no market.

Randolph (VA) proposed substitute language (now the first paragraph, Article VI).

The slave trade provision was again taken up. General Pinckney (SC) and Gorham (MA) moved to change the date to 1808; Madison said that 20 years would do all the mischief to be expected, and such a term was dishonorable. The motion carried.

Delegates

Dr. Johnson (CT) dined with Mr. Gerry (MA). He took a walk, and paid a laundry bill of 13 shillings and 2 pence.

General Washington dined with the club at Springsbury and spent the afternoon at his lodgings.

Governor Livingston (NJ) wrote from Philadelphia to his old friend John Tabor Kempe in London. (A Tory, Kempe had returned to England. Livingston was providing him evidence to support his claims against the crown for property seized from him by the Americans).

Sir Edward Newenham wrote a very long letter to Franklin on Irish, English and European affairs. He had arranged to have a "car" sent by Colonel Perss' car maker in the first ship sailing from Galway.

Economic Interpretation of the Constitution

ELBRIDGE GERRY, holder of more government debt than any other delegate, argued for payment of the face value of the debt, even though much of it could be bought at ten cents on the dollar or less. To what degree were the delegates motivated by personal economic considerations, and to what degree did their work reflect such considerations? These questions have intrigued historians since the appearance of Charles A. Beard's pioneering *An Economic Interpretation of the Constitution of the United States* in 1913.

To date, the questions have not been satisfactorily answered; they cannot be answered now and probably never will be answered. Not enough about the delegates is known to answer them.

Benjamin Franklin's chaise was probably similar to the conveyance called a "car" ordered from Colonel Perss's car maker and sent on the first ship sailing from Galway.

Considerations of direct personal economic benefit were not a primary motivation. If the Constitution did not specifically guarantee that Gerry's share of the public debt would be paid at face value, it did provide a government which would be financially capable of paying it. Gerry would oppose ratification. George Washington owned no government bonds. He did own land in western Virginia, western Pennsylvania and elsewhere which might be harder to sell if an effective central government was trying hard to sell its own western lands. He supported ratification, as he would have under any circumstances. Most, if not all, of the delegates were not influenced by their own short-term economic well-being.

Sunday, August 26, 1787

The day was cool, breezy and pleasant.

Convention

The Convention was enjoying its usual Sunday recess after a full week spent refining the draft Constitution.

The hard Windsor chairs in the stuffy closed-up Assembly Room were very uncomfortable after the

Delegates

Dr. Johnson (CT) worshipped at St. Paul's Episcopal Church (which stills stands on Third Street, south of Walnut), and dined at the Binghams. He wrote a short

delegates had sat in them for six hours without a break for lunch or any refreshment.

letter to his son Charles to give him some directions concerning his law practice.

General Washington rode eight or ten miles out into the country, dined at the Hills with the Morrises and spent the evening in his room writing letters. One of these was his weekly letter of instructions and questions to George Augustine Washington. Another to Alexander Spotswood recommended that Spotswood not try to get his son appointed a midshipman in the French Navy, but should he decide to, he would write to LaFayette.

James McHenry (MD) wrote his wife Peggy. "I am now going to drink tea at your aunt's, after which I propose to spend half an hour in the State House walks, and then return home to finish the evening with the political ingenious Haley. . . ."

Gerry (MA) wrote his wife in New York concerning servants, her health, mutual friends, etc. He noted . . .

You mistook my meaning, with respect to my Lodgings, I meant my situation as a delegate was uneasy: I am exceedingly distrait at the proceedings of the Convention, being apprehensive, I am almost sure they will if not altered materially lay the foundation of a civil war. This entre nous. . . . I never was more sick of anything than I am of conventioneering had I know what would have happened nothing would have induced me to attend, but here I am and must be patient a little longer.

The Delegates as Drudges

SHEER drudgery was required to produce the Constitution of the United States which is so familiar, so lucid, and so apparently (and deceptively) simple in its provisions.

During the thirteenth full week of the Convention, its sessions convened at 10 A.M. and adjourned at 4 P.M.—six hours a day without interruption for lunch or coffee break. So, for six hours the delegates sat in hard and uncomfortable Windsor chairs in a closed up and stuffy room. Worse, while sitting, delegates were required to perform two extremely difficult tasks.

By this time, the subjects were familiar and most of the thoughts expressed on each subject had been expressed before. How to define and punish treason, whether direct taxes should be apportioned among the states based on the number of representatives each state was allowed until the census could be taken, what role the federal government should have in controlling the militia, whether or not exports should be taxed, whether or not the slave trade should be prohibited, whether or not Congress should have authority to veto state laws and the other topics discussed in the past six days had been discussed over and over.

What might have been new and exciting in early June was old and boring in late August. Yet the delegates stuck with the task at hand, doing their best to think through every proposal.

Monday, August 27, 1787

Today was cool and rainy, with temperature in the 60s.

Convention

Consideration of Article X, Section 2, powers and duties of the Executive, was resumed. L. Martin (MD) moved to allow the president the power to pardon only after a conviction. Wilson (PA) pointed out the need to use pardons to obtain testimony, and Martin withdrew the motion.

Morris (PA) objected to having the Supreme Court try the president on impeachment and to having the president of the Senate succeed the president. Madison agreed, and suggested that when vacancies oc-

cured, the powers of the president devolve on the Council (Cabinet). Postponed.

Article XI, on the Judiciary, came up. Dr. Johnson (CT) suggested that the judicial power should extend to both law and equity. Read (DE) opposed, but the motion carried. Dickinson (DE) moved to judges removable by Executive on application of Congress. Consideration line by line continued and several clarifying amendments were approved.

Delegates

Secretary for Foreign Affairs Jay wrote from New York to his father-in-law, Governor Livingston, a

New Jersey delegate to the Convention in Philadelphia. In it he gave his opinion of Virginia delegate George Mason, and news of Livingston's extended family.

Since yours by Col. Mason I have recd. a letter from Mr. Ridley [who had recently married Livingston's daughter Caty] mentioning your having been there. He was much pleased with that mark of your attention and I am glad he received it for I believe him to be a worthy man. I thank you for introducing Col. Mason to me; he really is a man of Talents and an agreeable companion. There are few with whom on so short an acquaintance I have been so much pleased and I regret that it was not convenient to him to have remained longer in this city. Be pleased to present my compliments, to him, and assure him of my Respect and Esteem. The long Session of the Convention will I doubt not produce a System so well matured and wise as to have no Room for applying the moral of the old fable montes parteivient. When you return from Pha. we hope for the Pleasure of seeing you here, our little girls are well speckled with a sad Eruption which has given them & us much trouble [chicken pox], but which may perhaps have saved them from more serious Complaints. Peter [the Governor's grandson and favorite fishing companion] is now at Rye where I think it best to leave him a little longer, for at this Season the City is generally less healthy than that part of the Country.

The Philadelphia jail, or goal, was built by Robert Smith who built Carpenters' Hall. The seven-foot wall across the street enclosed the State House yard and contained the South Gate.

Debate on the Judiciary

ATTENTION TO DETAIL was typical in the debate on the judiciary as it was on almost every provision, and is illustrative of the delegates' thinking.

Dickinson moved to amend the section on tenure and salary to provide that judges may be removed by the Executive at the request of both houses of the legislature. At that point, a note of Madison is of interest

Mr. Gerry 2ded. the motion
Mr. Govr. Morris thought it a contradiction in terms to say that the Judges should hold their offices during good behavior, and yet be removeable without a trial. Besides it was fundamentally wrong to subject Judges to so arbitrary an authority.
Mr. Sherman saw no contradiction or impropriety if this were made part of the Constitutional regulation of the Judiciary establishment. He observed that a like provision was contained in the British Statutes.
Mr. Rutlidge: If the supreme Court is to judge between the U.S. and particular States, this alone is an insuperable objection to the motion.
Mr. Wilson considered such a provision in the

155

British Government as less dangerous than here, the House of Lords & House of Commons being less likely to concur on the same occasions. Chief Justice Holt, he remarked, had successively offended by his independent conduct, both houses of Parliament. Had this happened at the same time, he would have been ousted. The Judges would be in a bad situation if made to depend on every gust of faction which might prevail in the two branches of our Govt.

Mr. Randolph opposed the motion as weakening too much the independence of the Judges.

Mr. Dickinson was not apprehensive that the Legislature composed of different branches constructed on such different principles, would improperly unite for the purpose of displacing a Judge—

On the question for agreeing to Mr. Dickinson's Motion N.H. no. Mas. abst, Ct. ay., N.J. abst, Pa. no., Del. no, Md no., Va. no, N.C. abst., S.C. no, Geo. no., [Ayes-1; noes-7; absent-3.]

On the question on Sect. 2 art. Xi as reported. Del. & Maryd. only no—

Tuesday, August 28, 1787

Today was rainy and not as cool as yesterday, with temperatures in the 70s.

Convention

The judiciary article was approved, and the Convention moved on to Article XII which prohibited state coinage, state issued letters of marque, state treaties and state letters of nobility. Wilson (PA) and Sherman (CT) moved to prohibit the states from issuing bills of credit or making anything but gold or silver legal tender. The article passed.

King moved to prevent the states from interfering in private contracts. Sherman, Wilson, and Madison agreed; G. Morris (PA) and Mason (VA) thought this was going too far. Rutledge (SC) moved to prohibit bills of attainder and ex post facto laws.

Discussion proceeded to Article XIII:

No State, without the consent of the Legislature of the United States, shall emit bills of credit, or make any thing but specie a tender in payment of debts; nor lay imposts or duties on imports; nor keep troops or shops of war in time of peace; nor enter into any agreement or compact with another State, or with any foreign power; nor engage in any war, unless it shall be actually invaded by enemies, or the danger of invasion be so imminent, as not to admit of delay, until the Legislature of the United States can be consulted.

After debate and amendment, the article was agreed to. Article XIV, giving the citizens of each state all the privileges and immunities of citizens of the several states, was also approved.

Delegates

James McHenry (MD) wrote his "dear Peggy":

It is extremely distressing to me to be under the necessity to remain a day longer in this place, where I find no enjoyments whatever and am even without the satisfaction of knowing that what I am assisting those who sent me hither. . . .

Roger Sherman (CT) wrote to Colonel Wadsworth in Hartford, saying that the proceedings were still secret but he would inform Wadsworth when anything happened or he had the freedom to do so.

Hamilton (NY) wrote from New York to Rufus King:

Dear Sir,

I wrote to you some days since, that to request you to inform me when there was a prospect of your finishing as I intended to be with you, for certain reasons, before the conclusion. It is whispered here that some late changes in your scheme have taken place which give it a higher tone. Is this the case?

I leave town today, to attend a circuit in a neighbouring County, from which I shall return the last of the week, and shall be glad to find a line from

Independence Hall (as it appears today) was getting to be an unhappy reminder of the lack of progress that was being made in the Convention by the end of August.

you explanatory of the period of the probable termination of your business.

Voting in the Convention

RUFUS KING moved to prohibit the states from interfering in private contracts [no state shall pass any ". . . Law impairing the obligation of Contracts. . . ." Article II Section 10]. King seems to have felt strongly about this issue. Yet when the vote came, Massachusetts did not vote. What happened? Alexander Hamilton, who favored a strengthened federal government as much as any man, felt free to absent himself for weeks at a time. Why?

The answer to both questions lies in this fact: each state decided at the time it elected delegates how many of its delegates must be present to cast the state's vote. A single delegate could cast the votes of Connecticut and Maryland; New Hampshire, North Carolina, South Carolina and Georgia required at least two; Massachusetts, New Jersey, Delaware and Virginia required three; and Pennsylvania, four. New York did not specify, but the Convention seems to have assumed that a majority of the three member delegation two was required.

On this day, Strong had gone home to North Hampton, leaving only three Massachusetts delegates. Thus, if Gerry, Gorham or King were ill, or attending to personal business, Massachusetts could not vote. Since Lansing and Yates had gone home in mid-July, New York had had no quorum and hence no vote. Hamilton could influence the Convention only by his powers of persuasion, and his attendance, except on key occasions, wasn't worthwhile. It is this variation within delegations which permitted Sherman and Johnson to "run off" a week before the July/August recess began (Ellsworth could cast Connecticut's vote; which permitted North Carolina's Davie and Alexander Martin to leave early, and which allowed William Pierce of Georgia to stay on at Congress while Gorham and King couldn't.).

Wednesday, August 29, 1787

It rained this morning, was cloudy in the afternoon, then cleared.

Convention

Article XVI, the "full faith and credit" clause came up. Williamson (NC) didn't understand the clause, and moved to substitute the language in the Articles of Confederation. Wilson (PA) and Johnson (CT) provided their interpretations. Charles Pinckney moved to commit and add a provision for uniform bankruptcy laws; Madison agreed. Randolph (VA) moved a provision for accepting state actions by other States. The resolutions were referred to a committee.

A committee recommendation not to require a two-thirds vote to pass acts regulating trade was brought up. A move to postpone this report and instead require the assent of two-thirds of the members of each house lost after debate; MD, VA, NC and GA aye; 7 no. The committee report was agreed to.

Butler (SC) moved to insert a provision for the return of fugitive slaves, which was agreed to. Agreement to this provision may explain South Carolina's vote for regulating trade by a simple majority. The Convention then moved on to consider admitting new states.

Delegates

Dr. Franklin presided at a meeting of Pennsylvania's Supreme Executive Council.

Elbridge Gerry (MA) wrote his wife for the fourth time this week.

What is the cause my dearest love that you are of late so liable to fainting? I am quite distressed about it. If you do not find releif soon, I shall quit the convention; & let their proceedings take their chance.

Indeed I have been a spectator for some time; for I am very different in political principles from my colleagues. I am very well but sick of being here; indeed I ardently long to meet my dear Nancy.

Sectional Differences

NAVIGATION ACTS debate was probably the clearest expression of differing state economic interests to be found in the Convention records. In

presenting his motion to require a two-thirds vote of the total membership of each House, to pass a bill regulating trade, Charles Pinckney:

> . . . remarked that there were five distinct commercial interests—1. the fisheries & W. Indian trade, which belonged to the N. England States. 2. the interest of N. York lay in a free trade. 3. Wheat & flour the staple of the two Middle States, (N.J. Penna.)—4. Tobo. the staple of Maryd. & Virginia

The map of Philadelphia in the eighteenth century shows the extent of the docks. The debate on naviga- *tion acts reflected the different state economic interests.*

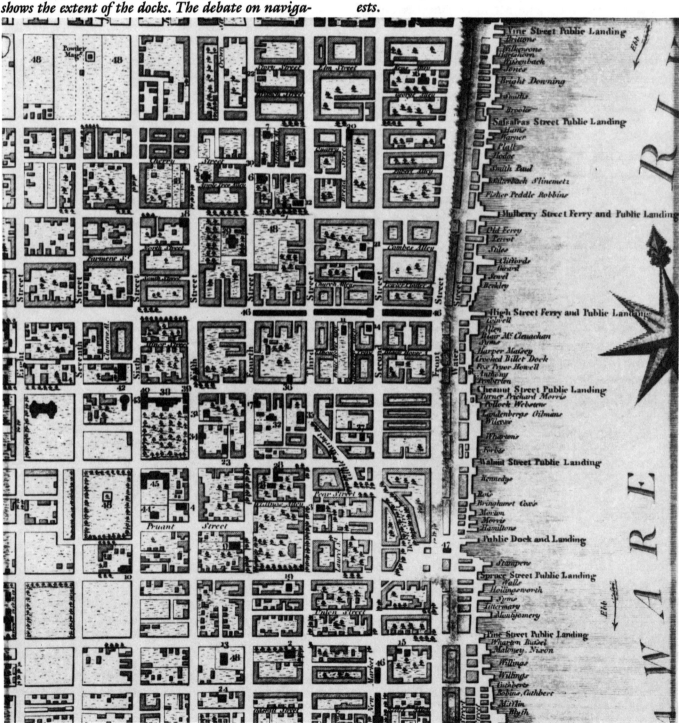

(& partly of N. Carolina.) 5. Rice and Indigo, the staple of S. Carolina & Georgia. These different interests would be a source of oppressive regulations if no check to a bare majority should be provided. States pursue their interests with less scruple than individuals. The power of regulating commerce was a pure concession on the part of the S. States. They did not need the protection of the N. States at present.

After L. Martin's (MD) second, Pinckney's older cousin, Charles C., said that the interest of the South was to have no commercial regulations, but the eastern States needed it, and had accommodated the South [on the slave trade] and he opposed fetters on regulating commerce. Clymer (PA) said the northern and middle states would be ruined if they couldn't retaliate against foreign regulation. Sherman (CT) observed that the divergence of economic interests among regions was itself security against abuse. Charles Pinckney observed that his five interests were minute—the great division was North and South.

G. Morris (PA) noted that preferences would increase American shipping, and a navy was essential to security. Williamson (NC) wanted a two-thirds requirement: "No useful measure he believed had been lost in Congress for want of nine votes." Spaight (NC) opposed the motion: the South could build ships for their own use if trade regulations were abused. Butler (SC) opposed the motion because he was "desirous of conciliating the affections of the East."

And so the debate went, with Mason (VA) and Randolph supporting the motion, and Wilson (PA), Madison (VA), Rutledge (SC) and Gorham (MA) opposing it, but no one disagreed that North and South had very different interests.

Thursday, August 30, 1787

Today was very pleasant and cool after a morning rain.

Convention

The Convention resumed debate on admitting new states, and specifically on Morris' motion to require the consent of a state before creating a new state. While the theoretical desirability of this requirement was obvious, practically, it might require the consent of Massachusetts, New York, Virginia, North Carolina and Georgia before Maine, Vermont, Kentucky, Ohio, Indiana, Illinois, Michigan, Wisconsin, Tennessee, Alabama and Mississippi could be admitted. Carroll (MD) and Luther Martin (MD) opposed the requirement; Rutledge (SC), Williamson (NC) and Wilson (PA) urged its necessity; and Sherman (CT) and Johnson (CT) sought a compromise. Eventually, Morris' motion, amended somewhat, passed: 8 aye; NJ, DE and MD no.

Article XIX, (The legislature to call a Convention for amending the Constitution upon application of two-thirds of the state legislature) was agreed to without opposition. Article XXI, requiring oaths to support the Constitution from federal and state officers came up. "Or affirmation" was added after "oath." Charles Pinckney (SC) moved to also add "but no religious test shall ever be required as a qualification to any office or public trust under the authority of the United States." Sherman (CT) thought that the prevailing liberation made the provision unnecessary; G. Morris (PA) and General Pinckney approved the motion, and it carried; NC no; MD divided.

Delegates

Dr. Johnson (CT) dined at Wilsons and posed for Robert Edge Pine, who was painting Johnson's portrait.

For the third day in a row, General Washington dined and spent the evening with his hosts, the Morrises. He wrote to William Hartshorne to introduce Major Baylies, of Massachusetts, a son-in-law of Washington's friend and colleague General Benjamin Lincoln.

At 54, the staid and proper John Dickinson (DE) was still writing love letters to his wife of 17 years, Mary Norris Dickinson.

My dearest Polly,
Your letter & the umbrella I have received. You grieve me with Complaints of my Absence, & more with accounts of your indisposition. It is one of the [illegible] Joys of my Soul to be loved by You, and I love you with the tenderest Affection. . . .

Elbridge Gerry (MA) also wrote his wife. He had not heard from her by the last post, and would be uneasy until the next one. He is well, but concerned about her fainting spell, and ". . . determined to leave no Stone unturned to prevent measures which if adopted will probably produce the most fatal consequences [the ratification of the Constitution]."

The Rev. John Lathrop, minister of Second Church, Boston, wrote Dr. Franklin to enclose a discourse delivered before the Human Society of Boston.

Religious Tests

RELIGIOUS DIFFERENCES in the twentieth century when Mormons, Catholics, Quakers, Baptists, Jews and others are routinely elected or appointed to national and state office, was a consideration in August 1787. By permitting federal and state officers to swear or affirm the oath to support the Constitution, the Convention opened the way to federal and state office for Quakers and others whose

Church steeples dominate this view from the East of Philadelphia. The delegates in the final draft of the Constitution banned any form of religious vows for federal and state officers.

religious beliefs precluded them from taking the oath, (Herbert Hoover, Dwight D. Eisenhower and Richard Nixon, had they followed their parents' beliefs, could not have taken the oath, but, since they could have taken an affirmation would still have served as President).

The Convention then went even further, and banned any form of religious test, somewhat to the dismay of Roger Sherman and over the objections of North Carolina. Delegates did this at a time when that most liberal of state constitutions, that of Pennsylvania, required members of its legislature to declare: "I do believe in one God, the Creator and Governor of the Universe, the Rewarder of Good and Punisher of the Wicked. And I do acknowledge the Scriptures of the Old and New Testament to be given by Divine Inspiration."

Friday, August 31, 1787

Clear and Pleasant.

Convention

Article XX1, on ratification, remained on the floor. King (MA) moved an amendment to confine the new government to the states ratifying it, which passed: only Maryland no. The entire day was spent debating how the proposed plan should be ratified. Maryland, as the act appointing its delegates required, sought to require all thirteen states to approve.

Late in the day, the report from the committee on treating the states equally in regulating trade came up. A clause forbidding preference to the ports of any one state was approved. A clause forbidding vessels bound to or from one state to enter or clear in another came up. Madison, Gorham (MA), and Langdon (NY) opposed it, pointing out cases where exceptions were desirable; Fitzsimons (PA) and the Marylanders strongly supported it and it passed: NH and SC only no.

Delegates

General Washington dined at Mr. Morris' (PA), then escorted Elizabeth Powel to Governor Penn's estate, Lansdowne, for tea.

Doctor Franklin replied to a letter of August 16 from the Treasury Board asking for Mr. Ross' accounts. Franklin had looked for them, couldn't find them, and thought he'd turned them over to Thomas Barclay. "However as soon as my Grandson returns from Albany, whom I expect in a week or ten days, and who knows better than I do the Arrangement of our immense Mass of Papers, I shall cause a more full Search to be made. . . ."

The Loyal Opposition

GEORGE MASON made it clear that he could not support the proposed Constitution as it stood. At the same time, he supported ratification by only nine of the thirteen states; a proposal which proved to be the key to ratification.

Of the fifty-five delegates who attended the Constitutional Convention, thirty-nine signed the Constitution, indicating their support of its ratification. Nine others left early for one reason or another, but subsequently supported ratification. Another three—Yates, Lansing and John Francis Mercer—came to oppose the plan soon after arriving in Philadelphia, and left shortly thereafter.

The four remaining delegates—Elbridge Gerry, Luther Martin, George Mason and Edmund Randolph—were still in this Convention on this day 200 years ago, although all four had decided they could not support the new plan of government. Martin had reached this decision very early, probably by June 16, and the death of the New Jersey Plan; Gerry had decided by August 21; and Mason and Randolph announced their opposition on this day. All, however, continued to work constructively to improve the document; none of them tried to make it less acceptable and thus less likely to be ratified. Mason's conduct is an example. It was he who moved and supported ratification by nine states, when a larger number would have made the Constitution's ratification less likely.

Cooking for the Convention delegates was done in open fireplaces, using stewing and roasting methods. *The kitchens were kept busy as the delegates dined in the various houses.*

Saturday, September 1, 1787

It rained most of the day and was cool.

Convention

Today's session was a brief one. As Madison noted it:

> *Mr. Brearley from the Comme. of eleven to which were referred yesterday, the postponed part of the Constitution & parts of Reports not acted upon, made the following partial report.*
>
> *That in lieu of the 9th. sect: of art: 6. the words following be inserted viz "The members of each House shall be ineligible to any civil office under the authority of the U.S. during the time for which they shall respectively be elected, and no person holding an office under the U.S. shall be a member of either House during his continuance in office.*
>
> *Mr. Rutlidge from the Committee to whom were referred sundry propositions (see Aug: 29), together with art: XVI, reported that the following additions be made to the Report—viz.*
>
> *After the word "States" in the last line on the Margin of the 3d. page (see the printed report)—add "to establish uniform laws on the subject of Bankruptcies" and insert the following as Art: XVI—viz "Full faith and credit ought to be given in each State to the public acts, records, and Judicial proceedings of every other State, and the Legislature shall by general laws prescribe the manner in which such acts, Records, & proceedings shall be proved and the effect which Judgments obtained in one State, shall have in another.*
>
> *After receiving these reports*
> *The House adjourned to IO A.M. on Monday next.*

Delegates

A thoroughly alarmed and depressed Elbridge Gerry wrote his wife:

> *I am distressed my dearest Girl exceedingly, at the information in yours of the 29th & 30th of your indisposition, & shall prepare myself to leave this city* on the arrival of the next post unless you are better. Indeed I would not remain here two hours was I not undr a necessity of staying to prevent my colleagues from saying that I broke up the representation [Strong had left, leaving MA with only the 3 delegates needed to cast its vote], & that they were averse to an arbitrary system of Government, for such it is at present. . . .

Louis XVI was reigning king of the French nation which was active in trade and cultural exchange with the Americans.

The French Connection

FRANCO-AMERICAN cultural exchange and trade had grown by 1787 from a trickle to a tidal wave. France began her love affair with Americans when introduced to our first ambassador, Benjamin Franklin, in 1776. Franklin always drew an admiring crowd in his public appearance.

By 1783 there was established a regular packet boat service between France and the United States. Robert Morris and William Blount were exporting substantial shipments of American tobacco to France.

Americans started visiting and living in France. Charles Bulfinch, the architect, John Trumbull, the artist, John Paul Jones, naval hero, and Thomas Paine, author and bridge builder—all visited Paris in the 1780s.

Philadelphia's own American Philosophical Society enjoyed high repute in Paris. Between 1784 and 1793 thirty-one Frenchmen were elected to the A.P.S. Boston's American Academy of Arts and Sciences, likewise, boasted a significant French membership. The Society of Cincinnati, the organization of Revolutionary War officers, included a Paris chapter of French veterans.

Our ambassador in Paris in 1787, Thomas Jefferson, faced the accusation of being too pro-French both in his term as Washington's Secretary of State and in his own term as our third president.

Sunday, September 2, 1787

After a cloudy morning, the sky cleared and the afternoon was sunny and pleasant.

Convention

The Convention was observing its customary Sunday recess.

Delegates

Dr. Johnson (CT) spent the day with Richard Peters, farmer and lawyer and former member of the Continent's Board of War, at the latter's country estate, Belmont. The doctor also wrote his wife of 38 years, Ann Beach Johnson, on family matters and private business.

General Washington rode out to Bartram's Garden and the country nearby, dined and drank tea at Gray's Ferry, and returned to Market Street in the evening. He wrote the usual long letter of instructions to his nephew, George Augustine Washington, among other things requesting that a full-size model of Mr. Young's plow be sent to Robert Morris (PA) so that Morris could manufacture others. He also wrote a brief note to John Paul Jones, and covered it with a note to Secretary of Foreign Affairs Jay, asking that he give the note to Jones or, if he had left, have it forwarded.

Richard Dobbs Spaight wrote John Gray Blount. Elbridge Gerry (MA) added a postscript to the letter to his wife he had written yesterday:

Yesterday I dined with General Pinckney & Mrs. Pinckney made particular inquiry for you & the baby. There was considerable company & she was very agreeable & attentive. The General is as we always thought the cleverest being alive. I love him better every time I meet him. Mrs. Pinckney says Mrs. Butler proposes to return to New York from Newport, having been there some time without being introduced to a person. I am sorry for this, but she should not have gone or remained there without letters to some of the citizens. . . ."

William Roberts wrote from Fredericksburg, VA, to General Washington asking the General to reemploy him and loan him 10 pounds.

Cash Problems

DELEGATES, as a whole, were well off financially, and several were very wealthy. However, most of them had problems getting cash. Today's letter from the North Carolina delegate, Richard Dobbs

Spaight, to John Gray Blount is typical:

PHILADELPHIA 2d September. 1787

Dear Sir,

I have for a long time past flattered myself that every post would bring me a letter from you, in answer to those I have wrote you, but have not—as yet been favored with a single line. My situation here is extremely distressing; as I expected when I came away only to stay six weeks or two months at farthest, I made a money provision merely for that term, and out of that, forty one dollars, still remain in the hands of Mr. Blackledge who was to send them after me, but I have not heard from him since I left N. Carolina. I have now overstayed the term I counted upon, two months, and shall be here till tomorrow week, when I hope to get away provided I can get money to pay off my Accounts here and bear my expences home, which I have no other means of doing than by borrowing, and no other way of doing that, then to get some friend to lend me his name to a note for thirty days, and get it discounted at the bank, and depend for the payment of it on the remittance I expect you will make for me. You will therefore do me an essential service, by remitting on the best terms you can such monies as you have received upon my Account as speedily as possible. I suppose you will send the remittance to Stuart & Barr. I will there leave directions with them to whom to pay it.

The Convention will I imagine finish their business by next Saturday in that case. If I can be supplied with cash I shall leave this the Monday following. I am with regard & Esteem

> *Your Most Ob. Ser.*
> *Rich. Dobbs Spaight*
> *John G. Blount esquire*

The Woodlands, a country estate visited by many delegates, was the home of a leading horitculturist and had over 10,000 varieties of plants. The delegates as a group were very wealthy and many owned estates of such size.

Monday, September 3, 1787

Convention

Today's session opened with debate on the "full faith and credit" article. G. Morris (PA) and Madison (VA) proposed amendments which were approved, and the result ["Full faith and credit shall be given in each State to the public acts, records and judicial proceedings of every other State . . ."] was approved without a vote.

The Bank of the United States, in addition to many other financial institutions, was built after the Convention because of the economic powers implied in the Constitution.

The clause giving Congress the power "to establish uniform laws on the subject of bankruptcies" was taken up. Sherman (CT) observed that, in England, some bankrupts could be punished by death, and he didn't want Congress to have the power to pass a law like that. Morris (PA) saw no danger of abuse. The clause was agreed to: 9 aye; CT only no.

Next was debated the provision that members of Congress be ineligible for other federal offices. The proposal simply prohibited a member of Congress from holding any other federal office during his term, and any federal office holder from serving in Congress

while holding office. Charles Pinckney (SC) moved to postpone this and take up a motion which would restrict members of Congress from accepting a salary for holding another office. "He considered the eligibility of members of the Legislature to the honorable offices of Government, as resembling the policy of the Romans, in making the temple of virtue the road to the temple of fame." He lost: PA and NC aye; 8 no.

After debate and amendment, this provision was finally approved.

Delegates

General Washington "Visited a Machine at Doctr. Franklin's (called a Mangle) for pressing, in place of Ironing, clothes from the wash. Which Machine from the facility with which it dispatches business is well calculated for Table clothes and such Articles as have not pleats & irregular foldings and would be very useful in all large families. Dined, drank Tea, & spent the evening at Mr. Morris'."

Governor Randolph (VA) wrote Philadelphian Tench Coxe, who was temporarily out of the city, to find out "when you will return, as I shall be very anxious to press forward to Virginia."

John Tabor Kempe wrote from London to inform William Livingston (NJ) that the copies of New Jersey papers Kempe needed to support his claims against the Crown for losses caused by his loyalty had not arrived and that he was anxious about them.

Ineligibility and the Parliamentary System

PARLIAMENTARY SYSTEM adherents ignore American history and culture. The first settlers in Virginia and Massachusetts began moving away from a parliamentary system towards one of checks and balances. By the 1700s in most of the colonies fighting the governor was the legislature's favorite activity.

On this day 200 years ago, the Convention voted to make members of Congress ineligible for positions in the administration. While this proposal was hotly debated, the debate was on how far to go. No one questioned the concept.

Tuesday, September 4, 1787

Convention

Chairman Brearly (NJ) of the Committee on Unfinished Parts made a partial report. The first clause of the report, the fateful "The Legislature shall have power to lay and collect taxes, duties, imposts and excises, to pay the debts and provide for the common defense and general welfare", was agreed to without opposition. The power to regulate commerce with the Indian tribes was also approved without opposition.

That part of the report recommending election of the president by an electoral college was then taken up and discussed for the rest of the session.

Delegates

Dr. Johnson (CT) "Din'd Lewis'." This is almost certainly William Lewis, distinguished Quaker lawyer and defense counsel in many of Philadelphia's Revolutionary War treason trials—at this time resident at the south west corner of Third and Walnut.

James Madison (VA) wrote his father to inquire about his health and about events in Virginia and to send along rumors of disturbances in Greenbrier Country and elsewhere. He noted that the price of good tobacco in Philadelphia was forty shillings Virginia money.

Governor Livingston (NJ) wrote an affectionate letter to his son-in-law, John Jay, asking whether Jay had forwarded the papers to John Tabor Kempe that Livingston had sent him. He wished a reply by next Monday, "because I hope to exchange noise, bustle and formality, for tranquility, blackfish and Sincerity."

Choosing the Executive

POWER TO PROVIDE for the general welfare was approved by the Convention with no debate and apparently without thought. This very broad grant of power has led the federal government into a host of activities which the delegates could not have foreseen.

Conversely, a proposed method of electing the president was debated for the entire day, a debate which would resume. In fact, over the entire Convention, and except for whether people or states were to be represented in Congress, the method for choosing the Executive occasioned more debate than any other issue.

This unique proposal provided that in elections where no candidate had a majority, the Senate would choose the president from the five with the most votes. The Convention delegates assumed that most elections would result in such a Senate selection for the Executive. But there were deep reservations about the Senate selecting the president and a growing preference to shift the choice to the House, as James Wilson's summary of the election process (as recorded by Madison) indicated:

This subject has greatly divided the House, and will also divide people out of doors. It is in truth the most difficult of all on which we have had to decide. He had never made up an opinion on it entirely to his own satisfaction. He thought the plan on the whole a valuable improvement on the former. It gets rid of one great evil, that of cabal & corruption; & Continental Characters will multiply as we more & more coalesce, so as to enable the electors in every part of the Union to know & judge of them. It clears the way also for a discussion of the question of reeligibility on its own merits, which the former mode of election seemed to forbid. He thought it might be better however to refer the eventual appointment to the Legislature than to the Senate, and to confine it to a smaller number than five of the Candidates. The eventual

The home of William Lewis at Third and Walnut was where Dr. Johnson dined on this day. Wilson was a distinguished Quaker lawyer and defense counsel.

169

election by the Legislature wd. not open cabal anew, as it would be restrained to certain designated objects of choice, and as these must have had the previous sanction of a number of the States: and if the election be made as it ought as soon as the votes of the electors are opened & it is known that no one has a majority

of the whole, there can be little danger of corruption. Another reason for preferring the Legislature to the Senate in this business, was that the House of Reps. will be so often changed as to be free from the influence & faction to which the permanence of the Senate may subject that branch

Wednesday, September 5, 1787

The day was cool and pleasant, with partly cloudy skies.

Convention

Chairman Brearley (NJ) of the Committee on Unfinished Parts reported five additional powers to be given Congress. One was the power to raise and support an army, provided that no appropriation would be valid for more than two years. Gerry (MA) objected to allowing appropriation for an army to run two years: "it implied there was to be a standing army which . . . [was] dangerous to liberty, as unnecessary even for so great an extent of Country as this, and if necessary some restriction on the number and duration ought to be provided." Sherman (CT) remarked that appropriations were permitted, not required, and Congress might not be in session when money was needed if appropriations ran only one year. The proposal passed without further debate.

Discussion of the electoral college resumed, with objections centered on having the Senate elect from the five leading candidates when no one had a majority. Among those objecting were Charles Pinckney (SC), Rutledge (SC), Mason (VA), Williamson (NC) and Randolph (VA); Morris thought that the Senate would decide less often than those objecting. A number of amendments to alleviate the problem were proposed and defeated before the Convention adjourned for the day.

Delegates

General Washington dined at Mrs. House's and drank tea at Mr. Bingham's. Like Madison (VA), Read (DEL) and Dickinson (DEL), who were boarding at Mrs. House's, the General was a long-time acquaintance of Mrs. House and her family.

Nathaniel Gorham (MA) borrowed 36 pounds lawful money from fellow delegate Robert Morris (PA) to pay his board bill and for the trip home.

James McClurg (VA) wrote from Richmond to give Madison some long-distance medical advice. "I am not surprised that you have been indisposed, at this season, with such a weight of business upon you. I am more surprised that you have been able to perservere in the application, which that business required. I hope you will never take a moment either from that, or from the relaxation which it renders necessary, on account of such a correspondent as myself; who would readily give up the satisfaction he takes in your letters, for the pleasure of hearing that you are in health."

Robert Fenning wrote a long letter from London to General Washington, outlining his experience at horticulture and estate management, giving as references "Mr. Laurence [Henry Laurens] of Charles Town, South Carolina and Mr. Samuel Chase of Maryland in America," and asked whether he could be of use to the General, or to any Gentleman in America. It is typical of Washington that he responded briefly but courteously, in January 1788.

Militia or Standing Army

DISTRUST of a standing army may seem strange. However, while Gerry's distrust may have bordered on paranoia, all of the delegates shared his concern. All were aware of ancient and modern examples of military takeovers, and particularly Cromwell's military dictatorship over Great Britain in 1653–58. All remembered the unwelcome presence of a standing army in the American colonies before the Revolution. No American has ever been more aware of the need for civilian control of the military than Washington, who, as commander of the Continental Army and as president did much to ingrain that principle.

However, while most of the delegates, even Roger Sherman, recognized that a small standing army would be necessary, Gerry did not. Not having fought, and basing his judgment on Concord and Bunker Hill, Gerry would have relied for defense on militia. Washington, with a different experience, would have agreed with the definitive assessment of militia made by Virginia Militia General Edward Stevens to Governor Thomas Jefferson in February 1782:

If the Salvation of the Country had depended on their [militia whose time of service was up] staying Ten or Fifteen days, I don't believe they would have done it. Militia won't . . . Their greatest Study is to Rub through their Tower [tour] with whole Bones.

Much debate at the end of the Convention concerned the power of Congress to raise and support a standing army. Many of the delegates who had never fought preferred to rely on militia for defense, whereas General Washington, because of his experience, knew the necessity for civilian control of the military.

Thursday, September 6, 1787

Convention

Either before the session began or shortly after, McHenry (MD) spoke to Morris (PA), Fitzsimmons (PA) and Gorham (MA) about adding a power to build piers to protect shipping in the winter. One of them, either Morris or Gorham, thought it could be done under the words "provide for the common defence and general welfare," a thought that shocked McHenry.

The Convention resumed debate on the electoral college on the provision that when no candidate has a majority, the Senate would choose from among the five with the most votes.

This topic consumed the rest of the day, finally concluding with the passage of a resolve which gave the House, with one vote per state delegation, the responsibility of selecting the president when the electoral college vote didn't turn up a majority candidate.

Delegates

General Washington dined with Dr. James Hutchinson, a professor of medicine at the University of Pennsylvania, and spent the afternoon and evening at Mr. Morris'. Secretary Jay wrote to the General to report that he had given Commodore Jones the letter Washington had sent. William Gordon, English-born minister and historian, also wrote him from London that his history would soon begin printing, that he has sent larkspur seed "to make the garden (at Mr. Vernon) gay," and to be optimistic about the work of the Convention.

James Madison (VA) wrote his friend Minister to France Jefferson.

> As the Convention will shortly rise I should feel little scruple in disclosing what will the public here, before it could reach you, were it practicable for me to guard by cypher against an intermediate discovery (use of codes in private correspondence was not unusual in the 18th century) . . . [but] this is the first day which has been free from Committee service both before and after the hours of the House, and the last that is allowed me by the time advertised for the sailing of the Packet.

John Jay wrote from New York to his father-in-law, William Livingston (NJ), to report that he had forwarded the papers to Mr. Kempe in London, and to report that "Mrs. Jay and our little folks are well."

Presidential Elections

ELECTING THE PRESIDENT, when no candidate had a majority in the electoral college, was a consideration of the Convention. The method—election by the House with each state delegation having one vote—obviated strenuous objections to the original proposal, objections which might have alienated several delegates and would certainly have worked against ratification.

The issue was simple. The members were in agreement with the electoral college concept as the least objectionable of the many possible methods of selecting the president. However, most of them thought that, once Washington was no longer available, very few elections would produce a candidate with a majority of the electors' votes.

The report from the Committee on Unfinished Parts had recommended that when no candidate had a majority of the electoral college, the Senate choose from among the five with the most votes. But the Senate appointed subordinate officers, conducted trials on impeachment, approved treaties, and so forth. If it also chose the president, that officer would be a creature of the Senate, not an independent executive capable of checking legislative excess. Yet, the small states were convinced that the large states would dominate the electoral college. If ties were broken by the Congress as a whole, or by the House of Representatives, the large states would always predominate, and Langdon (NH), Sherman (CN), Read (DE), McHenry (MD) would have no chance of being elected. Both problems were avoided by Williamson's suggestion to let the House decide the matter, with one vote per state delegation.

In fifty presidential elections, not one has failed to produce a majority vote, although one produced a tie between two candidates, each of whom had a majority. The Convention thus resolved a problem which to date has never occurred.

The Philadelphia Academy later became part of the University of Pennsylvania. Many public speeches and meetings were held here during the Convention. Dr. James Hutchinson, with whom Washington dined today, was a professor of medicine here.

Friday, September 7, 1787

Today was clear, cool and pleasant.

Convention

The Convention resumed consideration of the presidency. On a motion of Randolph (VA) and another of Madison (VA) and Morris (PA), the Legislature was authorized to declare by law who would serve as president if the president and vice president were dead or disqualified.

Gerry (MA) moved to require that, when the House elected the president, each state should have at least three members present [the purpose was to preclude election by a small minority of members]. Madison seconded, Read objected. The decision was to require the concurrence of a majority of the states. Requirements that the president be thirty-five, a natural-born citizen and resident for fourteen years passed without opposition.

"And may require the opinion in writing of the

principal officer in each of the Executive Departments" came up, and Mason (VA), renewed his motion for a council to advise the president. Franklin seconded. Wilson (PA), Dickinson (DE) and Madison favored the motion, while Morris thought a Council would be useless. The motion lost, and the clause under discussion was agreed to: NH only no.

Delegates

Dr. Johnson (CT) dined with his contemporary, former Chief Justice of Pennsylvania Benjamin Chew, at Chew's house on Third Street.

General Washington rode a few miles, and spent the afternoon at home. Part of the time was spent writing Charles Pettit [former aid to Franklin's son William, former assistant quartermaster general, and Jared Ingersoll's father-in law] to send the dimensions of three more fireplaces for which the General wanted iron castings. He may also have received and read the letter written to him this day by Jonas Phillips, merchant and ". . . one of the people called Jews of the City of Philadelphia." The letter called attention to the oath required by office holders by Pennsylvania's constitution and asked that the Convention leave out such

wording in any oath it might require. The letter was well aimed—Washington seems singularly devoid of the prejudice against Jews and Catholics which characterized many of his contemporaries—but too late. The Convention had ruled out any religious tests for federal office weeks before.

Secretary Jay wrote again from New York to his father-in-law William Livingston (NJ). He had received Livingston's letter to Kempe by the London packet. Jay added that his son Peter. Livingston's favorite grandchild, ". . . is now with us, and on your Return I will carry him to Eliz: Town, and let him share with me the pleasure of passing a day or two with you."

The Cabinet

GREAT DEPARTMENTS of the federal government—Defense, State, Treasury, Agriculture, In-

The fireplaces in the colonial kitchens were huge and open hearth to permit access for cooking. The other rooms all included fireplaces for heating purposes. On this day Washington is asking for the dimensions of three fireplaces so that he can order iron castings for them.

terior, Justice, Commerce, Education, Energy, Health and Human Services, Housing and Urban Development, Labor, Transportation—and the secretaries who direct them and advise the president on the great concerns facing the nation are provided for in one brief clause of the Constitution: ". . . he [the President] may require the Opinion, in writing, of the principal officer in each of the executive departments, upon any subject relating to the Duties of their respec-tive Offices . . ."

This clause was adopted by the Convention without substantive debate. If any delegate had questions about how many departments there should be, their jurisdiction, the responsibilities of their principal officers, whether or not they should meet with the president periodically and so forth, the questions were not asked.

Saturday, September 8, 1787

The day was, like yesterday, clear and pleasant.

Convention

Resuming discussion of the Committee on Unfinished Parts report, the Convention heard King (MA) move to include once again treaties of peace in the required two-thirds Senate approval. This motion was defeated.

The clause providing that the Senate conduct trial of impeachments against the president for treason and bribery was taken up. Mason asked why it was limited to treason and bribery, and the provision was amended.

Mr. Williamson (NC), seconded by Hamilton (NY), moved to increase the number of representatives. Sherman (CT) opposed. Hamilton strongly argued in its favor. "He was seriously of the opinion that the House of Representatives was on so narrow a scale as to be really dangerous, and to warrant a jealousy in the people for their liberties." The motion, however, lost: PA, DE, MD, VA and NC aye; 6 no.

Delegates

Dr. Johnson (CT) dined with General Mifflin (PA), and spent the evening at a meeting of the Committee on Style. He bought 40 shillings worth of books.

General Washington dined at Springsbury with the club, and spent the evening at home. Elizabeth Powel sent him a reflecting lamp for the hall at Mt. Vernon. She well knew "your delicacy on the subject of accepting the smallest present even from yor best friend," but

pointed out that lamps such as this would save oil and money. The General wrote a brief but unusually sprightly thank you note.

The reflecting lamp, with which you have been so obliging as to present me, I shall highly esteem. The benefits which will flow from the general use of such Lamps, are too apparent for the light of them to be long hid from the American World. Neat simplicity, is among the most desireable properties of the one you have sent me, but that which stamps the highest value thereon, is the hand from which it comes.

While we don't think of him in that light, the General could be a charmer when he wished to be.

John Dickinson wrote Tench Coxe about the property he had donated to the Pennsylvania Society for the Encouragement of Manufacturers. Katteuha, the Beloved Woman of Chota, wrote Dr. Franklin on behalf of the Cherokee delegation, enclosing a present of tobacco.

High Crimes and Misdemeanors

TREASON, BRIBERY, or other high crimes and misdemeanors were decided to be grounds for impeaching and convicting the president, vice president and all other civil officers of the United States. What the Convention did not decide, and what is still undetermined, is what "other high Crimes and Misdemeanors" are, and who decides what they are.

The Virginia Plan provided for impeachment of national officers, with the trial of the impeachment conducted by the Judiciary, but did not specify grounds for the action. The Committee of the Whole decided on "mal-practice or neglect of duty" as the grounds. During the debate the delegates gave numerous reasons for impeachment, among them a president's abuse of power, incapacity, negligence or perfidy, betrayal of trust, or corruption of his electors." Franklin, not entirely facetiously, argued that impeachment was desirable to prevent the assassination of bad leaders as the only means to rid the nation of them. The Committee of Detail amended the provision to give as grounds for impeachment "treason, bribery, or corruption." The Committee on Unfinished Parts reduced it to treason and bribery. It was at this point, after Madison (VA) moved to add "misadministration" and Mason objected that the word was too vague, that the change was made to add high crimes and misdemeanors.

"Treason" and "bribery" have relatively precise legal meaning, and treason is defined in the Constitution itself. "High Crimes and Misdemeanors," on the other hand, while lifted verbatim from British laws for removing and punishing executive and judicial officers, had vague connotations. However, in the minds of Randolph, Madison, Franklin, Morris and Mason an officer could be impeached for actions which were not in violation of a law, as based in English precedent.

Since the Constitution's ratification in 1789, some fifty impeachment proceedings have been initiated in the House, but only twelve articles have been approved, two of which the Senate has dismissed for lack of jurisdiction, including articles voted by the House against Convention delegate William Blount. Six articles resulted in acquittal, and four resulted in conviction including articles brought against John Pickering,

General Washington could be very charming. This side of his personality shows in the note of appreciation he wrote to Elizabeth Powel in thanks for a small gift.

a Convention delegate from New Hampshire, who never attended. Of those convicted, all federal judges, only one was clearly guilty of a criminal offense. The Convention debate, English precedent and American experience together indicate that high crimes and misdemeanors are any action which leads Congress to a reasonable determination that a person is unfit to hold office.

Sunday, September 9, 1787

Once again, the weather was cool and pleasant.

Convention

As the Convention enjoyed its customary Sunday recess, even the most pessimistic of the delegates must have felt that its work was nearly complete. The Convention had worked itself through the report of the Committee on Style and Arrangement except for the provisions for ratifying and amending the document, had debated the work of the Committee on Unfinished Parts, had finally agreed on a method of electing the Executive which most delegates could support, and had appointed a committee to put the new frame of government in final form. Probably most delegates assumed that this would be their last Sunday in Philadelphia. If so, none of them regretted that possibility.

Delegates

Dr. Johnson (CT) visited John Penn at his country seat, Lansdowne, and McPherson, probably John McPherson. He paid 15 shillings for a chair—one assumes a sulky-like buggy used in getting to and from the city. He does not indicate that its Committee on Style met, although its members may have worked on an individual basis.

General Washington made a visit to Don Diego Gardoque, the minister from Spain to the United States, who had come down from New York to visit Washington. He then dined at the Morrises'. He spent the evening writing George Augustine Washington. At the same time, John Paul Jones was writing from New York to express the honor he felt in having the bust of himself he had given Washington placed with

that of the General and to say that he could not catch the September packet to Paris and had not forwarded Washington's packet of letters to France by any of the other passengers.

James McHenry (MD) wrote his wife: "I shall soon I hope rejoin the home as it is likely the convention will finish their business in about eight days."

George Washington: A Letter Home

GEORGE WASHINGTON does not come across to us today so much as a man, but as the remote, marble bust-like father of his country. Today's letter to George Augustine Washington, his nephew and plantation manager, may help to bring Washington alive for us:

Dear George,   *Philadelphia Septr 9th 1787.*
This, in acknowledgement of your letter of the 2d of this month, is probably the last letter I shall write you

This slate-roofed house was one of the finer town houses in Philadelphia; William Penn lived here sporadically. Many of the delegates were guests in the finer homes during the months of the Convention.

from this place; as the probability is, that the Convention will have compleated the business which brought the delegates together, in the course of this Week. God grant I may not be disappointed in this expectation, as I am quite homesick.

As Mr McPhearson's glass (if good) is cheaper than the first cost here of that article, independently of the Comn, [Commission] freight, & ca; I request that you will get what may be necessary for the Green house, from him, that the building may be finished.

I had no idea, nor can I see the necessity, for stripping the Shingling from the Cupulo, in order to fix on the top [Weather vane—the work seems to have been well done, since the vane is still in place] which was sent from this place; As nothing more than the Iron spire is to pass through it, surely taking away the laths & plaistering on the inside would have been sufficient for the purpose of fixing the foot thereof— and this, instead of requiring a fortnight, would scarcely have been the business of a day; but it is too late now, I expect, to offer this opinion, as the work (some way or another) will have been nearly, if not altogether, compleated before this letter will have reached Mt Vernon.

I am very glad to hear of the interruptions your field work has met with from.the Rains which have lately fallen. If the weather should be warm, and the fall fine; they may facilitate the growth of every thing—the new meadow, so abundantly productive of weeds, ought to have been mown, as well for the sake of the young grass, as to prevent the seeds of the weeds from maturing and stocking the ground. I have but little expectation however, I must confess, that the

latter Corn will come to much; and less that Pumpkin, which are now only in blossom, can come to any thing. Of the Pease, from your acct of them much may be expected; but should be glad to know whether the vines cover the ground well (those in broad cast I mean) and whether they bear well? What is the general height of the Buck Wheat, how the ground is covered with it, & whether it is generally in blossom? If the Potatoes are so slow in forming, I fear not much is to be expected from the yield of them neither. I had expected, till your letter held up the contrary idea, that there would have been more than a sufficient of old rails at Morris's to have enclosed the fallen field, especially as they were aided, or to be aided, by a ditch. There is not a right understanding with respect to doors opening to the right or left for sure I am that the hinges I last sent were, according to the conception here for a door opening to the left—however I will get another pair contrary, if I can, to those last sent.

Inclosed I send a letter (to whom I offer best wishes) to Mr Lear [Tobias Lear, the General's personal secretary]. It came under cover to me from the Eastward. I hope Mathews model will be exact, and arrive soon; accompanied by the Spring Wheat I wrote for (I believe) im my last. My love to Fanny, [GAW's wife] & with affectionate regard I am Yours

G. Washington

P.S. If the Flax has not been spread to rot, it is time it should be—It ought to be returned, well watched, & taken up as soon as it is sufficient rotted and this can only be known by frequent examination after turning.

Monday, September 10, 1787

Today was clear and very warm—82°.

Convention

The Convention began its final week with Gerry's motion to reconsider the amending process, and particularly that provision whereby Congress could call a convention to amend the Constitution by request of two-thirds of the states. After debate, the Convention voted to retain the provision: DE no; NH divided.

Gerry then moved to reconsider the provisions for ratifying. He wanted to reinsert the requirement for Congress to approve the document. Hamilton (NY) agreed, and proposed that each state legislature should

New Market was the location of market stalls. As the delegates packed their belongings to depart from Philadelphia, much of their correspondence mentions items purchased or that they wish to purchase before they leave.

also vote on whether to accept ratification by only nine states. Gorham (MA) objected to the letter. Fitzsimmons (PA) observed that congressional approval had been deleted to avoid the embarrassment of asking Congress to violate its own charter. Randolph (VA) announced his opposition to the entire plan. Wilson (PA) and King (MA) opposed reconsideration. Sherman (CT) endorsed the method proposed but wanted it taken out of the Constitution and placed in a transmittal letter. Eventually, the clause was approved without change.

Delegates

General Washington dined and drank tea at the Morrises', and wrote shipping instructions to his business agent, Clement Biddle:

> *I have received both your Notes of this morning, and thank you for Notice of the Vessel's Sailing. The Books, I perceive, are only small treatises upon education, referred to by Doctr. Rush, which I can get, and carry in my Trunk. Remember the Clothes baskets. I send a small box containing a Lamp, it is a present, but could not have cost 20l. If the hounds presented to me by Captn. Morris are not provided for, will it not be neccessary to lay something in for them? I think of nothing else at this time; therefore, if you will let me know how the Acct. stands between us I would wish to square it.*

In a brief note, Abraham Baldwin (GA) "presents his compliments to his Excellency the President [Franklin] and will with pleasure wait on him at dinner on Wednesday."

Gerry wrote to Baltimore merchant Samuel Purviance to thank him on behalf of Mrs. Kearney "for the measures taken to detect the robbery." His objections to signing the Constitution held. The immigration to Louisiana and Florida [both Spanish territory] would drain us of inhabitants unless measures were taken to prevent the evil.

James McClurg (VA) wrote from Richmond to James Madison (VA). The report of a tendency to insurrection in parts of Virginia had some basis. The state seemed disposed to accept the plan of the Convention whatever it was.

Robert Morris wrote from Philadelphia to Constable Rucker and Co. about 191 hogheads of tobacco, and about getting mortgages on farms in Dutchess County, New York, he had sold recorded.

Edmund Randolph

EDMUND RANDOLPH has come down to us as a singularly indecisive, and therefore unsuccessful, politician. As governor of Virginia, he had led the state to reiterate the Annapolis Convention's call for the Convention and to appoint delegates. He had helped formulate, lent his name to and introduced the Virginia Plan, and had spoken often in Convention debates. Now, in the last week, he announced his intention not to sign the Convention's product.

Randolph's general concerns and the remedy he proposed are well stated in the first of two speeches he gave on this day.

"He had from the beginning he said been convinced that radical changes in the system of the Union were necessary. Under this conviction he had brought forward a set of republican propositions as the basis and outline of a reform. These Republican propositions had, however, much to his regret been widely, and in his opinion, irreconcileably departed from–in this state of things it was his idea, and he accordingly meant to propose, that the State Conventions should be at liberty to offer amendments to the plan—and that these should be submitted to a second General Convention, with full power to settle the Constitution finally- . . ."

Later in the day, he spelled out his objections; to the Senate trial of impeachments; to requiring three-fourths instead of two-thirds to override a veto; to the small number of representatives; to the lack of limits on a standing army; to "the general clause concerning necessary and proper laws"; to the lack of limits on navigation acts; to the authority to intervene in state civil disturbance on the request of the state executive; to the lack of a clear boundary between the national and state legislatures and judiciaries; to the unqualified power of the president to pardon treasons and to the lack of some limit on the Legislature when determining its own salary.

In the end, he did support the Constitution. However, he never quite lived down the reputation for indecisiveness his stand on the Constitution gained for him.

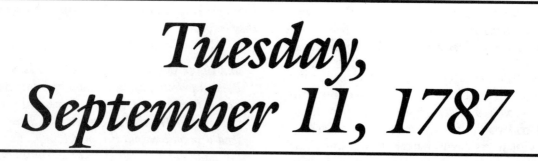

Tuesday, September 11, 1787

It was exceedingly warm.

Convention

Secretary Jackson recorded in the Journal: "The House met—but the Committee of Revision not having reported, and there being no business before the Convention "The House Adjourned."

Delegates

General Washington dined at the Morrises with Spanish Minister Don Diego Gardoqui and many others.

William Livingston (NJ) wrote his son-in-law John Jay in New York to thank him for forwarding the packet of papers to John Tabor Kempe in London.:

. . . as it will be of real importance to him if he receives it before the commissioners he mentions have finally reported relative to his confiscated property in the State of New Jersey. I am also obliged to you for your promise of paying me a visit on my return to Elizabeth Town, & the more so as there is another

promise to it, of bringing with you a certain little gentleman [grandson Peter Jay] whom I greatly long to see. I shall inform you of my arrival without loss of time. But my hopes of returning by the time expected are a little clouded by reason of there being certain creatures in this world that are more pleased with their speeches than they can [prevail] upon any body else to be.

The Committee of Style

FIVE MEMBERS of the Committee of Style—William Samuel Johnson (CT), Alexander Hamilton (NY), Gouverneur Morris (PA), James Madison (VA) and Rufus King (MA)—completed their report for presentation. Between the afternoon of September 8 and the evening of this day, the committee had reorganized and compressed the preamble and twenty-three articles into a preamble and seven articles of remarkable force and clarity.

Little is known about how the committee proceeded. Dr. Johnson's diary indicates that he met with the committee after dinner on September 8, and met them again on the 10th and 11th. It seems likely that the committee met on the 8th, worked out an outline, agreed on where each of the twenty-three articles fit into the new outline and assigned a member or members to do a draft. The draft was probably prepared on Sunday the 9th, reviewed and reworked as necessary on the 10th, and given any needed final touches on the 11th. All of the available evidence points to Gouverneur Morris as the draftsman, although the other four members wrote exceptionally well.

They gave us the language we have cherished, and been governed by, for two centuries. As an example, they took:

We the people of the States of New-Hampshire, Massachusetts, Rhode-Island and Providence Plantations, Connecticut, New York, New-Jersey, Pennsylvania, Delaware, Maryland, Virginia, North-Carolina, and Georgia, do ordain, declare and establish the following Constitution for the Government of Ourselves and our Posterity.

Article I

The stile of this Government shall be, "The United States of America.

Article II

The Government shall consist of supreme legislative, executive and judicial powers.

and turned it into:

WE, the People of the United States, in order to form a more perfect union, to establish justice, insure domestic tranquility, provide for the common defense, promote the general welfare, and secure the blessings of liberty to ourselves and our posterity, do ordain and establish this Constitution for the United States of America.

While historians have suspected that Gouverneur Morris, through careful selection and arrangement of words and punctuation marks, artfully bent the meaning of some provisions closer to his personal views (and he later claimed as much), this was not a convention which could be easily tricked. What Morris did do is present the Convention's work in language which has endured.

William Jackson, as secretary of the Convention, made notes of each day's proceedings.

Wednesday, September 12, 1787

Today was oppressively hot.

Convention

Dr. Johnson (CT) from the Committee of Style reported a digest of the plan, printed copies of which were ordered to be furnished to the members. A letter of transmittal to Congress was also reported.

Mr. Williamson (NJ) moved to require a two-thirds vote instead of a three-quarters vote to override a veto. Requiring a three-quarters vote gives the president too much power. Morris (PA) opposed, noting the difference amounted to only two votes in the Senate and no more than five in the House, and that it was too many laws, not too few, which was to be feared. Sherman (CT), Gerry (MA), Charles Pinckney (SC) and Mason (VA) spoke in favor of the motion, with Mason noting for Morris' benefit that "little arithmetic

In keeping accurate records, Jackson would have had to use similar materials. The cross-hatched paper would have been necessary to keep track of the votes.

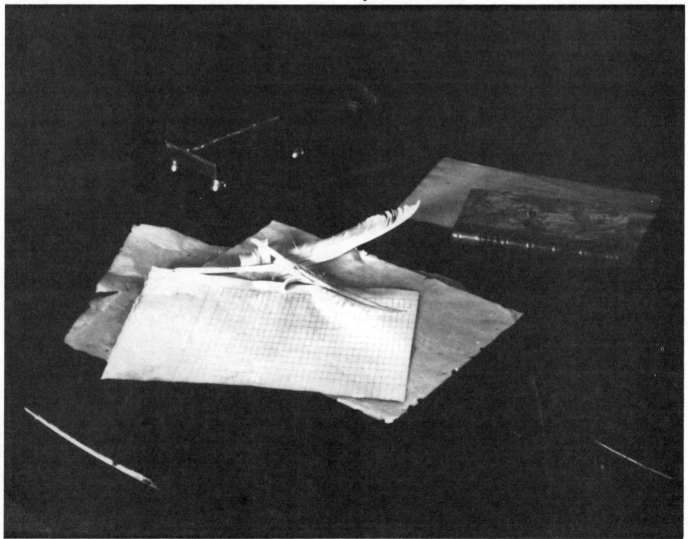

was necessary to understand that three-fourths was more than two-thirds, whatever the number of the Legislature might be." Hamilton (NY) and Madison (VA) joined Morris in opposing the change. The motion carried; 6 aye; MA, PA, DE and VA no; NH divided. Debate turned to other issues.

Delegates

General Washington, Abraham Baldwin (GA) and perhaps other delegates dined at President Franklin's. The General had tea with artist Robert Edge Pine.

After meeting with the Committee on Style, Dr. Johnson dined with Secretary Jackson, then called on his compatriot, Noah Webster.

Governor John Sevier of the State of Franklin [what is now Tennessee] wrote Dr. Franklin to thank him for his letter of June 30 and the kind advice contained therein.

No Bill of Rights?

NO BILL OF RIGHTS was contained in the Constitution written in Philadelphia. The ten amendments which spell out those basic freedoms in the Bill of Rights were added in 1791, after the Constitution had been ratified and the new government placed in operation.

Why wasn't a Bill of Rights included in the document produced by the Convention? Most of the state constitutions had one, and the delegates were familiar with the concept. We don't know. Thanks to the secrecy observed by the delegates, we don't even know enough to speculate.

Those delegates who were still present on September 12 had come to Philadelphia to help fix a government which wasn't working. Very early in the Convention, they were presented a plan for a complete restructuring. Right off, the Virginia Plan became the focus even of those delegates who thoroughly disapproved of it, and this focus may have worked to keep the delegates from thinking much about guarantees against governmental abuse of power.

Then, more than three months after the Convention began, and two weeks after the delegates had begun pinpointing September 15 as the day they would finish, the first motion to include a Bill of Rights was made. It was rejected by all ten of the states present. Later, federalists explained that, since the Constitution only gave the federal government the powers specified, there was no need to specify individual rights it had no power over.

But the Convention had been at work over three months. All of the delegates had other interests, most had families, and most had businesses, legal practices or state political offices which required their presence at home. One wonders if, when Mason (VA) moved for a committee to prepare a Bill of Rights, most delegates simply weren't physically or psychologically prepared to stay on in Philadelphia even an extra day, and therefore rejected a motion they simply couldn't consider.

Thursday, September 13, 1787

Today was rainy and cool.

Convention

As the Convention began the day's session, Mason (VA) again moved to appoint a committee "to report articles of Association for encouraging by the advice, the influence and the example of the members of the Convention, economy, frugality and American manufacture." Johnson (CT) seconded, the motion passed without debate or dissent, and Mason, Franklin, Dickinson (DE), Johnson and Livingston (NJ) were elected to the committee.

Next, Mason renewed his proposal to permit the states to collect export taxes to cover the costs of

commissioners to examine the claims of those who had bought land within Pennsylvania claimed by Connecticut, and the commissioner seemed disposed to do justice. One suspects that the letter might have been suggested by Sherman's fellow elder statesman, the president of Pennsylvania, Benjamin Franklin.

Gouverneur Morris

GOUVERNEUR MORRIS was in 1752 born at the manor of Morrisiana New York, to Lewis and Sarah Gouverneur Morris. From his French Huguenot mother he inherited his graceful manner, humor, and cynical detachment. At sixteen Gouverneur was graduated from King's College, today's Columbia University. Admitted to the bar at nineteen, he rapidly built up an extensive legal practice.

His legal career took a back seat to politics in the 70s. He with John Jay and Robert R. Livingston drafted New York's constitution in July 1776. His aristocratic family was divided by the revolutionary war. One half-brother, Lewis, signed the Declaration of Independence, while another half-brother, Staats Long Morris, was a major general in the British army. From 1778 to 1779 Gouverneur sat in the Continental Congress. Defeated for reelection in 1779 Morris moved to Pennsylvania. In 1780 Robert Morris (no relation) invited Gouverneur to become his assistant superintendent of finance.

Gouverneur Morris was elected to represent Pennsylvania in the Convention. As a firm believer in a strong central government Morris participated in debate more than any other delegate. After the Convention he purchased the family manor from his brother and retired to New York. He agreed to assist Robert Morris in collecting claims in France and stayed there for a decade. In 1792 Washington named him minister to France. He remained in Paris during the Reign of Terror, the only foreign diplomat to do so. He was recalled at France's request in 1794 over the Citizen Genet affair.

In 1809 he married Anne Carey Randolph. The fifty-seven-year old groom moved decisively to disperse rumors surrounding his new bride. Anne Carey Randolph, or Nancy, had been accused in 1792 of helping her brother-in-law Richard Randolph murder a new-born child. The child was widely believed to have been theirs. With the powerful assistance of

inspecting and storing such commodities as tobacco. He proposed a clause for that purpose. There was no debate, and the motion carried.

The Convention moved on to the report of the Committee of Style. Several minor changes in Gouverneur Morris' masterful draft were approved.

Delegates

After the Convention adjourned, Dr. Johnson met with the Committee on Style, "Din'd Tilghmans', and paid Robert Edge Pine another six guineas toward the portrait Pine was painting of him. He dined with Edward Tilghman, one of the most eminent lawyers of his day and the son-in-law of Provincial Chief Justice Benjamin Chew.

General Washington dined with the vice president of Pennsylvania, Charles Biddle, and drank tea at Mr. Powels.

Roger Sherman (CT) wrote from Philadelphia to Zebulon Butler in Wilkes Barre. In an obvious effort to help quit conflict between Pennsylvania and the Connecticut settlers in the Wyoming Valley, Sherman informed Butler that Pennsylvania had appointed attorneys, Patrick Henry and John Marshall, Richard and Nancy were acquitted.

In February 1813, Gouverneur Morris, Jr., was born. Morris, Sr., died on November 6, 1816. Nancy survived him by twenty-one years.

Friday, September 14, 1787

A violent thunder gust cooled the extreme heat.

Convention

Consideration of the draft constitution reported by the Committee of Style resumed, as the Convention went through it virtually line by line. As an indication of the consideration given each item, here are about one-fourth of Madison's notes for this day.

Art. 1. Sect. 5. "Each House shall keep a Journal of its proceedings, and from time to time publish the same, excepting such parts as may in their judgment require secrecy."

Col: Mason & Mr. Gerry moved to insert after the word "parts" the words "of the proceedings of the Senate" so as to require publication of all the proceedings of the House of Representatives.

It was intimated on the other side that cases might arise where secrecy might be necessary in both Houses—Measures preparatory to a declaration of war in which the House of Reps. was to concur, where instanced.

On the question, it passed in the negative: N.H. no. (Rh. I. ab:.) Mas. no. Con: no. (N.Y. abs) N.J. no. Pen. ay. Del—no. Mary. ay. Virg. no. N.C. ay. S.C. divd. Geor. no [Ayes 3; noes 7; divided 1.]

Mr. Baldwin observed that the clause. art. 1. sect 6. declaring that no member of Congs, "during the time for which he was elected; shall be appointed to any Civil office under the authority of the U.S. which shall have been increased during such time". would not extend to offices created by the Constitution; and the salaries of which would be created, not increased by Congs. at their first session—The members of the first Congs consequently might evade the disqualification in this instance.—He was neither seconded not opposed; nor did any thing further pass on the subject.

Art. 1. Sect. 8." The Congress "may by joint ballot appointed a Treasurer"

Mr. Rutlidge moved to strike out this power, and let the Treasurer be appointed in the same manner with other officers.

Mr. Gorham & Mr. King said that the motion, if agreed to, would have mischievous tendency. The people are accustomed & attached to that mode of appointing Treasurers, and the innovation with multiply objections to the System.

Mr. Govr. Morris remarked that if the Treasurer be not appointed by the Legislature, he will be more narrowly watched, and more readily impeached—

Mr. Sherman—As the two Houses appropriate money, it is best for them to appoint the officer who is to keep it; and to appoint him as they make the appropriation, not by joint, but several votes:

Genl Pinckney. The Treasurer is appointed by joint ballot in South Carolina. The consequence is that bad appointments are made, and the Legislature will not listen to the faults of their own officer.

On the motion to strike out

N.H.—ay. Mas. no. Ct. ay. N.J. ay. Pa. no. Del—ay—Md ay. Va. no. N—C. ay. S.C. ay. Geo—ay. [Ayes 8; noes 3.]

Delegates

General Washington dined at City Tavern at an entertainment given for him by the First Troop, City Cavalry, and spent the evening at Mr. Samuel Merediths. Henry Knox wrote to him from New York "to congratulate you on the termination of your arduous business & to wish you a happy sight of Mrs. Washington and your family."

This day was the forty-fifth birthday of James Wilson (PA).

James Wilson

JAMES WILSON'S intellect and personality were well understood by William Pierce when he wrote this characterization of the delegate:

> *Mr. Wilson ranks among the foremost on legal and political knowledge. He has joined to a fine genius all that can set him off and show him to advantage. He is well acquainted with Man, and understands all the passions that influence him. Government seems to have been his peculiar Study, all the political institutions of the World he knows is detail, and can trace the causes and effects of every revolution from the earliest stages of the Greecians commonwealth down to the present time. No man is more clear, copious and comprehensive than Mr. Wilson, yet he is no great Orator. He draws the attention not by the charm of his eloquence, but by the force of his reasoning. He is about 45 years old.*

Born in Carskerdo, near St. Andrews, Scotland, Wilson attended the Universities of St. Andrews, Glasgow and Edinburgh before migrating to New York in 1765. While he may not have had an undergraduate degree, he soon found work as an instructor in Latin at the College of Philadelphia, and began reading law under John Dickinson. Admitted to the bar in 1767, he then moved to Reading, then on to Carlisle. In 1771, after the Rev. William White's fiancee had written in his behalf, Wilson married Rachel Bird, sister of a Berks County iron master. Rachel died in 1786, leaving Wilson with six children.

From the beginning a very successful lawyer, Wilson soon got into politics, chairing the Carlisle committee of correspondence, representing the county at the first provincial congress, and serving as a delegate to the continental Congress in 1775, 1776, and 1777. An early and outspoken opponent of Pennsylvania's new state constitution, he was dropped from the congressional delegation in 1777, and moved to Philadelphia in 1778. In 1779 his house at the southwest corner of Third and Walnut Streets was attacked by an armed mob. Wilson, assisted by Robert Morris, George Clymer, Thomas Mifflin and others, beat the attackers off. In spite of this episode, his legal practice thrived, and he was returned to Congress in 1782, 1785 and 1786.

Wilson's stature in 1787 may be indicated by the fact that it was he rather than Robert Morris, Clymer or Ingersoll whom Franklin asked to read his speeches. As a delegate, he ranked third only to Madison and Gouverneur Morris in frequency of speaking.

Early in the Convention, Wilson set forth his desire "that a federal Government may be established that will insure freedom and yet be vigorous." Almost alone among the delegates, he supported direct popular election of representatives, senators and the president, and opposed qualifications of age, citizenship, years of residence or wealth which would limit the voters' choices. While he urged a continuance of the states, he supported a federal veto of state laws. He also favored giving the president an absolute veto, and opposed providing an executive council. As a member of the Committee of Detail, Wilson played an important role in organizing the work of the Convention through July 26, flashing out that work from such sources as the Articles of Confederation, and producing a draft from which today's document derived.

Of the fifty-five delegates, perhaps Wilson would be the least surprised by, and the most satisfied with, the document as it had evolved.

James Wilson was a consistent spokesman for a strong central government. He supported voting in Congress on the basis of population and the direct popular election of the President, Representatives, and Senators.

Saturday, September 15, 1787

Today was cool and pleasant.

Convention

Daniel Carroll opened the day by moving for a committee to prepare an address to the people to accompany the Constitution. Rutledge (SC) and Sherman (CT) pointed out that such an address would be improper before Congress acted on the document. The motion lost.

Langdon (NH) then moved to add an extra representative each for North Carolina and Rhode Island. Sherman (CT) supported one to North Carolina. King (MA) was against changing and said he wouldn't sign if Rhode Island's representation was increased. Charles Pinckney (SC) and Gunning Bedford (DE) favored the motion. Rhode Island and North Carolina were voted separately. Each lost: 5 aye; 6 no.

Section by section, the Convention continued to work through the document, debating several points and making changes. Randolph (VA) Mason and Gerry then stated their objections, and Randolph moved for a second convention to respond to the issues raised during ratification. At that point, Madison records:

> On the question on the proposition of Mr. Randolph. All the States answered—no.
>
> On the question to agree to the Constitution, as amended. All the States ay.
>
> The Constitution was then ordered to be engrossed. And the House adjourned.

Delegates

General Washington noted the day's events as follows: "Concluded the business of Convention, all to signing the proceedings; to effect which the House sat till 6 o'clock; and adjourned till Monday that the Constitution which it was proposed to offer to the People might be engrossed and a number of printed copies struck off. Dined at Mr. Morris' and spent the evening there." He also wrote Philadelphia merchant Clement Biddle to find out the price of the best Dutch striped blankets and the status of their accounts.

James Madison, in preparation for his return to New York as a Virginia Congressman, borrowed $100 from John Blair (VA), who would be going home and who apparently had part of his expense money left.

Thomas Fitzsimons (PA) wrote Noah Webster to start writing on behalf of the new federal system.

John Dickinson (DE) sent two notes to George Read (DE). In the first he announced that a headache had kept him from attending the Convention yesterday, and that he was about to leave for home. He had heard the delegates were going to give an entertainment at City Tavern for the Philadelphians who had entertained them, and enclosed a bank bill to pay for his share. A little later, he had another thought, and wrote asking Read if the members were to sign the document, to sign for him.

A letter from Alexander Hamilton (NY) in response to one from friends of Governor George Clinton appeared in the *New York Advertizer*. As with many eighteenth century letters to the editor, it would lead to a libel suit.

John Fitch, who had recently demonstrated his steamboat for the edification of the delegates, wrote his fellow Connecticut Yankee William Samuel Johnson (CT) to protest a report to Congress on a petition from James Rumsey, who also claimed a workable steamboat. Fitch was not unique in contacting well-placed acquaintances; Rumsey had written General Washington upon occasion.

Gunning Bedford

GUNNNING BEDFORD, Jr., born in Philadelphia, was the son of a carpenter, alderman, and militia captain. Bedford attended the College of New Jersey (Princeton) where he and his classmate James Madison and Hugh Brackenridge excelled. Bedford married Jane Parker of New York during his college years (the date of the wedding is uncertain, probably 1770). The couple eventually had three children. On the occasion of his commencement, as he delivered the valedictory, his wife looked on, having made the journey on horseback with their first baby.

Upon graduation, Bedford settled in Philadelphia and studied law under Joseph Read. The Bedfords then moved to Dover, Delaware, in 1779, when Gunning was appointed attorney general. Because of the "unhealthyness" of Dover, they moved to Wilmington, and Bedford continued to pursue an extensive career in public service. From 1783–1785, he attended the Confederation Congress, and in 1784, he served as a delegate to the Delaware Assembly. Bedford was elected to the Annapolis Convention in 1786, but failed to attend. The following February, the Delaware legislature named him a representative to the Federal Convention in Philadelphia.

Having gained a reputation as an outspoken politician and a fine orator, the tall, handsome, somewhat, "corpulent" man made his presence known during the Convention. Bedford as well as the other delegates recognized the need for a stronger, more efficient central government. As a representative from a small state, though, he was on guard against the intrigue and ambitions of the larger states. To that end, he fought vehemently for equal representation in the Senate, and did not hesitate to announce to the delegates of Virginia, Pennsylvania, and Massachusetts; "I do not trust you gentlemen." In another speech, Bedford went so far as to mention that the small states would seek foreign alliances. Once, however, the Convention adopted the Great Compromise with the clause of equal representation in the Senate, Bedford assented to the Constitution, albeit with some objections including his intense opposition to appointment of federal judges. After he signed it, Bedford then pushed for ratification in the Delaware Convention in

Gunning Bedford served on the Connecticut Compromise Committee and supported small states' interests.

December 1787, where the Constitution was first ratified.

Following the institution of the new government, Gunning Bedford overcame his prior opposition to judicial appointments and accepted President Washington's nomination as a U.S. district judge for the state of Delaware.

Sunday, September 16, 1787

The day was cool and pleasant.

Convention

The Convention was in recess as its members prepared for the trip home, and Secretary Jackson sorted his papers. Jacob Shallus, assistant clerk to the General Assembly of Pennsylvania, spent much of the day engrossing the Constitution on parchment for the delegates to sign.

Delegates

General Washington spent the forenoon writing letters [the General did not attend church very frequently], dined with Robert and Mary Morris at their country place, The Hills, and returned to Philadelphia in the evening. Among the morning's letters, one was to Chastellux, introducing Mr. Charles Pinckney, who intended to visit France. Three agents in southwestern Pennsylvania wrote concerning the land Washington owned there, and his efforts to either sell to the squatters who occupied it or to have them evicted.

Franklin's old friend the British economist George Whately wrote to him from London, to discuss paper money, the inapproachability of American Minister John Adams and so forth. According to Whately, ". . . Contention for the Emission of Paper money without a Suficient Foundation can but be deem'd a Roguery."

George Wythe

GEORGE WYTHE, a Virginia delegate to the Convention, was a half century old when he signed the Declaration of Independence. By 1776 Wythe had practiced law for thirty years and served in Virginia's House of Burgesses. In 1779 with Governor Thomas Jefferson, Wythe established the first professorship of law in the United States at the College of William and Mary. Wythe held that chair until 1790. The youthful Jefferson had studied with him as would a leader of a future generation, Henry Clay.

In 1779 Wythe and Jefferson, members of the Second Continental Congress, joined with Edmund Pendleton, delegate to the First Continental Congress, and revised the laws of Virginia. James Madison led the campaign to pass those laws through the House of Burgesses.

Wythe became Chancellor Wythe in 1778 when he

George Wythe began as chairman of the committee that prepared the Convention's rules, but left the Convention early in June when his wife became gravely ill.

was appointed to Virginia's high court of chancery. It was the illness and death of his wife that led Wythe to leave the Convention prior to adoption of the new Constitution. He did, however, become a member of Virginia's ratification convention. Indeed, Wythe introduced the ratification resolution.

George Wythe's death was a tragic irony. His grand-nephew poisoned him to inherit Wythe's estate. The grand-nephew, George Wythe Sweeney, was acquitted because the only witness was a black servant. Under the laws of Virginia, which George Wythe had written, a black person could not testify against a white person!

Monday, September 17, 1787

Convention

The Constitution was read. James Wilson read for Franklin the latter's plea to approve the document. Dr. Franklin moved that the form for signature be: "Done in Convention, by the unanimous consent of the States present . . ."

Gorham moved to increase the number of representatives by changing the minimum number of people per representative from forty to thirty. He was supported by Mr. King, Mr. Carroll, and in complete violation of parliamentary procedure, by Chairman George Washington. The change carried and the document was agreed to by the ten states present and Mr. Hamilton of New York. Randolph, Gouverneur Morris, Williamson, Hamilton, Blount, Gerry, General Pinckney and Ingersoll spoke on their reasons for signing or not signing, and Franklin's proposed form was approved by ten states, with South Carolina divided. A motion by King to deposit the Convention's papers with its president carried: 10 yea, Maryland no; the members present signed, and then adjourned sine die.

The delegates, in Washington's words "adjourned to the City Tavern, dined together and took a cordial leave of each other."

Delegates

Dr. Johnson spent the evening paying bills—Moyston's bill for meals at City Tavern, 29 shillings; washing, 25 shillings; servants, 5 dollars. He also paid 1 shilling 6 pence for watch repair, and bought $22 worth of buckles.

After dining with his colleagues, General Washington returned to his room, did some business, received the Convention's papers from Secretary Jackson, and "retired to meditate on the momentus work which had been executed, after not less than five, for a large part of the time six, and sometime 7 hours sitting every day, Sundays & the ten days adjournment . . . [except] for more than four months." The business he did included recommending coachmaker Clark to William Washington and his friends, signing forty diplomas for Rhode Island members of the Society of the Cincinnati, and accepting a John Pine engraving from Robert Edge Pine.

George Mason drew a bill of exchange on Lt. Governor Beverly Randolph in favor of Robert Morris for fifty pounds current money of Virginia to pay money loaned Mason by Morris so the former could get home.

The Words of a Wise Man

FRANKLIN'S SPEECH to the Convention was long, some of its phrasing seems archaic, and it did not persuade Gerry, Mason and Randolph to sign. But in it, a very wise man drew on eighty-one years of experience for advice which is as valid now as it was then:

Mr. President
    I confess that there are several parts of this constitu-

tion which I do not at present approve, but I am not sure I shall never approve them: For having lived long, I have experianced many instances of being obliged by better information of fuller consideration, to change opinions even on important subjects, which I once thought right, but found to be otherwise. It is therefore that the older I grow, the more apt I am to doubt my own judgment, and to pay more respect to the judgment of others. Most men indeed as well as sects of Religion, think themselves in possession of all truth, and that whereever others differ from them it is so far error. Steele, a Protestant in a Dedication tells the Pope, that the only difference between our Churches in their opinions of the certainty of their doctrines is, the Church of Rome is infallible and the Church of England is never in the wrong. But though many private persons think almost as highly of their own infallibility as of that of their sect, few express it so naturally as a certain french lady, who in a dispute with her sister, said "I don't know how it happens, Sister but I meet with no body but myself, that's always in the right"—Il n'y que moi qui a toujours raison."

In these sentiments, Sir, I agree to this Constitution with all it's faults, if they are such; because I think a general Government necessary for us, and there is no form of Government but what may be a blessing to the people if well administered, and believe farther that this is likely to be well administered for a course of years, and can only end in Despotism, as other forms have done before it, when the people shall become so corrupted as to need despotic Government, being incapable of any other. I doubt too whether any other Convention we can obtain may be able to make a better Constitution. For when you assemble a number of men to have the advantage of their joint wisdom, you inevitably assemble with those men, all their prejudices, their passions, their errors of opinion, their local interests, and their selfish views. From such an Assembly can a perfect production be expected? It therefore astonishes me, Sir, to find this system approaching so near to perfection as it does; and I think it will astonish our enemies, who are waiting with confidence to hear that our councils are confounded like those of the Builders of Babel; and that our States are on the point of separation, only to meet hereafter for the purpose of cutting one another's throats. Thus I consent, Sir, to this Constitution because I expect no better, and because I am not sure, that it is not the best. The opinions I have had of its errors I sacrifice to the public good—I have never whispered a syllable of them abroad—Within these walls they were born, and here they shall die—If every one of us in returning to out Constituents were to report the objections

and securing happiness to the people, depends on opinion, on the general opinion of the goodness of the Government, as well as well as of the wisdom and integrity of its Governors. I hope therefore that for our own sakes as a part of the people, and for the sake of posterity, we shall act heartily and unanimously in recommending this Constitution (if approved by Congress & confirmed by the Conventions) wherever our influence may extend and turn our future thoughts & endeavors to the means of having it well administered.

On the whole, Sir, I cannot help express in a wish that every member of the Convention who may still have objections to it, would with me, on this occasion doubt a little of his own infallibility—and to make manifest our unanimity, put his name to this instrument.

he has had to it, and endeavor to gain partizans in support of them, we might prevent its being generally received, and thereby lose all the salutary effects & great advantages resulting naturally in our favor among foreign Nations as well as among ourselves, from our real or apparent unanimity. Much of the strength & efficiency of any Government in procuring

Tuesday, September 18, 1787

Convention

Although Pennsylvania Convention delegates were also members of the state assembly, they did not believe that today was the appropriate time to offer a motion to elect a state ratifying convention. George Clymer reserved that action for several days later. Yet, Benjamin Franklin hinted that the Constitution would be ratified by suggesting that the Assembly should set aside ten square miles of land within the state for a new capital. Article I, Section 8, stated that a new capital would be created on land ceded by one or more states. Franklin obviously believed Pennsylvania should be that state.

The North Carolina delegation sent a copy of the Constitution with an explanatory letter to Governor Richard Caswell. They noted "that no exertions have been wanting on our part to guard and promote the particular interest of North Carolina" during the four months of deliberations. Further, they pointed out the particular advantages for their state when the Constitution was ratified. Many fellow statesmen did not share their instructions—North Carolina was one of the last states to ratify.

Delegates

After the long Philadelphia summer, the delegates were anxious to return home. Edmund Randolph remained in Philadelphia for a week waiting for his wife to recover from a minor ailment. Some delegates took care of personal business then returned home.

Others, who were also members of Congress, resumed their duties in New York.

George Washington sent letters and copies of the Constitution to Thomas Jefferson and the Marquis de LaFayette, and enjoyed an early dinner with Robert and Gouverneur Morris. He was escorted to Grays Ferry by Morris and left Philadelphia with John Blair as his traveling companion. They spent their first night in Chester, Pennsylvania.

The Rising Sun Chair

JAMES MADISON recorded in his *Notes of Debates* this memorable moment in American history as the members of the Convention were signing the Constitution on September 17, 1787:

Doct. Franklin looking towards the Presidents Chair, at the back of which a rising sun happened to be painted, observed to a few members near him, that Painters had found it difficult to distinguish in their art a rising from a setting sun. I have said he, often and often in the course of the Session, and the vicisitudes of my hopes and fears as to its issue, looked at that behind the President without being able to tell whether it was rising or setting: But now at length I have the happiness to know that it is a rising and not a setting sun.

The only documented relic of the Constitutional Convention is the Rising Sun Chair in which the president, George Washington, sat. On December 3, 1779, the Pennsylvania Assembly paid cabinetmaker John Folwell for fashioning a replacement for its speaker's chair that had been destroyed during the British occupation of Philadelphia. The new furniture was a grand celebration of cosmopolitan taste. Inspired by contemporary fashion and enhanced by imported materials, Folwell's creation has a Gothic back, a red leather seat, and the oversized proportions of public seating furniture. Sixty-one inches high, it provided the ideal prop for Washington's imposing presence on the speaker's platform.

On the center of the chair's top rail is a carved and gilded device, a half-sunburst topped by a Phrygian Liberty cap on a pike. Perhaps a spirited public servant, perhaps Folwell himself, introduced this unique decoration. The cap and pike, an ancient Roman symbol of freedom, bespoke Pennsylvania's foundation of religious freedom and equality for its inhabitants. At the close of the Federal Convention, September 1787, Benjamin Franklin expanded the symbol's scope, so that now 200 years leater, we refer to Folwell's piece as "The Rising Sun Chair."

The Rising Sun Chair is the only documented relic of the Constitutional Convention.